Economics of Changing Age
Distributions in Developed Countries

The International Union for the Scientific Study of Population Problems was set up in 1928, with Dr Raymond Pearl as President. At that time the Union's main purpose was to promote international scientific co-operation to study the various aspects of population problems, through national committees and through its members themselves. In 1947 the International Union for the Scientific Study of Population (IUSSP) was reconstituted into its present form.

It expanded its activities to:
- stimulate research on population
- develop interest in demographic matters among governments, national and international organizations, scientific bodies, and the general public
- foster relations between people involved in population studies
- disseminate scientific knowledge on population

The principal ways through which the IUSSP currently achieves its aims are:
- organization of worldwide or regional conferences
- operations of Scientific Committees under the auspices of the Council
- organization of training courses
- publication of conference proceedings and committee reports.

Demography can be defined by its field of study and its analytical methods. Accordingly, it can be regarded as the scientific study of human populations primarily with respect to their size, their structure, and their development. For reasons which are related to the history of the discipline, the demographic method is essentially inductive: progress in knowledge results from the improvement of observation, the sophistication of measurement methods, and the search for regularities and stable factors leading to the formulation of explanatory models. In conclusion, the three objectives of demographic analysis are to describe, measure, and analyse.

International Studies in Demography is the outcome of an agreement concluded by the IUSSP and the Oxford University Press. The joint series is expected to reflect the broad range of the Union's activities and, in the first instance, will be based on the seminars organized by the Union. The Editorial Board of the series is comprised of:

John Cleland, UK   Henri Leridon, France
John Hobcraft, UK   Richard Smith, UK
Georges Tapinos, France

Economics of Changing Age Distributions in Developed Countries

edited by
RONALD D. LEE
W. BRIAN ARTHUR
GERRY RODGERS

CLARENDON PRESS · OXFORD

Oxford University Press, Walton Street, Oxford OX2 6DP
Oxford New York
Athens Auckland Bangkok Bombay
Calcutta Cape Town Dar es Salaam Delhi
Florence Hong Kong Istanbul Karachi
Kuala Lumpur Madras Madrid Melbourne
Mexico City Nairobi Paris Singapore
Taipei Tokyo Toronto
and associated companies in
Berlin Ibadan

Oxford is a trade mark of Oxford University Press

Published in the United States
by Oxford University Press Inc., New York

© IUSSP 1988
First published in hardback 1988
First issued in new as paperback 1995

British Library Cataloguing in Publication Data
Economics of changing age distributions in
developed countries.—(International
studies in demography)
1. Age distribution (Demography)
I. Lee, Ronald D. II. Arthur, W. Brian
III. Rodgers, Gerry IV. Series
304.6'1 HB1531
ISBN 0–19–829503–0
ISBN 0–19–828887–5 (Pbk)

Library of Congress Cataloging in Publication Data
Economics of changing age distributions in developed
countries.
Bibliography: p.
Includes index.
1. Age distribution (Demography) 2. Age
distribution (Demography)—Great Britain. 3. Age
distribution (Demography)—Israel. 4. Age distribution
(Demography)—Japan. 5. Age distribution
(Demography)—United States. I. Lee, Ronald Demos,
1954– . II. Arthur, W. Brian. III. Rodgers, Gerry.
HB1531.E28 1987 304.6'2'091722 86–25098
ISBN 0–19–829503–0
ISBN 0–19–828887–5 (Pbk)

Printed in Great Britain
on acid-free paper by
Biddles Ltd., Guildford and King's Lynn

Preface

Most of the chapters in this volume were originally prepared for a seminar on Economic Consequences of Changing Population Composition in Developed Countries, organized by a committee of the International Union for the Scientific Study of Population (IUSSP). The seminar was jointly sponsored by the International Institute for Applied Systems Analysis, which hosted the meeting at its headquarters in Laxenburg, Austria, in December 1983. Editorial responsibility was shared by Ronald Lee, who had overall responsibility and who edited the first part; by Brian Arthur, who edited the second part; and by Gerry Rodgers, who edited the third part. The other members of the IUSSP committee, Allen Kelley, Juan Carlos Lerda, and T.N. Srinivasan, played an important role in organizing the seminar, as did Georges Tapinos, the General Secretary of the IUSSP.

Contents

Contributors

Ronald D. Lee	University of California, Berkeley
Yoram Ben-Porath	The Hebrew University of Jerusalem and the Maurice Falk Institute for Economic Research
Kevin Murphy	University of Chicago
Mark Plant	University of California, Los Angeles
Finis Welch	University of California, Los Angeles
Linda G. Martin	University of Hawaii and the East–West Population Institute
Naohiro Ogawa	Nihon University, Tokyo
John Ermisch	Policy Studies Institute, London
W. Brian Arthur	Stanford University, California
Nathan Keyfitz	International Institute for Applied Systems Analysis, Laxenburg, Austria
Robert J. Willis	University of Chicago and National Opinion Research Center
Alessandro Cigno	University of Hull, England
Gerry Rodgers	International Labour Organization, Geneva
Frank T. Denton	McMaster University, Hamilton, Canada
Byron G. Spencer	McMaster University, Hamilton, Canada

Introduction to Volume

RONALD D. LEE

The demographic situations of the currently developed countries (DCs) share important features which distinguish them from the less-developed countries (LDCs) and from their own pasts prior to the nineteenth or twentieth century. Fertility is now very low, typically below the level needed for long-run demographic replacement. It is at a third or a half of its historical levels, which were similar to those now prevailing throughout much of the Third World. Life expectancy has risen from around thirty years at birth prior to the nineteenth century to well over seventy years now. These two aspects of DC demography together determine a third: the secular ageing of the populations, with low proportions of children and high and rising proportions of the elderly, often in need of support by the working-age population.[1] Historically, the now-developed European countries had about 5 per cent of their populations over 65 and a median age of about 26 years.[2] Contemporary LDCs, on average, have populations that are younger still, with a median age of 21 years and less than 4 per cent over 65.[3] In such young populations, the problem of providing for support in old age may loom large in the life cycle planning of individuals, but from the point of view of total social resources the problem is quite minor. In today's DCs, on the other hand, an average of 11 per cent of the population is over 65, and the median age is 32 years. Even if fertility rises to replacement level, these countries can expect in the long run to have over 17 per cent of their populations above the age of 65, and median ages in the neighbourhood of 40 years.[4] In such circumstances the problem of old-age support is far greater on the societal level as well as on the individual level, while the resource burden of rearing, educating, and providing health care for the young, currently a major concern in the LDCs, assumes much smaller proportions. As fertility declines in many of the LDCs, they too will have to confront the disadvantages of an older population, along with the advantages.

Fertility in DCs is not only very low by historical standards, but it is also much more variable, at least over the medium term. In the past, both fertility and mortality fluctuated strongly under the influence of harvest and epidemic, but this variability was short-run, and fluctuations tended to be self-cancelling across the span of a few years. In the twentieth century, by contrast, the extreme short-run volatility has all but vanished, and has been replaced by steady mortality and longer, smoother fluctuations in fertility —baby booms and busts—which do not average out from year to year, and which consequently have a greater impact on the general shape of the age distribution. Therefore age distributions today, compared to those in the past, are less jagged in the small, but more irregular in the large.[5] Until the fertility declines of the last two decades, the same comparison would hold in relation to the age distributions of most LDC populations.

Population growth rates in the DCs are generally well below 1 per cent annually, and for some countries are negative. Except for frontier regions, and periods of demographic recovery, however, growth rates have never been much above 1 per cent in the past few centuries. In LDCs, growth rates over 3 per cent have been common in recent decades, and rates over 4 per cent have occasionally been observed. But while aggregate growth rates in the DCs are low, the growth rates of specific age groups can be very high: for example, in the US, the age group 30–4 grew at 4.3 per cent per year between 1970 and 1980, while the 5–9 group decreased at −1.8 per cent, an example of the age distribution distortions just discussed for DCs.

The numbers of households have grown more rapidly than the population in many countries, as the average size of household has declined. Changes in fertility and mortality account for much of the reduction in household size: lower fertility has an obvious direct effect, and a less obvious indirect one, since the elderly are less likely to have a surviving child in a position to take them in. Due to lower mortality, couples live more years after their grown children have left home, and the large difference in male and female life expectancy, which appears to be a feature of all DCs, means that women spend many years as widows, often living alone. Other changes contribute less mechanically to the decline in household size: people marry later and more remain single, and people are choosing more often to divorce and live alone, in part because they can now better afford to.

Other important demographic changes in DCs are less closely tied to the long-run decline in fertility and mortality. In recent decades many DCs have relied on migrant workers, doubtless in part because of the declining rate of growth of their indigenous labour forces, which in turn reflects the low fertility of previous years. DCs have become ethnically more diverse as a result. Patterns of geographic dispersion have also changed. Initially, of course, DC populations became increasingly urbanized, but more recently these trends have slowed, and in some countries there has been a mild reversal, with smaller proportions of the population living in metropolitan areas.

The fundamental demographic differences between DCs and LDCs have, not surprisingly, given rise to quite different sets of concerns about economic consequences. DCs worry about the secular ageing of the population, the vitality of the labour force, and the burden of supporting the aged retired population. LDCs worry about the burden of providing health, education, and jobs for their children. DCs have worried that slowed population growth rates might cause reduced investment demand, leading through Keynesian 'demand-side' problems to economic stagnation; the LDCs have worried about the difficulty of investing at a sufficient rate to overcome the supply-side problems caused by rapid labour force growth. DCs have worried about the difficulties of adjusting to fluctuating age group sizes, while until recently LDCs have not had to. DCs are far less concerned about their agricultural sectors than are the LDCs, since they account for a far smaller fraction of employment and total output. Urban size and growth are of little concern in DCs, but in LDCs these are the aspects of population which give governments the greatest concern.

In this volume, rather than trying to be comprehensive, we have focused on a few issues, choosing ones which combine policy importance with current activity at the forefront of research. This led us to stress problems arising from the changing age composition of the population, both its secular ageing and its fluctuations, and issues arising from the changing household composition. Specifically, this volume deals with three broad problems: the impact of age distribution fluctuations on the earnings and unemployment experience of young workers; the way in which intergenerational transfers, and particularly the pension problem, are affected by the secular ageing of the population; and the effects of changing population composition, both by age and household composition, on the structure of consumption demand, particularly housing demand.

This volume is thus principally concerned with the economic consequences of changing demographic composition in the developed countries. The analysis of the effects of changing demographic composition can be carried out in practice at several different levels. At the most basic level, one assumes that the age-specific rate of some form of economic behaviour, let us say labour force participation, remains fixed over time at current or historical levels. Then, given an actual or projected change in the population age composition, one can derive the implications for the size and age composition of the labour force. This approach has many variations, including those in which an age profile such as labour force participation is broken down into constituent elements, such as male and female, with allowance for differing numbers and ages of children; then the overall profile may change in shape as a result of a change in fertility, although all the constituent rates remain fixed. This sort of analysis may frequently be very useful, for example by providing an estimate of the amount by which the labour supply schedule will shift as the result of demographic change. On the other hand, as a forecast of future labour force size it may be misleading, since demographic change is only one of many relevant ingredients, and may itself interact in systematic and predictable ways with other variables to produce the final outcome. Because the potential for adjustment by the system is ignored, such analyses often make demographic influences appear unrealistically powerful *ex ante*, when *ex post* their influence may turn out to have been quite minor. This could happen because independent events swamp the demographic influences, or because the economic system adjusts smoothly, altering the age-specific rates which were assumed constant in the calculation, and forestalling the dramatic consequences which were foreseen.

A more ambitious approach might consider both labour supply and labour demand, and attempt to predict the equilibrium outcome in the labour market, taking into account the likely effect of variations in demand and supply on the market wage, and thereby on labour force participation itself. Most such attempts take the shape of the age profile as fixed, but allow the level of the profile to vary according, let us say, to the wage level. This is a second level of analysis, far more sophisticated than the first. A third approach, more sophisticated still, is to allow the age profiles of economic behaviour to be fully endogenous, so that their shapes as well as their levels may vary in response to other influences. Such an approach is difficult to implement with a rich theory of underlying motivations, since it requires some sort of optimization over the life cycle; however, there are many ways to introduce simplifying assumptions, thereby making the problem more tractable. This kind of analysis has been applied most extensively to life cycle labour supply, life cycle consumption and saving, and life cycle birth spacing. In this volume, both the second and third kinds of analysis are represented, although only the chapters by Willis and Cigno analyse full-blown general equilibrium models.

The volume is divided into three parts, each one dealing with one of the areas mentioned earlier. The first part contains empirical studies of the impact of population age distribution fluctuations on the labour market, particularly on age-specific earnings and unemployment. The second part addresses a set of problems centred on intergenerational transfers, fertility, and economic growth. It is inevitable in an undertaking of this kind that some of the chapters sit more comfortably together than do others. In this volume, the third part is less cohesive than the other two; one chapter discusses demographic aspects of housing problems, and another considers the effects of endogenizing fertility in a macroeconomic simulation model. Each of the three parts commences with a brief introduction that provides some background on the issues and places the chapters in the context of the broader literature.

Endnotes

1. Low fertility is the main cause of demographic ageing, while reduced mortality initially makes the population younger rather than older. Once life expectancy rises above the mid-60s, however, survival to the age of reproduction is affected very little, and further gains do lead to an ageing of the population.
2. Assuming that life expectancy was about 30 years, and the intrinsic rate of natural increase was

zero. In the US, with higher fertility, lower mortality, and an annual growth rate of 3 per cent, the median age was 16 years and the proportion over 65 was only about 2 per cent.

3. These figures are taken from standard United Nations sources, and refer to the DCs and LDCs as totals or averages; of course, there are very wide variations within each of these categories.

4. This assumes that life expectancy at birth is 75 years, and fertility is such that the intrinsic rate of natural increase is zero.

5. Only occasionally do we have direct observations of historical age distributions on the national level, so the assertion is based only on indirect inference from what is known of the behaviour of the vital rates.

Part 1

Cohort Size, Wages, and Unemployment

Introduction: Demographic Fluctuations and Labour Markets

RONALD D. LEE

The secular growth of population has not generally appeared to depress economic well-being in today's developed countries. One reason may be that to a considerable extent the demographic growth has itself been induced by economic progress, and has therefore played a passive rather than disruptive role. This passive role has obscured the causal relations among trends and made identification of population's independent influence very difficult.

But if Malthusian forces have not appeared to dominate the long-run trends, they may have exerted a more visible influence over medium-length fluctuations. Some authors have suggested that nineteenth-century Kondratieff cycles arose from oscillations of labour supply about its equilibrium growth path, and the swollen sizes of post-World War II birth cohorts in many developed countries are frequently blamed for economic difficulties experienced by these cohorts as they entered the labour market. Causal relationships are more easily untangled empirically over such fluctuations, because variations in the sizes of entry-aged cohorts, if indeed they are of economic origin at all, were induced by economic conditions at the birth of the entering cohorts about two decades earlier, and therefore are exogenous in relation to contemporaneous conditions. Since economic and demographic fluctuations are measured relative to underlying trends, they are also more nearly independent of the causal links binding these trends. For these reasons, the influence of age distribution fluctuations on earnings and unemployment by age appears to be not only an interesting subject for empirical research on the consequences of population change, but also a feasible one.

But the subject is certainly not only methodologically convenient and empirically promising; it is also of considerable importance for policymakers, for labour economists, and for economic demographers. Policymakers are concerned about the economic situation of the young, and about wage levels and unemployment generally. There are also implications for educational policy: to what extent do the much-reduced returns to investment in education for recent cohorts represent a long-run decline, perhaps due to 'overeducation', and to what extent do they merely reflect the temporary impact of the baby boom generations? As many LDCs experience sharp fertility declines, leading to age distribution perturbations, these issues become more relevant for them as well.

Labour economists question whether the age profile of earnings can be modelled purely from a human capital perspective, or whether the age profile may 'twist' in response to changes in the relative supply of workers at each age. Similarly, they question whether the worsened relative position of the baby boom generations will be a permanent feature of their experience, reflected in the lower level of their cohort's age–earnings profile but not its shape, or whether earnings will be depressed only at the stage of labour market entry, the effect wearing off as the workers age and gain experience.

Economic demographers have been particularly interested in these issues as they bear on the 'Easterlin Hypothesis', which asserts that large cohorts experience lower relative income, leading them to reduce their fertility so sharply that as a group they give birth to a smaller than normal cohort, which in turn does unusually well, has unusually high fertility, and produces an oversized cohort, continuing a self-generating cycle forty or fifty years long. Easterlin did the pioneering work on the effects of cohort size fluctuations on economic well-being in the early 1960s.

The data requirements for this kind of study are fairly stringent, as one needs time series of age-specific real wages, and these are rarely available. Indeed, the US appears to have by far the richest data in this regard among those countries studied, and its data none the less leave much to be desired. There are also important theoretical and econometric issues to be addressed. For example, one must decide whether the educational attainment and the labour force participation of the workers can be treated as exogenous in the analysis (as is usually done), since presumably the decisions whether to work, continue in school, or do neither are taken with reference to prevailing unemployment rates and earning differentials, and are therefore endogenous.

It is also not clear how best to treat age in the analysis. The most common approach is to group workers together into 'young' and 'old', and then to examine the ratio of numbers of workers (or of the base population) in relation to the ratio of their wages. But it is obvious that any dividing line for age groupings must be arbitrary, and have possibly serious implications for the analysis. The study by Murphy, Plant, and Welch takes an interesting approach, viewing workers of different ages as possessing quantities of certain useful attributes in different mixes. Young workers, for example, might have more energy and creativity, but less wisdom, reliability, and experience, relative to older workers. These attributes are not measured directly, nor need they be; instead, factor analysis is used to identify implicit characteristics which vary with age. This allows a more flexible treatment of age composition in the analysis, but at the same time suffers from the difficulties of theoretical interpretation which often afflict this statistical procedure.

Over the past two decades, there has been a considerable amount of research on these issues, but it has been largely, if not entirely, confined to the experience of the United States. In this volume we present studies for three other countries—Israel, England, and Japan—in addition to a new study of the United States. The study for the US, by Murphy, Plant, and Welch, documents once more the negative effect of cohort size on earnings, using an interesting and powerful new method. The effect of a large single-year cohort on its own and the nearby cohorts' earnings is very small, but a long run of unusually large cohorts, such as occurred in the baby boom, has a large cumulative effect. For Israel, Ben-Porath reports that immigration as well as fertility played an important role in creating a severely distorted age distribution. Large cohorts did apparently suffer lower earnings and higher unemployment, but it was also notable that public sector actions served to reduce the economic impact of the demographic fluctuations: many of the young were absorbed in the military, and many others in the educational sector. There was a similar phenomenon in the US, where the impact of the baby boom on labour markets was delayed and attenuated by the timing of increases in the army, and in enrolments in higher education.

For Japan, Martin and Ogawa found that secular ageing of the labour force proceeded very rapidly, but that the age distribution fluctuations about this trend were smaller and of shorter duration than in the US or Israel. The analysis again reveals a negative influence of cohort size on earnings, but it is small, and less important than the influence of fluctuations in aggregate demand on the relative earnings of the different age groups. In England, Ermisch found that relative cohort size seems to have made very little difference in the labour market, with wage trends generally moving in the opposite direction to that predicted by the hypothesis. To the extent that negative consequences of cohort size emerge, they show themselves in unemployment rates. Institutional changes appear to have played an important role in relative wage movements, particularly in the 1970s.

1 Market, Government, and Israel's Muted Baby Boom

YORAM BEN-PORATH

Rapid changes arouse curiosity, and this chapter is motivated by such curiosity. There is a great deal of variety in the rapid changes that we observe: in cohort size, age distribution, entry of women into the labour market, the level of education, ethnic composition, and so on. Some of these changes are exogenous to the contemporary economic, demographic, or social scene, some may result from other changes; some are expected and some come as a surprise.

Generally, a problem is defined and a research programme is designed around endogenous variables. In seeking explanations for a phenomenon we construct hypotheses, propose theories, or make speculations about its causes which either predispose one towards specific independent variables or impose a preselection of such variables. It is less clear how to chart a research project around an exogenous change: here is an exogenous variable which may affect everything (or nothing) under the sun. If it appears in many equations, what are we after?

One argument in favour of focusing on large-scale changes is that they may generate findings sufficiently robust to show up even if the analysis fails to take many other variables into account, so that they provide more dramatic experiments for dealing with conventional questions. Another is that rapid changes can reveal different aspects of social and economic systems from those we learn about in the normal course of events; in other words, they invite different types of questions. What we ask and what we hope to learn has to do with the adaptability of society to rapid changes: the assessment of the capacity to absorb shocks, and the identification of bottle-

This chapter was written while I was visiting the National Bureau of Economic Research and supported by a grant from the Mellon Foundation to the NBER. I draw here on work which was done at the Falk Institute as part of a project on the Israeli economy after 1967, and also on some work I did while visiting the Population Council. N. Sicherman, Y. Yacob, J. Lotan, and R. Sendek provided research assistance and programming at various stages of the work. I thank M. Eisenstaedt for her valuable editing and Richard Freeman, Robert Gregory, Zvi Griliches, Simon Kuznets, and Ron Lee for useful comments on an earlier draft.

necks and rigidities. This is a question of dynamics; the emphasis is not on a particular variable but on the phenomenon of rapid change. Now it also makes sense to compare different cases of rapid change and ways of adjusting to them. While the exogenous shocks may stem from diverse causes, the sets of protagonists and the relevant bottlenecks in each case may have much in common.

Several studies have examined the specific effect of cohort size on wages and unemployment (Freeman, 1979; Wachter, 1976; and Welch, 1979). Detailed documentation and arguments for the US presented by Easterlin (1980) and Russell (1982) trace the history and discuss the consequences of the American baby boom. Easterlin (1980) and Jones (1980) focus on the unique experience of the baby generation. Louise Russell (1982) argues that on the whole the baby boom was not a very important phenomenon; her judgement relates not to the presence or absence of partial effects but to the robustness or dominance of the phenomenon.

Israel experienced a baby boom in the 1950s. In view of the keen interest in the American baby boom, one wonders whether the Israeli version had any effect. The sources of the Israeli baby boom were analysed by Friedlander (1975). The potential significance of the rapid change in age structure was pointed out by Kop (1980).

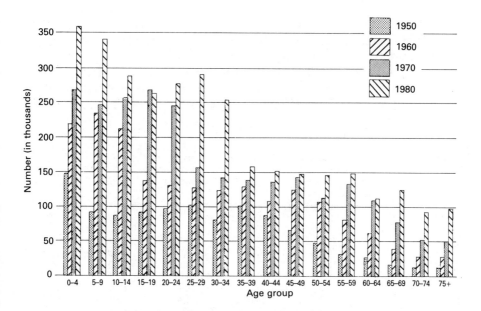

Figure 1.1.   Mean Jewish population, men and women

The Boom

The Jewish population of Israel is based on immigrants, most of whom arrived in the past century. Immigration occurred in waves, inducing uneven growth in the total population. The single most significant wave occurred in 1948–51, when the population doubled. Subsequent immigration rates fluctuated, but were much lower; between 1951 and 1973 the Jewish population grew at 3.8 per cent annually, of which immigration directly contributed 47 per cent. Between 1974 and 1980 the population grew at an annual rate of 2.1 per cent, the migration balance contributing only 20 per cent.

Looking at the age structure of the population in 1955, we see that the age group 0–4 numbered 214,000, while the age group 10–14, i.e., those aged 0–4 in 1945, numbered only 122,000 (Figure 1.1 and Appendix 1.1). Obviously, the jump in the size of cohorts is translated into big spurts in the rate of increase over time of particular age groups (see Table 1.1). The dramatic change was brought about by a combination of the large and concentrated immigration, the higher fertility of immigrants, a baby boom among immigrants (Friedlander, 1975), and perhaps some making up of births delayed abroad prior to immigration (Ben-Porath, 1980).

The greater part of the Jewish population in Palestine before 1948 was of European origin (EA); only approximately one-tenth originated from the Arab countries of the Middle East (AA: Asia–Africa). Mass immigration was more equally divided between these two groups. AA women bore far more children than EA women: in 1951 total fertility of AA women was 6.31 per cent, while that of EA women was 3.16 and that of Israel-born women was 3.56.[1] To these compositional differences there was added a baby boom within the migrant population. The figures on age structure in 1950 for the European-born (not shown) indicate a deficiency in the size of the 5–19 age group (i.e., those born in 1931–45); the largest deficiency is for people born in 1941–45, which partly reflects the effect of the war and the holocaust on births and the creation and resumption of family life after the war.[2]

Table 1.1. The Jewish population by age group, 1950–80

	1950–5 (percentage change)	1955–60	1960–5	1965–70	1970–5	1975–80
0–34	41.0	21.2	20.6	11.3	16.0	10.8
0–4	45.2	1.7	10.0	11.7	24.8	7.6
5–9	101.7	25.4	4.0	0.8	15.2	21.1
10–14	39.2	73.9	22.5	– 3.7	2.9	11.7
15–19	26.7	18.1	72.4	12.5	0.3	– 2.0
20–4	22.6	9.3	19.4	58.1	17.5	– 4.0
25–9	13.1	9.9	9.9	12.1	61.1	15.4
30–4	45.4	4.5	10.6	2.9	12.1	60.9

Source: Appendix 1.1.

Table 1.2.   Changes in the birth-rate of the Jewish population

	1955–60	1960–5	1965–70	1970–5	1975–80
1. Actual change	– 3.20	– 1.07	1.32	1.08	– 3.02
Contribution of:[a]					
2. Age-specific birth-rates	– 2.35	– 1.07	– 0.32	– 0.29	– 3.12
3. Age structure of women 15–49	– 0.80	– 1.36	0.19	2.04	0.50
4. Share of women aged 15–49 in the population	—	0.07	0.97	– 0.12	– 0.46
5. Origin	1.84	1.20	0.20	0.14	0.44
7. Marriage rate	—	—	– 1.26	0.14	– 0.65
8. Age-specific birth-rates of married women	—	—	0.28	– 0.43	– 2.41

[a] The contribution of each variable to the change in the birth-rate from period t to $t + 5$ ($B_{t+5} - B_t$, line 1) was calculated in the following manner: B_{t+5} is the predicted birth-rate for $t + 5$, if x were not to change from t to $t + 5$. The contribution is $B_{t+5} - B_{t+5}$. In this way, the interactions are included with the partial effect.

The subsequent changes in cohort size are a result of reduced immigration and fertility, and are an echo of the first boom. The crude birth rate declined sharply in the 1950s, increased between 1965 and 1975, and declined again from 1975 to 1980 (Table 1.2). The decline in the 1950s was largely a result of the steep decline in age-specific fertility coupled with a sharp drop in the share of women of the main child-bearing age (20–34) in the population. These outweighed the change in the composition of women by continent of origin, which, by itself, should have raised fertility: because of the composition of immigration, the share of women from AA among women of peak child-bearing age, which must have been less than 10 per cent before 1948, rose to 22 per cent in 1950, 35 per cent in 1955, and 43 per cent in 1960. This is only part of the story. The decline in age-specific fertility rates continued throughout the period, mostly among the immigrants from Asia and Africa whose fertility converged down towards the levels of the European immigrants; only in recent periods was there a decline also among the latter. Between 1965 and 1975 we observe the echo of the original baby boom. The number of women aged 20–34 rose from 215,000 in 1965 to 347,000 in 1975, an increase of 60 per cent, while the total population of women rose by only 30 per cent. Children aged 0–4 increased in this period by 39 per cent.

There has been a trend towards postponed marriages, which accounted for some of the decline in age-specific fertility rates. The marked decline in the proportion married between 1965 and 1970, coupled with a sharp narrowing of age differentials between brides and grooms, reflects the coming of age of large cohorts of nubile women with some scarcity in the older male cohorts. Ben-Moshe (1984) has found that the marriage squeeze brought about a decline in the age-specific marriage rates of women and an increase in the marriage rates of men.

The School System

The relevant age group for elementary school is roughly 5–14, and the one relevant for high school is roughly 14–17. The evolution of these groups' sizes is shown in Table 1.3.

Table 1.3.   Evolution of the 5–17 age groups in Israeli society

	1950 (thousands)	1955	1960	1965	1970	1975	1980
5–14	180	308	445	502	502	539	629
14–17	n.a.	90	118	199	208	203	213
As percentage of total population							
5–14	16.3	19.8	23.6	22.1	19.8	18.4	19.4
14–17	n.a.	5.8	6.3	8.8	8.2	8.2	6.9

Friedlander (1975) has demonstrated the effect of mass immigration and the baby boom on Israel's school system by citing the absolute number of children aged exactly 6 (in thousands): 1947—1.5; 1952—31.1; 1957—45.0; 1962—47.2. During the 1950s the proportion of pupils out of this rapidly growing population increased steeply, converging towards full coverage in elementary schools by the end of the 1950s. Among those aged 14–17 the proportion enrolled in schools rose from 43 per cent in 1952 to 60 per cent in 1960, fluctuated for several years when the population grew at peak rates, and then resumed its growth in the mid-1960s to reach 80 per cent in 1980. (Note that elementary education has been free and compulsory in Israel since 1949; secondary schooling has been free since 1978.)

The most surprising thing was noticed at the very start. There were 125,000 pupils in the Hebrew educational system (excluding higher education) in 1948/9. In 1951/2 the number reached 284,000, an increase of 126 per cent (or an annual rate of increase of 31.3 per cent). At the same time, the number of teachers' posts increased by 123 per cent, so that the average number of pupils per teaching post hardly changed! This, in a country whose total population had doubled, and where the immigrant population was illiterate—at best in the language of the country and often illiterate in general—or had relatively low levels of schooling. The increased supply of teachers therefore had to come from the absorbing population. It is well known that this rapid expansion took its toll in terms of a deterioration in teachers' qualifications; it is, in fact, remarkable that the response in quantities was so close to perfect and that all the pressures translated into quality reduction. It would have been reasonable to suppose that the quality–quantity trade-off would be more evenly balanced: a higher teaching load borne by few, but better-qualified teachers. A similar picture appears in the US baby boom, where the certification standards of teachers were lowered, and the student–teacher ratio reflected only small pressures (Russell, 1982, p. 30).

Let us now examine this response in greater detail. The wave of increase between 1948/9 and 1951/2 affected elementary and secondary schools more or less to the same degree, with very little change in the student-teaching-post ratio (Table 1.4). In the following years the number of elementary school pupils kept rising, though at a decreasing rate, until around 1964/5. During this period of rapid growth, which also included the entry of the baby boom cohorts, the number of teaching posts and classrooms increased proportionately with practically no change in the student-teacher–classes ratios. During the next twelve years of stability (or some decline) in the number of pupils—1964–76—the number of teaching posts kept rising, sharply reducing the ratio of pupils to teaching posts. This reduction continued when the growth of the student population resumed in 1976–82, the echo of the first baby boom.

The growth of the student population in secondary schools also decelerated gradually, but was none the less quite high throughout the period. In the 1950s a significant part of this growth was caused by the increase in the rate of school enrolment among teenagers (secondary school enrolment rates for the 14–17 age group rose from 23.4 per cent in 1952 to

Table 1.4.   Students, teaching posts, and classrooms in the Hebrew Education System

| Year | Students per | | Annual rates of growth of | | |
	Teaching post	Classroom	Students	Teaching posts	Classrooms
1. Elementary schools					
1948/9	21.9	—	} 29.8	31.4	—
1951/2	21.2	29.4^c	} 6.2	6.2	5.9^c
1963/4	21.2	29.2	} −0.7	4.2	0.8
1969/70	{ 15.9^b	26.8^a	}	3.4^b	0.8
	{ 16.3^a	26.7^b	} −0.2^b		
1975/6	12.9^b	25.1	} 2.6^b	4.0^b	1.8$^{b,\,c}$
1981/2	11.9^b	25.8^d			
2. Secondary schools					
1948/9	10.8	—	} 34.7	33.2	—
1951/2	11.2	27.1^c	} 12.0	8.5	6.4^c
1958/9	14.0	36.9	} 14.5	15.6	14.9
1963/4	13.3	36.3	} 2.9^b	7.2^b	7.7^b
1969/70	10.5^a	27.8^b	} 4.0^a	8.5^a	8.6^a
	10.3^a	28.0^a	} 4.6^a	6.7^a	4.6^a
1981/2	8.1^a	20.2^d			

^{a} Including new intermediate school (in a 6:3:3 system).
^{b} Excluding intermediate schools.
 Figures for 1969 and subsequent years with slightly different coverage.
^{c} 1953/54.
^{d} 1981.
Source: CBS, *Statistical Abstracts*, various years.

46.5 in 1959). This is the only period in which the pressure of students was not met by a proportional increase in teachers and classrooms (Table 1.4). The early 1960s marked the arrival of the large cohorts to secondary school age. The age group 14–17 increased from 107,000 in 1959 to 200,000 in 1965. These new cohorts also differed by origin: a higher proportion were of Asia–Africa origin. For the secondary school system this growth meant several years in which school enrolment remained fairly stable, probably due to the change in the composition of the teenage population by origin rather than a supply constraint on the part of the system itself. The figures in Table 1.4 show that the slightly higher rate of increase of students in this period (compared to 1952–9) was matched by an increase in the numbers of both teachers and classrooms. When cohort size and composition stabilized, the increase in enrolment rates was renewed (46.1 per cent in 1964, 64.4 in 1979), which mean that the number of inputs (teachers, classrooms) rose faster than that of students, improving the relevant input ratios.

It is probably no accident that a reform that broke down the two-tier system of eight years of elementary and four years of secondary school into a 6 : 3 : 3 system was introduced in the late 1960s after the pressures exerted by the growing number of pupils had subsided.

With regard to teenage employment, in the late 1950s approximately two-fifths of the boys and one-third of the girls aged 14–17 were in the labour force. This meant leaving school early and starting work, being interrupted at the age of 18 by army service for two or three years, and then returning to the labour market. The rate of labour force participation of the 14–17 age group was on the decline between 1955 and 1960. In 1959 the growth of the 14–17 age group began accelerating, and, as noted, this influx was associated with a change in composition by origin and with a temporary halt in the increase in school enrolment. It was also associated with a halt in the declining trend of teenagers' labour force participation. Between 1960 and 1965 the number of teenage workers doubled and their proportion in the labour force increased from 3.2 to 5.6 per cent for boys, and from 6.3 to 9.7 per cent for girls. Still, the rate of unemployment of the group did not increase in response to this influx. 1967 was the trough of a depression and teenage unemployment reached 30.4 per cent (whereas the normal level before that was 12–14 per cent), the size of the group stabilized, and the rate of labour force participation resumed its rapid decline; teenage employment gradually disappeared (less than 2 per cent of employment in 1980).

On the Reaction of the Public Sector

The above discussion indicates that in terms of the rough physical indicators there has been a very responsive accommodation of the change in cohort size by the public sector. There was one period in which pressure was felt in the secondary schools, and there was also an improvement in quantitative standards when pressures subsided. Of course, the quality aspect is not discussed here; the deterioration in teachers' quality in the period of undiscriminating recruitment may have affected the quality of education received by children who went to school in the 1950s.

There is no generally accepted framework within which the reaction of the public sector can be analysed. Various models of the public sector can be examined: (*a*) a bureaucratic machine that has some quasi-firm responses to changing prices or demand pressures, but also stickiness in certain parameters (budgets or various indicators of performance); (*b*) a benevolent maximizer of a perceived social welfare; (*c*) a political entity intent on maximizing support or moved by self-seeking politicians and bureaucrats. For any particular government response, one could find a rationale in more than one view.

Large-scale demographic changes cause large changes in the number of clients the government serves: in schools (in the case of the baby boom), in health services (for the elderly), and so on. Such pressures can be expected to lead to a deterioration of services for a variety of reasons. A quasi-firm argument is based on upward-sloping (and perhaps short-run) inelastic supply curves of the factors used to provide the services. A bureaucratic argument is based on short-term stickiness of budget allocations which would impart an elasticity of -1 to the curve relating expenditure per client to the number of clients. From a static political economy point of view, if rapid pressures sharply increase the marginal cost of satisfying a particular group of supporters, there is an argument for seeking the support of others. A benevolent government, too, would shift the distribution of its efforts in response to changes in relative costs. There are therefore many reasons to expect a short-run downward-sloping curve relating government services per client to the number of clients.

What if the government copes swiftly with certain aspects of crises and shocks with little or no decline in the level of services, that is, has a short-term elastic curve relating expenditures or performance to clients? This may reflect some bureaucratic or public attachment to certain parameters, it may reflect real social priorities of a benevolent government, or it may reflect a political system which has an in-built bias towards handling crises. We can describe the political process in the following terms. Governments seek support, which is presumed to depend on government actions. The support of most people is quite inert in the short run, and unresponsive to government activities in many fields, including thinly spread changes in taxation or the quality of services (see Olson, 1982, and Peltzman, 1976).[3] However, at different times certain topics can become political issues, that is, the way in which the government handles a problem will significantly affect the support it gets. This may be so either because the topic is high on the minds of the public at large, or because a particular group in the population will sway its support based solely on the way a specific issue is resolved. The issues more likely to get government response are those where the group of beneficiaries is well defined while the cost is spread out thinly, because of the inert reaction described above. Obviously, there are advantages to government expenditures that have a public good property and thus satisfy more than one group. Particularly notable is the convergence of interests of clients of services and their suppliers.

Demographic structure and changes fit well into such a framework. For example, the elderly are likely to be highly responsive to how the government treats them because of their relatively high dependence on government support, which should afford them some protection against the adverse effects of their size. Shocks of the sort discussed here are a natural source of issues. By definition, they create problems relating directly or indirectly to well-defined groups in the population. (Often there is also an interested party of government employees.) The problems associated with a rapidly growing group may become an issue over which that group's support could easily sway, depending on government action. This may make the government's short-run 'demand curve' more elastic, that is, it will make an extra effort to minimize the reduction in the services that it provides. In fact, there are indications here that such a mechanism may make the government *overly* responsive to major challenges, under the supposition that politically induced rapid adjustment entails neglect of other, less dramatic issues that the government is supposed to take care of, neglect of less visible aspects of the problem, and so on.

The same rationale carries over to the role of government as an employer. When young men or large numbers of women flood the labour market and the government steps in to employ them, this too is open to interpretation on several levels: (*a*) as the response of a quasi-firm moving along a downward-sloping demand curve for the factors it uses to produce services for the population; (*b*) as the response of a bureaucracy intent on keeping a claim to certain budgetary allocations slanting demand towards unitary elasticity; (*c*) as the political concern of a government with the ramifications of sharp declines in relative incomes or the emergence of unemployment in groups that it is concerned about, providing some kind of employment/income insurance through its functions as an employer. This ties in with our earlier comment on the double-barrelled effect of expenditures that both serve clients and provide government employment. Certainly the most dedicated opponents of cuts in social budgets include social workers, and the staunchest (if not always successful) defenders of budgets for research and higher learning are university professors.

What happens when the tide ebbs? Is there symmetry in the reaction? Or should we expect the level of services to continue to increase after the number of clients has declined (or growth has levelled off)? The quasi-firm argument probably says yes. The initial pressure on specific factors supplying the services may create lagged supply response shifting relative costs in

Table 1.5.　National expenditure on education

| | As percentage of GNP | Share in current expenditure | | | | |
		Total	Kindergarten	Elementary schools	Secondary schools	Post-secondary
1962/63	6.0	100.0	6.4	38.7	25.8	12.9
1964/65	6.7	100.0	6.8	36.3	27.3	13.6
1969/70	7.3	100.0	6.2	32.3	27.0	21.9
1974/75	8.3	100.0	7.3	31.3	26.4	24.2
1979/80	8.8	100.0	8.8	25.6	25.9	23.3

Source: Central Bureau of Statistics, *Statistical Abstract of Israel*, 1982, p. 618.

favour of improvements in areas previously under pressure. Bureaucratic arguments would predict the same: budgets eventually respond to pressures and are certainly downwardly sticky. The political argument works in the same direction: where government employment was rapidly created to meet the growth in demand, the group of suppliers has been strengthened. This asymmetry in the response to rising and falling needs imparts an upward bias to public sector expenditures. The figures on national expenditure on education are consistent with our conjecture (Table 1.5): the shares of the different levels change in response to changing pressures, but this is done by upward pressure on total expenditure, accompanied by an increased share of GNP being allocated to education. Ofer (1983) has shown how the real expenditure per student in elementary and secondary education related to per capita GNP rose from 12.9 per cent in 1962 to 19.3 in 1978. His figures for the post-secondary level show a slight decline in expenditure per student (deflated by GNP per capita) when the system expanded (from 66.0 to 62.7 per cent between 1962 and 1972, respectively), and a sharp increase afterwards (it reached 73.7 per cent in 1978). As we shall see below, the higher education system also reacted swiftly to the increase in its clientele.

In the case of the education system, the employment aspect of an expansion in this system should be discussed in conjunction with the increase in women's labour force participation. The tremendous increase in women's participation, particularly through the 1970s, could be viewed as a quasi-shock in its own right (see Ben-Porath, 1983). But unlike the changes in cohort size, there is some ambiguity in ascribing this shock to purely exogenous causes. One hypothesis is that what we observe is largely a long-term increase in demand that encouraged women's investment in schooling, stimulated their entry into the labour force, and led to associated changes in family planning strategy. Alternatively, one could place the responsibility on various supply-side factors like schooling or people's attitudes. There may also have been some sort of income effect from the direction of young men, which would fit in with the decline in fertility observed in the late 1970s and be consistent with Easterlin's interpretation (1980). Either way, the gestation period of schooling may create excess supply in the short run.

The government certainly played a major role in expanding the opportunities for higher education by financing a large fraction of the growth of that system. More to the point here is its role on the demand side: the public sector is the major employer of women, and it employs a high proportion of those women new to the labour force. This was accomplished partly by the expansion of employment in public services and partly by the substitution of women for men. The public sector had a fairly elastic demand curve and was thus ready to provide employment to the women whom it helped educate. The growth of employment in the public sector occurred at a time when such growth is more naturally interpreted as a response to supply than to demand (see Klinov, 1983).

The school system is an important element here. There has been a strong feminization of the teaching profession, demonstrated by these figures: women's share of teaching posts rose from 52.5 per cent in 1948/9, 58.3 per cent in 1959/60, and 63.7 per cent in 1969/70 to 73.9 per cent in 1981/2. The decline in the student–teacher ratio, noted above, occurred when the student population had stopped growing (in elementary and secondary schools) and while more and more educated women were entering the labour market. These are probably connected. There is no operational difference between the view that the government reacted to the increased supply of women as a quasi-firm, with a fairly elastic demand curve, and the hypothesis that this elastic demand curve was designed to protect the level of employment and relative wages of an important part of the population.

A similar phenomenon occurred in another sphere of demographic change, the increase in the number of the elderly. The rates of growth of old-age support per recipient, provided by Israel's National Insurance Institute, and of the number of recipients, are shown in Table 1.6.

Table 1.6.   Annual rates of growth of old-age support

	Population of recipients	Support per recipient in real terms	Total old-age support
1960–6	10.1	– 1.4	8.5
1966–77	8.4	5.8	14.9
1977–9	3.6	5.2	6.2
1979–82	2.2	12.4	16.6

Source: National Insurance Institute, *Statistical Abstract*, various years.
National Insurance Institute, *Quarterly Statistics*, various issues.

This is, however, a tentative picture and should be studied further. Another case from a different field has to do with defence expenditure. Berglas (1983), who analysed the evolution of defence expenditure in Israel, noted a step function marked by a series of wars. While the increases may have been inevitable, the absence of downward adjustment is part of the same asymmetry.

Entry into Adult Activities

The baby boom of the 1950s had a dramatic effect on the age structure of the adult population in the 1970s. This can be appreciated by comparing the Israeli figures with those describing the American baby boom; these are shown in Table 1.7.

Table 1.7.   Ratio of age group 15–29 to age group 30–64

	1960	1970	1975
Israel	54.5	76.5	85.3
US (Easterlin, 1980)	50.2	66.3	74.0

Adult activities consist of work and higher education, generally following army service.

This section refers mainly to the male population. For some general background on the role of age changes and participation rates consult Appendices 1.2 and 1.3, which show (*a*) that the ratio of employed persons to the population aged over 14 has been on the decline since 1955, but more emphatically so in 1965–75, and (*b*) that this was due to the change that occurred in age structure, mostly in the period 1960–70, and to significant reductions in labour participation in 1965–75. The main trends of the employment history of young men are presented in Table 1.8 and Figure 1.2. The participation rate of the 18–24 age group dropped in three steps: from 1966 to 1967, from 1968 to 1970, and from 1973 to 1974. Over the whole period 1965–75 the drop was from 52.6 to 34.9 per cent, a truly remarkable change for such a short period. The result was that in spite of a 66 per cent increase in the mean population aged 18–24 the number employed rose only moderately from 1965 to 1973, and in 1980 was more or less equal to what it was fifteen years earlier.

The most rapid increase in the size of the 25–9 age group occurred between 1970 and 1975. Our data allow us to observe only the group aged 25–34, where we see a significant decline in participation (4.9 percentage points (p.p.)), more pronounced than before 1970 or after 1975.[4] The annual data show that the decline occurred between 1968 and 1975 (7.8 p.p.). This was against a background of some, but milder, decline in the participation of older men.

Thus the major part of the story of the demographic shock is that entry into the labour market was delayed. The army played an important role

Table 1.8.   Men aged 18–34, population, labour force, and employment (Jewish men)

	1955	1960	1965	1970	1975	1980
1. Levels						
Share in population						
18–34	38.4	35.2	32.9	36.7	39.2	41.0
18–24	—	—	15.5	20.2	19.5	17.0
25–34	—	—	17.4	16.5	19.7	24.0
Share in employment						
18–34	37.8	34.6	31.3	33.3	36.2	39.9
18–24	—	—	10.0	11.3	9.9	8.1
25–34	—	—	21.3	22.0	26.3	31.8
Labour force participation rate						
Total	80.3	78.3	75.5	68.5	64.2	63.5
18–34	79.7	77.7	73.5	63.5	60.4	63.4
18–24	—	—	52.6	41.8	34.9	34.7
25–34	—	—	92.0	90.5	85.6	84.0
Unemployment rate						
Total	6.7	3.5	3.3	3.4	2.4	4.0
18–34	7.3	4.6	5.5	5.3	4.1	6.8
18–24	—	—	10.7	10.9	8.9	16.2
25–34	—	—	2.8	2.1	2.2	4.1
35–54	4.6	2.2	1.2	1.3	1.0	1.9

	1955–60	1960–5	1965–70	1970–5	1975–80
2. Changes					
Percentage growth of population					
Total (14 +)	17.0	24.5	14.6	15.4	9.3
18–34	*7.5*	*16.2*	*28.0*	*23.2*	*14.6*
18–24	—	—	*49.2*	*11.4*	*– 4.4*
18–19	—	—	32.5	0.8	– 5.8
20–4	11.1	20.3	58.1	16.2	– 3.9
25–34	*5.0*	*12.0*	*9.0*	*37.6*	*33.4*
25–9	11.9	11.3	13.5	59.9	16.0
30–4	– 1.6	12.9	4.5	12.9	61.7
Percentage growth of labour force					
Total (14 +)	14.1	14.5	4.0	8.1	8.2
18–34	4.8	6.0	18.2	24.6	23.4
18–24	—	—	18.4	– 7.0	– 4.8
25–34	—	—	6.7	30.8	30.9
Share of age group in net addition to employment					
18–34	16.3	14.9	88.0	67.1	97.4
18–24	—	—	46.7	– 6.1	– 19.1
25–34	—	—	41.3	73.2	116.5

Source: All data are based on Labour Force Surveys except the breakdown for age 20–4 and 25–9, which are from the population estimates, and the data for age 18–19, which are the difference between 18–24 as in the Labour Force Statistics and 20–4 in the population estimates.

here. Military service is compulsory and universal for both men and women (though exemptions are granted, mainly to women, on religious grounds). There is also a career army, and many conscripts sign up for an extended term of duty before going on to work or study. This is clearly a powerful

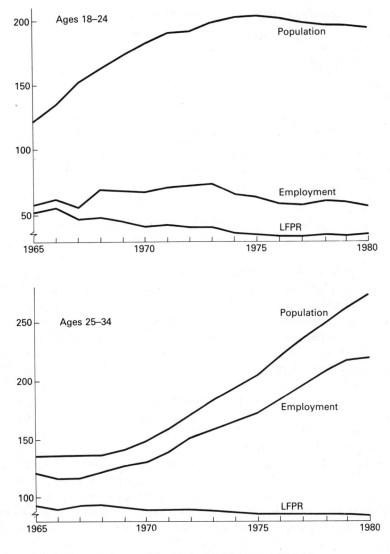

Figure 1.2. Labour force participation, Jewish men, 1965–80

instrument with which the public sector can affect the impact of changing cohort size on the rest of the system. Two of the sharp declines in the partici- pation rate of the 18–24 group coincide with the wars fought in 1967 and 1973, both of which were followed by increase in the size of the army. While we have no reliable estimates, there is a basis for arguing that a significant portion of the delay occurred through army service. Obviously, the shift in demand by the military was autonomous; the ability to satisfy this demand

Table 1.9.   Students and teachers in academic institutions

	1964/5	1969/70	1972/3	1974/5	1977/8–8/9
Percentage of university students in the Jewish population					
Both sexes	3.8	6.3	7.1	7.2	6.8
Men	5.4	7.0	7.9	8.0	7.3
Women	2.8	5.6	6.2	6.3	6.4
All students in academic institutions	18,368	36,246	45,365	51,000	55,360
Academic staff	2,628	5,977	7,681	8,281	9,680
Student–teacher	7.0	6.1	6.5	6.2	5.7

Source: Central Bureau of Statistics, *Statistical Abstracts of Israel*, various years.

was, however, certainly enhanced by the demographic context.

The other obvious route to consider is schooling. The universities grew most rapidly in the late 1960s and early 1970s (in 1965–75 the number of students almost tripled). The share of students in the population aged 20–9 increased sharply from 1964/5 to 1972/3, and declined slightly after 1974/5. For the 20–4 age group, most of the increase in the enrolment rate occurred between 1965 and 1969, while for the age group 25–9 it continued until 1972/3. The expansion was strongly reflected in resource allocation: as already indicated, 12.9 per cent of the national expenditure was allocated to post-secondary and higher education in 1962 and 16.4 per cent in 1965, peaking in 1975 at 25.1 per cent, and then slowly declining (Table 1.5). During the period of highest pressure the ratio of students to academic staff did not deteriorate, and as the number of students stabilized the academic staff increased further (Table 1.9). As in the case of the lower educational levels, the impact was absorbed with an elastic response, and improvement occurred after the pressure subsided, when inputs continued their growth.

It should be noted that the activities described here may not have exhausted the adjustment. There was an increase in emigration after the 1973 war (Lamdany, 1982): it may well be that extended periods of absence from the country before entering the labour market or university served as a buffer.

In the US between 1960 and 1970 the size of the age group 16–19 increased by 44 per cent, and the number of employed increased by 11 per cent; the age group 20–4 increased by 49 per cent and employment by 26 per cent. The educational system absorbed much of the excess, but the armed forces were also a significant factor (see Office of Science and Technology, 1983, pp. 50–1).

Before we explore whether the baby boom had any impact on the labour market, we have to clarify the demographic and economic context in which the change took place.

Immigration

We have already noted the large and fluctuating waves of immigration. In Table 1.10 we break down the sources of growth in the population of Jewish men aged 20-64. We see how the contribution of the young, both Israel-born and foreign-born (lines 4 and 5), to the growth of the adult population rises abruptly between 1965 and 1970, while net immigration falls steeply and the more mature foreign-born grow older. The contribution of the Israel-born to the adult population increases over time and becomes dominant in the 1970s. The foreign-born contribution occurs first through immigration, then the weight shifts to the maturation of the foreign-born young, reaching a peak in 1965-70 when the foreign-born baby boom generation comes in. But at the same time growing numbers exit from the 20-64 category, so that in the 1970s the process of maturation of the foreign-born contributes *negatively* to the growth of the adult population: as net immigration slows down in the late 1970s, the foreign-born reduce rather than increase the adult population, offsetting part of the very high increase in the Israeli-born. The successive five years of growth of the 20-64 age group are less volatile than the rates of change for the total population.

The context of large and changing immigration has broader implications. It means that the system is accustomed to shocks, that the public sector has

Table 1.10. Sources of growth of the population aged 20-64 (Jewish men)

	1950-5	1955-60	1960-5	1965-70	1970-5	1975-80
1. Total change in per cent: All	39.2	20.8	20.1	10.9	15.2	10.6
2. Total change in per cent: 20-64	28.5	15.9	16.0	13.0	16.4	9.6
3. Total change	100.0	100.0	100.0	100.0	100.0	100.0
4. Israel-born	13.3	31.6	32.0	59.2	87.0	130.4
5. Foreign-born: maturing in	35.0	52.8	51.9	96.9	37.0	43.7
6. Foreign-born: maturing out	− 12.6	− 29.6	− 38.0	− 56.6	− 51.6	− 82.9
7. Net maturing	22.4	23.2	13.9	40.3	− 14.6	− 39.1
8. Net migration and mortality	64.3	45.2	54.0	0.5	27.5	8.7

Line (4): Change in the Israeli-born age 20-64.
   (5): Foreign-born aged 15-19 at the beginning of each period.
   (6): Foreign-born aged 60-4 at the end of each period.
   (7): (5) − (6).
   (8): 100.0 − (4) − (7).

always had to alter rapidly the level of services that it provides, and that the way it copes with the variety of social issues raised by immigration is a primary criterion by which it is judged.

Women

In assessing the impact on the labour force of the entry of larger cohorts of young persons it is important to note that at the same time there has been a change in women's employment.

As in many other countries, the period under review was one of significant increase in the labour force participation of women. When we examine men alone, the share of men aged 18–34 in the change of all employed men rises sharply after 1965, from approximately 16 per cent to between 66 and 100 per cent (Table 1.11 line 1). For both sexes the change is quite sharp (line 3) after 1965, but more moderate than for men alone because in the case of women there was significant increase in the number of women aged 25–44. Because of the jump from one-third to two-thirds in the share of women in the increase in employment after 1965 (line 5), the contribution of young men to the change in overall employment rises much more moderately than their contribution to the rise in *men's* employment (line 6). We see in Table 1.11 that while all women and young men contributed less than half of the net increase in the change in employment before 1965, they contributed 85–100 per cent of the change in 1965–80. At the same time the proportion of men aged 35–54 in employment declined.

Whether the influx of women aggravated or alleviated the position of young men depends on whether they were substitutes or complements in the labour force. Do young men compete with young women? With all women? The ratios of young men to young women and to all women declined

Table 1.11.   Men and women in the growth of employment

		1955–60	1960–5	1965–70	1970–5	1975–80	
1.	$\dfrac{\Delta YM}{\Delta EM}$	16.3	14.8	87.9	67.3	97.4	
2.	$\dfrac{\Delta YF}{\Delta EF}$	33.4	53.0	54.5	61.8	53.7	
3.	$\dfrac{\Delta Y(M+F)}{\Delta E(M+F)}$	22.0	29.0	66.5	64.0	68.8	
4.	$\dfrac{\Delta YF}{\Delta Y(M+F)}$	52.0	68.0	53.6	56.4	51.0	
5.	$\dfrac{\Delta EF}{\Delta E(F+M)}$	34.5	37.7	64.9	58.5	65.3	
6.	$\dfrac{\Delta YM}{\Delta E(F+M)}$	10.6	9.2	30.8	27.9	33.7	
7.	$\dfrac{AM}{E(M+F)}$	$\dfrac{1955}{33.9}$	$\dfrac{1960}{33.8}$	$\dfrac{1965}{30.1}$	$\dfrac{1970}{27.3}$	$\dfrac{1975}{26.2}$	$\dfrac{1980}{23.1}$

M—Male, F—Female, Y—18–34, A—35–54, E—Employed.

dramatically through the 1970s while the relative hourly earnings of young men and young women did not change. As the difference in schooling between men and women both aged 25–34 in the labour force did not change from 1970 to 1980, a high degree of substitution is suggested.[5]

Arabs from the Occupied Territories

A direct consequence of the 1967 war was the occupation of the West Bank and the Gaza Strip, and the entry of Arab labour from these territories into the Israeli labour market, increasing the supply of unskilled, manual labour. Again, this effect could go either way: the obvious substitution with unskilled domestic labour, or a complementary effect opening opportunities for low-level supervisory and middle-men positions for Jews. Amir (1981), who studied the changing returns to education, tends to argue that the effect was positive, that the unskilled Arab labour improved the opportunities among Jews for domestic low- and medium-schooling labour.

The Macroeconomic Picture

Israel experienced a continuous period of rapid economic growth until 1965. This was interrupted by a deep recession in 1965–7, with considerable unemployment. The young were hit particularly hard: the rate of unemployment of men aged 18–24 rose from 10.7 per cent in 1965 to 22.5 in 1967, and for men aged 25–34 from 2.8 to 7.8 per cent; the rate for men aged 45–54 rose from 1.1 to 4.9 per cent. The combination of continued slump and influx into the labour force of the young workers could have been disastrous. But following the 1967 war the country experienced a resumption of rapid growth until 1973. This created an environment that certainly eased the entry of new young cohorts into the labour force. Following the 1973 war and the energy crisis Israel was gripped by stagflation, which led to rising rates of unemployment towards the end of the decade. The deterioration in the relative position of the young in the late 1970s might reflect this change.

Wages and Employment

When we examine the impact on the labour market of a sudden change in cohort size our main concern is with the elasticities of substitution which reflect the uniqueness of particular types of labour. At the same time, unemployment rates are also of interest, particularly for the identification of short-term difficulties (see Freeman, 1979; Wachter, 1976; and Welch, 1979, 1983). In addition, some groups tend to be more sensitive than others to cyclical variations.

The delay in the entry of people aged 20–4 into the labour force was important enough in itself, but it also made an impact on the age

Table 1.12. Young and old wage-earners[a] relative to age group 35–64

	Annual earnings			Number of wage-earners		
	1970	Turning-point	1981	1970	Turning-point	1981
Men 18–24	0.59	—	0.39	0.20	*1972* 0.22	0.17
25–34	0.90	*1972* 0.95	0.86	0.42	*1980* 0.67	0.61
65 +	0.57	*1972* 0.64	0.48	0.06	*1978* 0.09	0.08
Women 18–24	0.67	*1975* 0.75	0.62	0.84	—	0.39
25–34	1.03	*1971* 1.09	1.06	0.47	*1979* 0.83	0.78
65 +	0.79	*1974* 0.96	0.56	0.02	—	0.02

[a] The data refer to all wage-earners, Jews and Arabs. These are ratios where the denominator refers to the age group 35–64.
Source: Central Bureau of Statistics, *Survey of Income*, 1981, Table 16.

composition of the labour force when these people did eventually enter it. In Table 1.8, part I, we can see that from 1965 to 1970 the share of those aged 20–4 in the population increased by 4.7 percentage points, while their share in employment rose by only 1.3 p.p. In 1970–80, however, the change in the population share of the 25–34 age group was 7.5 p.p., and among the employed it was 9.8 p.p.

As is well demonstrated in Table 1.12, the relative earnings of young men declined sharply during the 1970s. The relative earnings of men aged 25–34 and women aged 18–24 declined more moderately. The relative earnings of older people declined too (sharply for women). The relative number of men aged 18–24 did not increase and the relative number of young women actually declined sharply. It is the 25–34 group and older men whose numbers increased sharply during this period, which probably affected the relative earnings of young men.

Obviously, we have a change in the profile of earnings. This has been confirmed in a comparative cross-section study by Amir (1983), who estimated earnings functions for 1970–2 and 1978–80 within education categories and showed that the positive linear coefficient on experience and negative coefficient on experience squared both increased in absolute terms. The question is what caused that change, and, specifically, whether it is related to the change in the size of the age groups.

The series of regression equations presented in Table 1.13 reveal the following information.

First, the relative earnings of young cohorts are adversely affected by increases in the general level of unemployment (represented by the rate of unemployment of men aged 35–54).

Table 1.13.   Equation of relative earnings of young men, 1970–82

Independent	Age						
	18–24				25–34		
	(1)	(2)	(3)	(4)[c]	(5)	(6)	(7)
Rate of unemployment of men 35–54	−0.078 4.2	−0.089 4.3	−0.079 4.3	−0.078 4.2	−0.039 3.1	−0.042 3.7	−0.039 3.2
Relative size:[a] 18–34 M + F	−0.465 3.5				−0.138 1.5		
65 + M + F		−3.211 2.8				−1.413 2.2	
(18–34) + (65 +) M + F			−0.422 3.5	−0.457 3.7			−0.132 1.6
$\bar{R}^2$	0.74	0.67	0.75		0.51	0.59	0.52

Independent	18–24				25–34		
	(8)	(9)	(10)	(11)[d]	(12)	(13)	(14)
Rate of unemployment of men 35–54	−0.069 3.1	−0.083 4.2	−0.055 3.4	−0.046 2.3	−0.036 2.6	−0.039 3.4	−0.032 2.4
Relative size:[b] 18–34 M	−0.365 2.7			−0.522 4.0	−0.111 1.3		
65 + M		−2.164 2.8				−0.872 2.1	
Relative size:[b] 18–34 F			−0.416 4.9				−0.124 1.8
65 + F							
$\bar{R}^2$	0.67	0.71	0.83	0.78	0.48	0.58	0.54

[a] The ratio between size of the group of employed persons to the age group 35–64.
[b] The denominator in this regression is the number of *men* aged 35–64.
[c] Identical to (3) with an instrumental variable ratio of the age groups in the labour force.
[d] Identical to (8) with the ratio in the labour force rather than employment.

Second, young men's relative earnings are adversely affected by increases in their own share of total employment as well as by the increases in the share of other groups—young women and older men and women. This indicates a fair amount of substitution between these groups. Welch (1983), studying US data, also found that the relative wages of the young react to the proportion of the old. Indeed, fairly good results are obtained when we run relative wages on the proportion of young people of both sexes, and also the proportion in employment of the elderly (65 +) of both sexes. It is hard to separate out the effect of different demographic groups when the variables appear simultaneously, but when they appear separately the reaction of the young men's relative earnings to changes in the proportion of young women or older men are certainly no smaller than to their own numbers.

Third, the age group 18–24 responds adversely to the size of the *whole* group aged 18–34 rather than to its own size.

Fourth, the response of relative earnings of men aged 25–34 to changes in their share in employment is somewhat weaker than that of the 18–34 age group.

Similar results have been obtained when the dependent variable is hourly rather than annual earnings and where instead of the ratios of the age groups in employment we used as independent variables their ratios in the labour force and (alternatively) in the population both as independent variables and as instrumental variables (see regressions no. 4 and no. 11 in Table 1.13).

The age group 18–24 seems to have suffered in relative terms not when it was at its peak size but at the end of the decade, when it was smaller and when the whole 18–34 group was at peak size. This means that the vanguard of the larger cohort (aged 18–24 in the beginning of the 1970s), most of whom were in the 25–34 category in 1980, suffered much less than the following (somewhat smaller) class that found the entry positions in the labour market crowded with the very large 25–34 cohort.

The data for the labour force extend over longer periods. For the period 1955–80 there is a significant negative correlation between the employment rate of persons aged 18–34 (the ratio of employed to population) and the share of that age group in the population. For the period 1965–80 we can distinguish between age groups 18–24 and 25–34, finding large negative correlations for the latter. For the period 1965–80 we find that the rate of unemployment of the 25–34 age group (relative to age 35–54) is positively correlated with its share in the population and in the labour force, and negatively related to its rate of labour force participation. Several regressions show that the unemployment of the young rises more in absolute terms and less in relative terms than the rate of unemployment of men aged 35–54. In different variations it is also positively associated with the relative weight of the young (18–34) and of the old (65 +) in the labour force (Table 1.14).

In principle, the change in the age structure could have affected demand.

Table 1.14. Rate of unemployment of young men,[a] 1965–82

	Age group			
	18–24		25–34	
Constant	1.620	1.650	–0.060	–0.097
	7.53	6.8	0.2	0.3
Rate of employment of men 35–54	0.598	0.602	0.838	0.847
	11.0	10.4	10.5	10.5
Ratio in labour force of men: $\frac{18-34}{35-64}$	0.0090		0.012	
	2.9		2.6	
$\frac{65+}{35-64}$		0.0574		0.083
		2.5		2.6
DW	1.564	1.436	1.211	1.480
$\bar{R}^2$	0.877	0.863	0.866	0.864

[a] The dependent variable is the logarithm of the rate of unemployment.

Some indication of this is seen in the regressions where the proportion of the population aged 20–9 has a significant effect on investment in dwelling.[6] But it is quite clear that the net effect is supply effect.

Conclusions

The entry of large cohorts into the labour market affected both relative wages and unemployment. What merits attention is the larger role that the government played in meeting the baby boom. This was demonstrated here by following the evolution of the school system as it coped with the uneven arrival of students at different levels. The entry of the large cohorts into the labour market was delayed because of the expansion of the army, another silent role of government. We presented some tentative ideas on what could explain the behaviour of the public sector, suggesting that governments may be keen on responding quickly to big shocks but are unable to adjust downward once the pressure subsides. Whatever the correct model, it is important to unravel the role of the public sector and to pay more attention to its behaviour.

Endnotes

1. CBS, *Statistical Abstract of Israel*, 1982, p. 95.
2. The 1950 figures for EA are: age 0–4, 27,400; age 5–9, 11,242; age 10–14, 18,095; age 15–19, 35,856; age 20–4, 51,124. The 0–4 category does not include children born to EA women after immigration. While the figures are also affected by the selectivity of immigrants by age and family status, the large 0–4 group relative to the 5–9 group most likely reflects the effect of the war.
3. The inertia may be a result of the infra-marginal commitment because of ideology or interests, or it may reflect lack of information and care. See Olson (1982).
4. Within the 25–34 age group the weight of those 25–9 changed in the following manner: 1965—51.0; 1970—53.0; 1975—61.7; 1980—53.7. The change in weights by itself could account

for participation rates for the whole group (92.0, 91.7, 90.8, 91.7) for the corresponding years (assuming that the LFPR of men aged 30–4 was 97 in 1965, and for men aged 25–9 was 87). The sharp decline observed in 1970–5 is thus not just a matter of weighting.

5. The expected hourly earnings using the earnings of men by schooling in 1980 were (only the ratio matters):

	Men		Women				
	25–34 (1)	35–54 (2)	25–34 (3)	45–54 (4)	All women (5)	$\frac{1}{3}$ (6)	$\frac{1}{5}$ (7)
1970	11.6	11.0	12.3	11.0	11.5	0.94	1.0
1980	12.7	11.7	13.3	11.6	12.5	0.95	1.0

6. The dependent variable (DWELINV) is the ratio of gross investment in dwelling to the capital stock in dwelling, for the period 1951–82.

$$\begin{aligned} DWELINV = &-2.6 + 0.22 \ RGNPPC + 0.69 \ IMMIG - 0.58 \ EMIG \\ &(1.3) \quad (5.2) \qquad\qquad (2.9) \qquad\qquad (1.3) \\ &+ 0.215 \ AGE(20-9) + 0.68 \ DWELINV(t-1) \\ &\ (2.0) \qquad\qquad\quad (9.4) \end{aligned}$$

$$\bar{R}^2 = 0.856$$

RGNPPC: rate of growth of per capita GNP.
IMMIG: ratio of immigrants to Jewish population.
EMIG: ratio of 'emigrants' to Jewish population; 'emigrants' is the difference between immigrants and the net migration balance.
AGE 20–9: share of their age group in the population.

Appendix 1.1.   Mean Jewish population, 1950–80

	1950	1955	1960	1965	1970	1975	1980
(Men)							
Total	567,482	789,705	954,264	1,146,175	1,270,745	1,464,236	1,619,484
0–4	76,075	110,231	112,270	123,305	138,627	171,783	185,257
5–9	47,487	96,080	119,924	124,892	125,707	144,564	175,091
10–14	44,936	62,738	109,509	133,164	128,288	132,101	147,085
15–19	47,508	60,059	71,166	123,243	137,181	138,139	134,934
20–4	48,202	59,544	66,135	79,567	125,838	146,196	140,494
25–9	53,515	56,148	62,836	69,937	79,415	126,962	147,255
30–4	41,043	59,849	58,916	66,523	69,495	78,500	126,903
35–9	50,917	46,452	63,943	63,214	66,477	73,648	78,243
40–4	46,830	57,350	51,050	69,320	63,524	72,116	74,052
45–9	35,784	53,427	61,733	55,399	69,726	67,984	71,845
50–4	26,237	41,607	56,776	66,456	55,444	72,321	67,133
55–9	17,192	31,802	42,633	60,231	65,228	55,541	70,359
60–4	12,792	21,260	31,530	44,061	57,178	62,790	52,648
65–9	8,289	15,106	20,094	30,540	39,720	53,283	57,674
70–5	5,001	9,159	13,325	18,161	25,405	34,877	45,396
75 +	5,674	8,893	12,424	18,162	23,492	33,431	45,115
(Women)							
Total	535,523	765,606	928,321	1,123,634	1,256,941	1,466,979	1,629,915
0–4	71,631	104,243	105,946	116,838	131,692	163,138	175,108
5–9	44,802	90,102	113,634	118,006	119,142	137,536	166,466
10–14	42,489	58,985	102,126	126,091	121,569	125,023	140,062
15–19	44,623	56,662	66,680	114,472	130,227	130,812	127,961

Appendix 1.1. Continued

	1950	1955	1960	1965	1970	1975	1980
20–4	48,660	59,214	63,691	75,463	119,337	141,877	135,881
25–9	48,985	59,760	64,570	70,072	77,496	125,819	144,371
30–4	40,282	58,424	64,707	70,174	71,178	79,277	126,995
35–9	50,635	47,231	64,431	70,960	71,231	76,367	79,677
40–4	40,231	58,615	52,051	71,827	72,297	76,569	77,261
45–9	29,803	47,657	62,311	57,214	73,377	77,409	76,861
50–4	22,743	37,206	50,343	67,432	57,851	77,311	77,834
55–9	15,097	29,601	38,292	54,042	67,138	59,282	77,506
60–4	13,522	19,832	30,196	40,538	52,675	68,317	58,487
65–9	9,466	16,335	19,363	30,425	38,167	53,155	65,297
70–5	6,370	10,695	14,674	18,495	26,517	36,220	47,764
75 +	6,184	11,044	15,306	21,585	26,537	38,869	52,384

Appendix 1.2. Percentage growth of population and employment, 1955–80 (Jewish) contribution of changes in age structure, labour force participation, and unemployment rate

	1955–60	1960–5	1965–70	1970–5	1975–80
	Men				
Increase in:					
1. Population aged 14 +	17.03	24.53	14.63	15.43	9.28
2. Employment	18.04	20.04	3.89	9.20	6.41
Difference (2) – (1)	1.01	– 4.49	– 10.74	– 6.23	– 2.87
(a) Age structure	– 0.74	– 5.05	– 3.72	0.70	1.63
(b) Labour force participation rate	– 2.12	0.42	– 7.30	– 7.72	– 2.63
(c) Unemployment rate	3.91	0.19	– 0.14	0.62	– 1.85
Interaction between:					
(b) and (c)	0.05	0.34	– 0.11	0.19	– 0.04
(a), (b), (c)	– 0.09	– 0.39	– 0.42	– 0.02	– 0.02
	Women				
Increase in:					
1. Population aged 14 +	16.19	26.89	15.43	17.76	10.29
2. Employment	28.24	33.75	17.70	28.06	22.38
Difference (2) – (1)	12.05	6.86	2.27	10.30	12.09
(a) Age structure	– 1.39	– 4.87	0.95	0.55	0.01
(b) Labour force participation rate	10.13	9.98	1.52	11.18	15.23
(c) Unemployment rate	3.44	1.32	– 0.68	– 0.45	– 2.68
Interaction between:					
(b) and (c)	– 0.24	– 0.11	– 0.02	0.31	0.14
(a), (b), (c)	– 0.13	0.43	0.48	– 0.98	– 0.47

Appendix 1.3.   Rates of labour force participation by age and sex, 1955–80 (Jews)

	1955	1960	1965	1970	1975	1980	1955–60	1960–5	1965–70	1970–5	1975–80
Men (all)	80.3	78.3	75.5	68.5	64.2	63.5	−2.0	−2.8	−7.0	−4.3	−0.7
14–17	39.4	28.8	35.8	25.9	15.9	12.9	−10.6	7.0	−9.9	−10.0	−3.0
18–34	79.7	77.7	73.4	63.5	60.4	63.4	−2.0	−4.3	−9.9	−3.1	3.0
18–24			52.6	41.8	34.9	34.7			−10.8	−6.9	−0.2
25–34			92.0	90.1	85.6	84.0			−1.9	−4.5	−1.6
35–54	96.8	96.9	96.7	95.1	93.3	91.3	0.1	−0.2	−1.6	−1.8	−2.0
35–44			96.8	94.8	93.8	91.3			−2.0	−1.0	−2.5
45–54			96.6	95.4	92.9	91.4			−1.2	−2.5	−1.5
55–64	83.6	85.8	92.0	89.4	85.6	84.0	2.2	6.2	−2.6	−3.8	−1.6
65+	39.2	38.2	41.7	35.0	30.3	29.1	−1.0	3.5	−6.7	−4.7	−1.2
Women (all)	27.9	29.5	31.3	32.0	34.7	39.2	1.6	1.8	1.7	2.7	4.5
14–17	34.3	23.4	28.1	20.1	12.5	12.3	−10.9	4.7	−8.0	−7.6	−0.2
18–34	34.0	36.4	41.1	43.4	47.0	52.1	2.4	4.7	2.3	3.6	5.1
18–24			48.9	48.7	44.7	44.2			−0.2	−4.0	−0.5
25–34			34.7	37.3	49.3	57.6			2.6	12.0	8.3
35–54	27.4	31.7	32.5	35.7	42.3	51.3	4.3	0.8	3.2	6.7	9.0
35–44			31.9	35.4	45.1	56.9			3.5	4.7	11.8
45–54			33.2	36.0	40.0	45.8			2.8	4.0	5.8
55–64	17.9	19.7	23.9	23.4	23.6	27.6	1.8	4.2	−0.5	0.2	4.0
65+	5.3	8.1	6.3	5.5	6.4	7.0	2.8	−1.8	−0.8	0.9	0.6

Sources to Tables
  Central Bureau of Statistics, *Labor Force Surveys*.
    1955–61, Special Series 162; Jerusalem 1964, p. 7, Table 4.
    1963, Special Series 176; Jerusalem 1965, p. 7, Table 4.
    1964–6, Special Series 243; Jerusalem 1968, p. 12, Table 5.
    1965–72, unpublished data received from the CBS.
    1976, Special Series 564; Jerusalem 1978, p. 6, Table 3.
    1976, Special Series 564; Jerusalem 1978, p. 8, Table 2.
    1977, Special Series 611; Jerusalem 1979, p. 6, Table 3.
    1978, Special Series 653; Jerusalem 1981, p. 82, Table 3.
  1980: Central Bureau of Statistics, *Monthly Bulletin of Statistics*, supplement; Jerusalem, April 1981, pp. 66–7, Table 4.
  Population Figures: Statistical Abstracts and Files of the Central Bureau of Statistics.

References

Amir, Shmuel (1981), 'Changes in the Wage Function for Israeli Jewish Male Employees Between 1968/9 and 1975/6', *Bank of Israel Economic Review*, 52, Jerusalem.

—— (1983), 'Educational Structure and Wage Differentials of the Israeli Labor Force in the 1970s', Discussion Paper 83.11, Falk Institute for Economic Research in Israel, Jerusalem.

Ben-Moshe, Eliahu (1984), 'Marriage Squeeze and Marriage Patterns: The Case of Israel', unpublished manuscript.

Ben-Porath, Yoram (1980), 'Fertility and Child Mortality: Issues in the Demographic Transition of a Migrant Population' in R.A. Easterlin (ed.), *Population and Economic Change in Less Developed Countries*, University of Chicago Press for NBER.

—— (1983), 'Ms Jewish Mother Goes to Work: Trends in the Labor Force Participation of Women in Israel, 1955-1980', paper presented at a conference on Women's Work, Sussex, England.

Berglas, Eitan (1983), 'Defense and the Economy: The Israeli Experience', Discussion Paper 83.01, The Maurice Falk Institute for Economic Research in Israel, Jerusalem.

CBS, *Statistical Abstract of Israel*, various years.

Easterlin, R.A. (1978), 'What Will 1984 be Like? Socioeconomic Implications of Recent Twists in Age Structure', *Demography*, 15, 4 (November), 397-432.

—— (1980), *Birth and Fortune: The Impact of Numbers on Personal Welfare*, Basic Books, Inc., New York.

Freeman, Richard B. (1979), 'The Effect of Demographic Factors on Age-Earnings Profiles in the US', *Journal of Human Resources*, 14, 3, 289-318.

Friedlander, Dov (1975), 'Mass Immigration and Population Dynamics in Israel', *Demography*, 12, 4 (November), 581-99.

Jones, Landon Y. (1980), *Great Expectations, America and the Baby Boom*, Coward, McCann, & Geoghegan, New York.

Klinov, Ruth (1983), 'The Industrial Structure of Output and Employment in Israel, 1950-1980', mimeograph, Falk Institute, Jerusalem.

Kop, Yaacov (1980), 'Changes in the Age Structure and their Application for the Demand for Public Services', Discussion Paper D-6480, Brookdale Institution, Jerusalem.

Lamdany, Ruben (1982), 'Emigration from Israel', Discussion Paper 82.08, Falk Institute for Economic Research in Israel, Jerusalem.

Ofer, Gus (1983), 'The Civilian Public Expenditure in Israel', Discussion Paper 83.12, Falk Institute for Economic Research in Israel, Jerusalem.

Office of Science and Technology, Executive Office of the President (1983), *Youth: Transition to Adulthood*, report of the Panel on Youth of the President's Science Advisory Committee.

Olson, Mancur (1982), *The Rise and Decline of Nations*, Yale University Press, New York and London.

Peltzman, Sam (1976), 'Toward a More General Theory of Regulation', *Journal of Law and Economics*, 19 (August), 211-40.

Russell, Louise B. (1982), 'The Baby Boom Generation and the Economy', The Brooking Institute, Washington DC.

Wachter, Michael L. (1976), 'The Changing Cyclical Responsiveness of Wage Inflation', Brookings Papers on Economic Activity 1: 1976, pp. 115–59.

Welch, Finis (1979), 'Effects of Cohort Size on Earnings: The Baby Boom Babies' Financial Bust', *Journal of Political Economy*, Vol. 87, No. 5, part 2, (October), pp. S65–S97.

2 Cohort Size and Earnings in the USA

KEVIN MURPHY, MARK PLANT, AND FINIS WELCH

Baby boom figures are dramatic. There were 4.3 million babies born in the United States during the peak year, 1957. Eighteen years earlier, in 1939, there were 2.4 million births and eighteen years later, in 1975, there were 3.1 million. This later figure, 14.6 births per thousand of population, is a twentieth-century low. These familiar trends are plotted in Figure 2.1.

With appropriate lags as the baby boomers reached the age of work entry, labour markets have absorbed shocks in the age composition of workers that offer unusual opportunities for monitoring responses to rapid change. We

Figure 2.1.

This research was generously supported by the National Institute of Education. The authors would like to thank members of the UCLA Labor Economics Workshop for helpful suggestions. All errors are our responsibility.

have seen the US labour force first grow rapidly younger and then begin gradually to age as the crest of the baby boom passed and the number of new entrants reflected the gradual decline in numbers of births that followed the 1957 peak.

There is a natural curiosity about effects of change in the age composition of workers on the earnings capacity of people of different ages. First consider a population in a dynamic equilibrium where the age structure of the work-force is fixed. Presumably there is an associated profile showing average wage rates of people of different ages. Now change the age distribution of workers and observe the responding change in the wage profile. One suspects that if the fraction of workers of a given age rises, the wages of persons who are that age will fall. Wages of those in adjacent age intervals will probably also fall, but that is about as far as our simple intuition takes us. We do not know how far the wage waves spread or whether and where reversals occur. We don't know whether cohort size effects for young people are larger or smaller than for older workers. Also, when workers are partitioned into skill or education groups we don't know whether and how cohort size effects are related to skill levels. We also don't know how changes in the ages of workers at one level of education affect wage profiles at another.

All students of income patterns are aware that earnings capabilities have a life cycle of their own. New entrants typically start their careers earning less than they will at any time in the future. Thereafter, earnings rise, relatively smoothly, for thirty years or so. At the peak, earnings are almost twice as high as at entry. In comparison to the gains realized before the peak, the subsequent decay is not great. Workers approaching retirement earn 5 to 10 per cent less than those at the peak.

This is the pattern one sees in cross-sectional data when earnings are arrayed by age of workers. During periods of sustained growth, this cross-sectional pattern may not be reflected for any specific cohort. Begin with the typical cross-sectional profile and think of growth as shifting the profile upward each year. A cohort's life cycle of earnings can be traced by allowing one year's shift for each additional year of age. Given this, it would not be surprising, in periods of sustained growth, if retiring workers were earning more than at any time in their past. But, even in such periods, the cross-sectional profiles are as described.

These profiles are not the same for all groups. For example, one finds for college graduates that the peak is higher relative to the extremes than is true for those with less education.

The age composition effects that we questioned refer to the way the typical profiles bend or twist as the underlying age composition of workers changes. For example, during the early 1970s, as the baby boomers first entered the labour market, we found that new-entrant wages fell relative to those of peak earners. This observation of diminishing returns was hardly surprising, although quantification of the sensitivity of earnings to cohort size continues to absorb analysts.

One of the central questions concerns the life cycle of wage-depressing effects that large cohorts experience. The early work on this subject gave conflicting results. One of us, Finis Welch (1979*a*), argued that, like rocks tossed into ponds, the wage waves made by large entering cohorts are greatest at entry and that what begins as a wave becomes a ripple as the cohort is absorbed into its career. Mark Berger (1984), however, reports a contrary finding, which is consistent with results reported by Richard Freeman (1976, 1979).

The early work is based on shorter observational periods than are now available and each study of the life cycle of effects is an extrapolation based on the common observation that new-entrant wages dropped when the baby boom crest hit the labour market. Each study invokes arbitrary assumptions about the way the size of a cohort is to be measured; the fact that their predictions disagree testifies to what is too often the case, namely, that estimation results are driven too much by procedures used and too little by the data.

Our purpose here is to present results for a longer period, from 1967 to 1982, which is none the less so brief relative to job market careers that inferences must be viewed as speculative. The estimates are based on a new procedure which, superficially at least, imposes weaker constraints on estimation than is true of earlier work.

In the next section, we describe the underlying data and present summaries showing patterns of change, both in earnings and in the age of the work-force. We then outline the methods used for estimation. Results including simulations of life cycles of effects follow. The main conclusion supports Welch's earlier conjecture that cohort size effects on full career earnings are not particularly large and are considerably smaller than effects for new entrants. The final section summarizes what has preceded it.

The Data and the Empirical Setting

We used data from the March Annual Demographic Survey of the *Current Population Surveys* (CPS), 1968 to 1983, and restricted observations to white male civilians between 14 and 65 years old who were in the labour force and not in education. A major shortcoming is that women and male members of minority groups were excluded. The reason for excluding women was largely that we organized the data around estimates of years of labour market experience and CPS did not have enough information about work histories to permit useful inferences. Further, since 1964 employers in the US have faced constraints associated with affirmative action (or non-discrimination), which appear to have affected earnings patterns for women and minority men. A full treatment of these effects exceeded our purpose here and we opted for the simple expedient of excluding them.

The CPS is a survey of between 50,000 and 70,000 households and our annual samples of white men working for wages each contain more than 30,000 observations. To simplify the data-processing chore we worked with average wages and population counts where observations are grouped into work experience, school completion cells.[1] We worked with 40 single-year experience levels, four educational groups (8–11 grades completed, high school graduates, 1–3 years of college, and college graduates), for 16 years. This gave 2,560 aggregated observations.

The CPS surveys ask about labour market experiences during the previous calendar year, so our observations refer to the period 1967–82. The change in the age distribution of the male labour force in this period was remarkable. As the workers who were born in the baby boom began their working careers the labour force took on a much younger complexion. Table 2.1 illustrates the changing age distribution of the work-force by giving the percentage of men who are in their first five years of work experience since leaving school. Although we only reported four-year averages, the sixteen-year period begins with 14.5 per cent of all men in the labour force being in their first five years out of school. We arbitrarily restricted the work-force to the first 40 years of experience, and therefore the percentage in their first five years begins only slightly higher than the 12.5 per cent one would expect with the same number of entrants every year and zero mortality. By 1976, 22.6 per cent of the labour force was in this low-experience group. Thus in only nine years the share of the youth cohort grew by more than half. After this crest of the baby boom, the percentage of young workers began to decline so that by 1982 only 19.7 per cent of white male workers were in their first five years in the labour force. Relative to the stationary state, the 1982 labour force was still very young.

Because the baby boom cohorts had higher educational levels than preceding entrants, the pattern for college graduates is even more pronounced. Table 2.1 shows the four-year averages for college graduates in the third column. In 1967, 19.3 per cent of male college graduates were in their first five years in the labour force, and by 1975 this percentage had grown to 25.3 per cent, more than double the stationary state prediction. After this peak the percentage began to fall, reaching 17.9 per cent by 1982. For high school

Table 2.1. Percentage of men in the labour force who are in their first five years out of school

	All	High school graduates	College graduates
1967–70	15.8	16.2	20.7
1971–4	20.6	20.7	23.9
1975–8	22.2	23.1	23.5
1979–82	20.7	22.8	19.0

Table 2.2.   Average weekly wages of men in their first five years since leaving school as a percentage of wages for men in their 28th–32nd years

Year	High school graduates	College graduates
1967–71	64.2	61.9
1971–4	57.5	53.7
1975–8	56.7	52.5
1979–82	55.9	55.4

graduates the increased percentage of young workers reached a lower peak and fell off less rapidly as the baby boom exited the labour force.

It would be surprising if the labour market could digest such a large increase in the numbers of new entrants without reducing their average wage. Table 2.2 shows that such a reduction did occur. This table compares the average weekly wage of young workers (1–5 years of experience) to that of older workers (28–32 years of experience). As in Table 1.1, we report four-year averages of the annual figures. As noted in the chapter's introduction, a typical feature of age–earnings profiles is that earnings increase with time out of school for about thirty years until earnings are roughly 60 to 80 per cent higher than for new entrants. After the maximum at thirty years, wages decline gradually until retirement, at which time workers earn 5 to 10 per cent less than at the peak. In the early years of our sample, earnings for college graduates were 62 per cent of those for peak earners. They fell to 52.5 per cent during the 1975–8 period. Thus, compared to prime-age earnings, the earnings of new entrants dropped 15 per cent.[2] In Figure 2.2, we plot the cross-section experience profile of weekly wages for high school and college workers in 1967 and 1977, in constant dollars. These figures further illustrate the change in the wage distribution that occurred as the baby boom entered the labour force. For both education levels, the age earnings profiles became steeper, with younger workers taking a 10 to 15 per cent reduction in wages, and older workers receiving a higher relative wage. This shift in the age profile of earnings is particularly pronounced for college-educated workers.

In working with large samples, one typically observes considerable stability in wage comparisons across age and education groups. Swings such as those summarized in Table 2.2 and illustrated in Figure 2.2 are uncommon, and we suggest that there has been a real shift in the age structure of compensation. We, of course, think that this shift was primarily caused by the rapid increase in the fraction of all workers who are young, and it is the relationship between the age structure of earnings and the age structure of the population that we address. In particular, we wish to develop a theoretical and empirical methodology that will allow us to predict if the decreased relative wages experienced by workers in large cohorts will continue throughout their lives, or whether the life cycle wage effects are concentrated

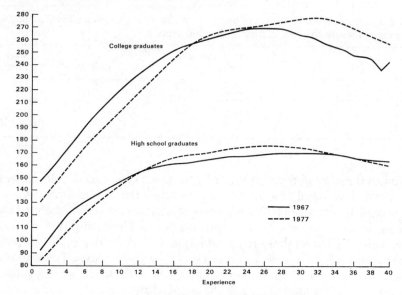

Figure 2.2.   Weekly wages (1967 dollars)

in the early years of the career. We review this methodology in the next section.

Empirical Methodology

The premise on which our empirical work rests is that a worker can be considered as a bundle of attributes or underlying factors of production. Each underlying factor has a well-defined market price determined by ordinary market forces. A worker's wage is the total compensation for these factors. For example, in a two-factor scheme, an individual's wage is the sum of the payments to the two factors, where each payment is the quantity of the factor held by the person times its price.[3] As a worker ages, quantities of some skills increase while others may decrease. Workers of differing education may have different initial bundles and different life cycle patterns as well.

The flexibility of this scheme as a descriptor is easy to see. Take, for example, a two-skill model and consider the life cycle path of two groups of workers. Call the skills A and B and the groups high school and college graduates. Suppose that recent high school graduates have only skill A and that as they mature the quantities of A increase. College graduates start with both A and B and as they age quantities of B increase while quantities of A decline. Thus A is the high school specific factor.

One implication of this simple scheme is that young high school and college graduates are better substitutes for each other than mature workers of the two groups. This, of course, assumes that the underlying skills, A and B, are not themselves perfect substitutes.

To see how a scheme like this can produce the kinds of patterns seen in the data, examine Figure 2.2. In it wages in 1977 are lower than in 1967 for college graduates with less than 18 years of work experience. The profiles cross at 18 years and 1977 wages exceed 1967 wages for older workers. Presumably the prices of A and B (the underlying factors) in a given year are the same for all workers but change between years.

The general upward drift in wages as workers age (for either year) is presumably caused by the dominance of the growth in B over the loss of A. Yet because young college graduates are relatively A-intensive the twist experienced between 1967 and 1977 could have resulted from an increase in the price of B alongside a falling price of A.

Now examine the high school profiles in Figure 2.2. The model just described assumes that high school graduates have only one factor, A, and that the life cycle path refers only to growth in the quantity of that factor. If so, a change in the price of A between 1967 and 1977 would result in a parallel shift in the earnings profile. Thus the crossing pattern observed for high school graduates is inconsistent with the one-factor model.

One alternative to the factor-analytic approach is to treat each level of experience and education as a separate factor of production, but then the implicit production function would have 160 labour inputs for our data set, so this approach is not feasible. Another alternative is to divide workers into age intervals to decrease the number of factors of productions, but such divisions are arbitrary and result in predictions of discontinuous changes in wage profiles.

Returning to the factor structure, suppose that there are M underlying factors, indexed by m, and consider a worker with i years of experience and e years of schooling. Our basic supposition is that this worker's wage is the value of his or her marginal product (VMP) in time t, $y(i, e, t)$, which is a linear combination of the VMPs of each factor. Specifically:

$$y(i, e, t) = \sum_{m=1}^{M} g(i, e, m) \, w(m, t)$$

where $w(m, t)$ denotes the VMP of each factor of production and $g(i, e, m)$ denotes that amount of factor m imbued in a worker with i years of experience and e years of education. Notice that the life cycle compositional path of a worker with education e is characterized by the pattern of weights $g(i, e, m)$, as i goes from 1 to I ($m = 1, \ldots, $ M). The time pattern of wages, holding experience and education constant, is based on the changing VMPs of the basic factors of production. If we array the observed wages of workers with a given level of education by level of experience and time we can then write

$$Y(e) = G(e)W$$

where $Y(e)$ is the $I \times T$ matrix of observed wages, $G(e)$ is the $I \times M$ matrix of factor weights, and W is the $M \times T$ matrix of the VMPs of the underlying factors, each for educational level e. Assuming that the factors underlying each education level are the same, we can stack the system so that

$$\begin{bmatrix} Y(1) \\ Y(2) \\ \cdot \\ \cdot \\ \cdot \\ Y(E) \end{bmatrix} = \begin{bmatrix} G(1) \\ G(2) \\ \cdot \\ \cdot \\ \cdot \\ G(E) \end{bmatrix} W$$

or, more succinctly,

$$Y = GW$$

where Y is the matrix with $(I \times E)$ rows and T columns, G is $(I \times E)$ by M, and the matrix W is M by T. Clearly such a characterization is not unique, since for any $M \times M$ non-singular matrix A we can write

$$Y = (GA^{-1})(AW)$$

or

$$Y = G^*W^*.$$

Given the number of factors, M, we must impose $M \times M$ normalizations on the factor-analytic representation of the wage data. Clearly, if $M = T$ the data can be described perfectly by the factor scheme. For any $M < T$ the fit in an empirical setting will not be perfect. Our stochastic model, then, is

$$Y = GW + U$$

where $M < T$ and U is a matrix of errors. We estimate G and W using weighted least squares.[4] As described elsewhere (see Murphy, Plant and Welch, 1984), we chose to use three factors to characterize our data, since additional factors contributed little to explaining the variance in factor profiles. For our sample T is 16, I is 40, and E is 4, so we explain Y, the 160×16 matrix of wages, by a matrix G of factor quantities which is 160×3 and a matrix W of factor loadings which is 3×16. We can think of an element of G, say $g(i, k)$, as representing the quantity of factor k for an individual in experience/education cell i, and an element of W, say $w(m, t)$, as the VMP of the mth factor in year t.

Let $p(i, t)$ denote the number of men in experience/education cell i in year t. Then $P = (p(i, t))$ is the 160 × 16 matrix that describes the experi-ence/education distribution of the population. Now define

$$X = G'P$$

where X is the M by T (3 × 16) matrix that represents the total quantity of each factor over the T (16) years of the sample.

Presumably the wage structure W will depend on the amount of every factor X. If the factors that we extract from our estimation process are the underpinning economic characteristics of workers then the wage of factor m should decrease when the amount of factor m present increases, *ceteris paribus*. Thus the wages W and the factors X represent a 16-observation data set, with wages being the dependent variables. We regress the wage of each factor on the quantities of all factors. With these regressions in hand we have a means by which we can calculate the effect of changes in the distribution of education and experience on the labour force. Specifically, let the estimated regression structure of factor wages W be

$$\hat{W}' = X'\hat{B}$$

where $\hat{B}$ is the matrix (3 × 3) of regression coefficients. Suppose that in a given hypothetical year the experience/education distribution is charac-terized by a 160 × 1 vector $\bar{p}$. Given $\bar{p}$, we want to know what the wage structure will be. The 3 × 1 vector of factor quantities is $\bar{x} = G'\bar{p}$, and the predicted factor VMPs are $\bar{w}' = \bar{x}\hat{B}$. Given these factor-predicted wages we can compute the wage structure $\bar{y} = G\bar{w}$. The factor decomposition gives us a means of predicting the wage structure across experience/education cells from any distribution of population among those cells. The factor loadings G and the factor wages W are arbitrary since we have chosen M × M normali-zations, but we show in Appendix 2.1 that the predictions $\bar{y}$ are not depen-dent on the normalization chosen. The factor-analytic decomposition has given us a means to characterize the sensitivity of wages to various changes in the composition of the labour force. By choosing appropriate hypothetical distributions, $\bar{p}$, we can isolate the effects of age, education, and business cycle changes on the wage distribution.

The factor decomposition we performed used three factors to explain the 160 × 16 matrix of observed weekly wages. Here we describe the factor loadings and factor weights generated; we present the actual results else-where (Murphy, Plant, and Welch, 1984). Within an educational level, the first factor is shaped like the mean experience–earnings profile, and as education increases the endowment of the factor increases. Alone, the first factor explains 99 per cent of the variation in the observed earnings profiles. If we analysed our data using this one factor, we could only explain variation in experience–earnings profiles as parallel shifts of this profile within education group, and we could not explain any change in the shape of the experience–earnings profiles. The second factor profile is primarily youth-intensive, with a peak between five and ten years of experience and a steady decline until the last few years of the profile, at which time it turns upward. Like the first factor, more highly educated groups have higher endowments, except that the men with between eight and eleven years of schooling have a higher endowment than high school graduates. The third factor profile is hump-shaped, peaking at around twenty years of experience. Young workers have negative endowments of this factor, as do the oldest members of the work-force, and endowments once again increase with increasing education. The second and third factors explain 80 per cent of the residual variance after the first factor is added.

The time pattern of the factor wages is critical in understanding how the factors change the wage profiles. The wage of the first factor increases throughout the period, essentially accounting for the steady upward drift of wages during the sixteen years. The second factor has a positive wage in the early years of the period, but by 1975 the wage is negative. Recall that the second factor is youth-intensive (and old-age-intensive), so that in the early years this factor flattens the wage profile by raising young and very old wages relative to prime-age earners. The third factor, which is prime-age-intensive, exhibits the opposite pattern, its wage being negative in the early years of the sample, positive in the middle years, and then turning negative in the late 1970s as the baby boom enters the middle years of its career. In the last two years of the sample, during the recession of the early 1980s, the youth-intensive factor has a large negative wage and the middle-age-intensive factor has a large positive wage. This indicates that there may indeed be some cyclical sensitivity in these wage patterns.

To explain the factor wage pattern, and to allow prediction of factor wages under various age and education structures of the population, we regressed the factor wages on the factor quantities and on the prime-age male unemployment rate. The dependent variables in the three-equation system of wage equations are estimated factor wages normalized by a constant-quantity price index. The prime-age male unemployment rate was included to pick up any fluctuations in factor wages due to the business cycle. We constrained the wage system so that it was homogeneous of degree zero in factor quantities, and the partial effects of quantities of factors on wages were constrained to be symmetric.

The regression results show that the partial effects of quantities of factors on own wages are large, negative, and significant. The cross effects are all positive (an increase in the number of workers of one factor lowers the wage of other factors, holding all else constant). The only insignificant coefficient is on the third factor in the second wage equation (and vice versa). The prime-age male unemployment rate has a negative and significant effect on the wage of the first factor, an insignificant positive effect on the wage of the second factor, and a significant positive effect on the wage of the third factor. Thus in bad economic times, when the unemployment rate is high, the average wage profile is lowered, but also the teenage-intensive factor (factor two) has a low wage and the middle-age-intensive factor has a high wage. This confirms the notion that teenagers suffer relatively more during recessions than do middle-aged workers. The importance of these regressions is that they allow us to generate a full 160 × 160 substitution matrix. We can compute the partial effect of a change in the quantity of workers of a particular experience and education on the wage of a worker of any other experience and education. We also have implicitly estimated the response of the wages of all 160 types of workers to changes in the prime-age male unemployment rates. Clearly, it is impossible to present all these partial effects in a succinct manner, so we summarize the implications of these results using simulations.

Simulation Results

The factor-analytic techniques reported here allow us to simulate wage profiles generated by any distribution of education and experience in the labour force. In particular, we can isolate effects of changes in the age structure of the work-force from those changes due to changing education or business cycle effects. In the simulations we present here, we hold the education distribution at its mean across the period 1967–82 and the prime-age male unemployment rate at its mean of 2.9 per cent.

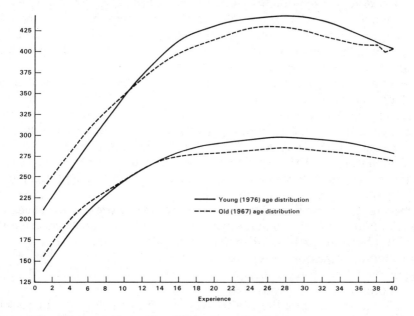

Figure 2.3.   Wage profiles under different age distributions

Figure 2.3 isolates the effects of a change in the age distribution on the cross-sectional wage profiles and relative wage profiles. In it we present the cross-sectional wage profiles for high school graduates and college graduates using the mean distribution of education under two age distributions: the 1967 age distribution and the 1976 age distribution. We held population constant at its mean for 1967–82. Note that in times when there are a large number of mature workers (1967), young workers do relatively better, and that mature workers do relatively better when they are more scarce. This complementarity between older and younger workers seems to lessen as workers enter the last five years of their careers. The substitutability between very young workers and very old workers is evident from the factor patterns described in the previous section.

The effect illustrated here—that an increase in the relative amount of any particular age cohort of labour will decrease their wages—has led authors such as Freeman and Berger to conclude that over their entire career the baby boom workers will suffer relatively lower wages. Berger, in fact, concludes that the relative wage effect will worsen as the baby boom reaches middle age. The simple simulations we have considered indicate that the more scarce a particular age group, the higher the wage paid to that group. The size of the effect in terms of lifetime income, however, cannot be ascertained from such cross-sectional simulations. To focus on the lifetime effects, we ran a simulation that tracked a synthetic baby boom generation throughout its career to see if the effects were indeed lasting. We began with the 1967 experience distribution, as a hypothetical long-run equilibrium value for the population. We then passed a 31-year 'V-shaped' baby boom through the population. Specifically, we introduced the first year of the baby boom by assuming a growth in the number of first-year workers of 2.6 per cent. The following year we aged the first workers to second-year workers and introduced a new first-year cohort 5.2 per cent larger than steady state. We continued in this fashion, increasing the percentage augmentation by 2.6 per cent per year until it reached a value of 39 per cent in the 15th year, and we then decreased the augmentation by 2.6 per cent per year until it reached zero in the 32nd year. Assuming the baby boom began in 1942, the peak year of birth rates in our simulation was 1957, when the cohort was 39 per cent larger than steady state. Throughout the simulation the education level was kept at its mean level in our sample, and was independent of year of birth. Thus we expect the effects reported to be smaller than those that would occur if the education distribution changed simultaneously. These figures roughly describe the actual observed pattern of population increase. We trace the wage distribution of the population from the time the first year of the baby boom enters the labour force until the last year exits the labour force, when the population returns to steady state.

In Figure 2.4 we plot the lifetime wage profile of college graduates who were born in 1957 and 1981 in our hypothetical simulations. As the results

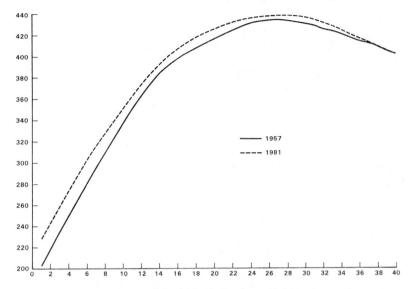

Figure 2.4.   Wage profile of college graduates born in 1957 and 1981.

indicate, these two years represent the extreme values in the present value of total lifetime earnings. Babies born in 1957 had the lowest earnings, and those born in 1981 had the highest. Recall that in our simulation 1957 is the peak of the baby boom. By the time the 1982 cohort reaches the labour market the 1957 cohort is in its 24th year of experience, so there is a relative shortage of young workers. The wage pattern shows that workers born in 1957 receive wages approximately 10 per cent lower than the cohort born in 1981 in the initial phases of their career. Until the last few years of the career the wage of babies in the large cohort is consistently less than that of the small cohort, but the percentage difference declines steadily. By the time the cohorts are at the peak earnings level the percentage difference is only 1 per cent. In Figure 2.5, we graph the ratio of the 1957 cohort earnings to the 1981 cohort earnings by year of experience. This figure reinforces our observation that at the beginning of the career workers in large cohorts suffer large wage losses, but as their career progresses and they are absorbed into the labour force the wage loss declines, and by the end of their career it vanishes altogether. These simulations belie the claim that the baby boom will suffer from increasingly large wage penalties as their careers proceed.

Since the large decrease in wages we see in the early phases of a large cohort's career does not last throughout the career, it is appropriate to ask what the lifetime effect on earnings might be. Assuming a 5 per cent real rate of discount, we calculate the present value of earnings of each birth year cohort relative to the present value of earnings in the steady state. This relative present value is plotted by birth year for high school graduates in

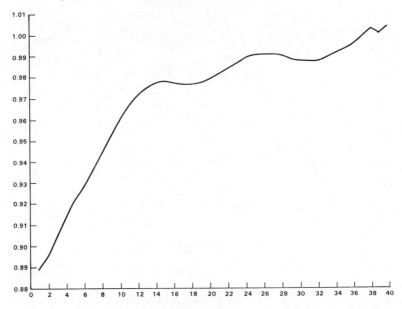

Figure 2.5.   Ratio of 1957 wage to 1981 wage, college graduates

Figure 2.6 and for college graduates in Figure 2.7. Recall that the synthetic baby boom begins in 1942, peaks in 1957, and ends fifteen years later in 1972. High school graduates who were born before 1947 experience an increase in relative wages, since they are prime-age workers when the baby boom enters the labour force. Their relative scarcity drives their wages up during the peak earnings years of their careers. Lifetime wages go below steady-state levels in 1947 and reach the lowest point for cohorts born in the late 1950s. Workers born in the 1970s and early 1980s receive a premium for being young workers during the time in which the baby boom are peak earners. The level of lifetime wages returns to its steady state when the last of the baby boom cohorts leaves the labour force—the year the babies born in 2012 enter the labour force. The story for college graduates is roughly the same as for high school graduates, except that the initial peak is much smaller, and the premium to those born in the 1970s and 1980s is much larger.

The most striking observation to be made about Figures 2.6 and 2.7 is that the difference in lifetime wages is very small. From peak to trough the difference is only about 3 per cent for high school graduates and 4 per cent for college graduates. High school graduates born in the least favourable year experience lifetime wages only 1.6 per cent less than steady-state levels, and for college graduates the discount is 2.5 per cent. This contrasts markedly with the initial impact of increased cohort size on young workers.

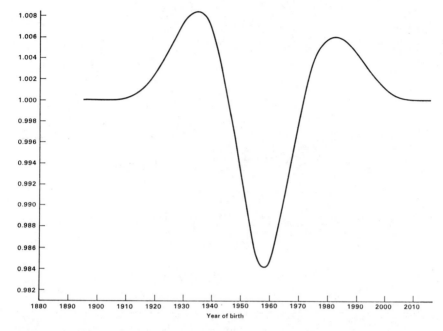

Figure 2.6. Relative present value of wages under simulated baby boom, high school graduates

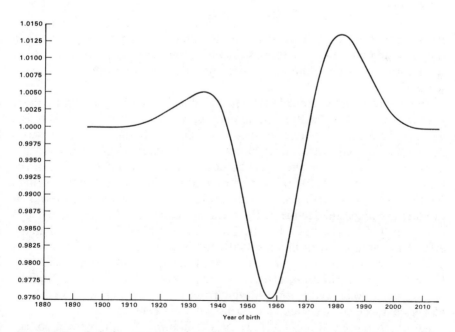

Figure 2.7. Relative present value of wages under simulated baby boom, college graduates

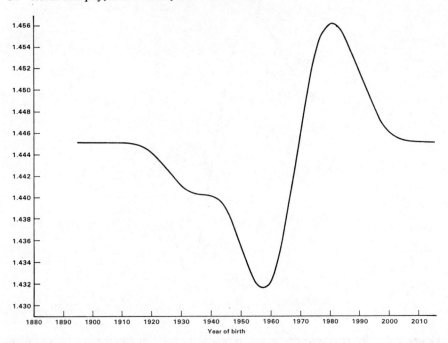

Figure 2.8.   Ratio of present value of wages, college to high school, under simulated baby boom

Recall from Figure 2.4 how we concluded that the impact of cohort size in the early stages of a large cohort's career is large, around 10 per cent in our simulation. However, the entire lifetime net effect is minimal for most workers.

Some authors have argued that college-educated workers are particularly hard hit by the recent changes in labour force composition, since there is a surplus of educated labour as well as young labour. In this simulation we do not change the education distribution, but the changing age distribution does have an impact on the return to education. In Figure 2.8, we plot the ratio of the present value of college earnings to the present value of high school earnings by birth year, given the simulated baby boom. In terms of lifetime earnings the decline in the return to education begins for persons born well before the baby boom. This demonstrates the notion that the effects of large cohorts increase with the level of education, which was evident from the increase in factor endowments as education increased. Once again these lifetime effects are relatively small, with the lifetime premium to a college education varying from a low of 43 per cent to a high of 45 per cent, the steady-state value being 44.5 per cent.

Although these estimated effects on the lifetime premium for a college education are relatively small, specific year effects can be quite large. In

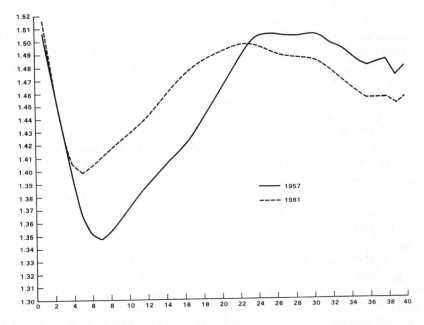

Figure 2.9. Ratio of college to high school weekly wages for cohorts born in 1957 and 1981

Figure 2.9, we plot the relative wages of college to high school graduates over their lifetimes for the 1957 birth year and the 1981 birth year. College graduates born during this simulated baby boom suffer from a lower educational premium than do their small-cohort counterparts, but by the end of their life the pattern is actually reversed: the rewards of education increase faster for the large-cohort babies and remain at higher levels for longer in their lives. The decreased premiums observed currently for the baby boom workers have led some authors to assert that these educated workers will suffer throughout their lives from 'overeducation'. Our analysis leads us to expect that the decreased relative wages of educated baby boomers is a temporary phenomenon and that their relative wages will increase in the course of their lifetime.

Conclusion

The labour force has undergone large changes in demographic and educational composition in the twentieth century. It is clear the demographic fluctuations have had an economic impact on workers, but the nature of that impact has been unclear. In order to attribute fluctuations in wages to fluctuations in labour force composition, it is necessary to develop an empirical framework in which the effects of composition on wages is well defined. In this chapter we developed such a framework by viewing workers as a composite of several productive factors: a worker's wage will change if the composition of factors changes or if the value of any of those factors change. This leads us to analyse the sixteen years of observed wage patterns using a factor-analytic technique. The advantage of such a technique is that it allows us to summarize the changes in the composition of the labour force succinctly in terms of a small number of underlying factors of production rather than having to resort to arbitrary divisions of workers into factor groups or to a complicated production technology with numerous factors and numerous restrictions to make the technology estimatable. In our estimation we saw that we could characterize most of the variation in wage patterns using three underlying factors of production. The first factor reflected the increase in skills that comes with experience. The second factor was a youth and old-age factor, and the third factor was a middle-age factor. In regressing the quantities of these factors on wages, we were able to build a structure that allowed us simulations of wage patterns given any educational or age distribution, holding constant business cycle effects. Although this structure enabled us to build a complete substitution matrix, that way of summarizing the interactions of 160 different productive types of workers was hardly succinct, so we resorted to simulations to illustrate results. The first simulation simply contrasted the wage patterns in a youthful population with that in an older population. These cross-section results showed that the rewards to scarcity of factors exist but are relatively small. We then went on to consider the effect of the entrance of a baby boom on lifetime earnings and found that although the depression of wages caused by large cohorts could be large during the initial stages of the large cohort's career, the wage differential diminished over the course of the career. The individual year effects in our simulations were as much as 10 per cent, but the effects on lifetime earnings were at most 3 per cent. Our evidence also indicates that a younger labour force does not lead to a large lifetime decrease in the return to college education nor to a permanent decrease in that return.

The list of potential avenues for future research is long. Of immediate concern is running simulations of the baby boom that accurately reflect the changing educational composition of the labour force as well as the changing age composition. We also recognize that the emergence of a large number of female workers may have had an impact on the wage structure during this period. Other outside influences such as affirmative action and the end of the Vietnam conflict and the draft have been omitted here. Our contribution has been both methodological and substantial, and we believe the methodology is sufficiently flexible to permit much more fruitful research.

Endnotes

1. A detailed description of procedures used to develop the data base is provided in Welch (1979*a*), and details of the experience calculation are in Gould and Welch (1976). The main point of the experienced imputation is that it is not the commonly used age–education–6 but is instead a probability distribution (conditional on age, education, and birth year) for each observation. The number of people in an experience cell is the sum of individual probabilities for that cell.
2. The detailed year-by-year data show a drop of 25 per cent from the peak in 1967 to the trough in 1976.
3. See Welch (1979*b*) for the basic reference of this topic.
4. Clearly, this estimation could be done using ordinary least squares, but recall that the observations on the wages are cell means. Thus a weighted scheme seems more advisable to account for the heteroscedasticity resulting from varying cell size. The cell sizes are computed by applying the experience weighting scheme described in Gould and Welch to the CPS weights given in the original sample. The weights reflect the expected number of males in the given experience cell in any given year.

Appendix: Insensitivity of Predicted Wage Profiles to Normalization

Suppose we decompose the wage matrix Y into

$$Y = (GA^{-1})(AW)$$

where A is a non-singular matrix chosen to normalize the factors and factor loadings. Define

$$G^* = (GA^{-1})$$

and

$$W^* = (AW)$$

so

$$Y = G^*W^*.$$

We regress $W^{*\prime}$ on the matrix $X = P'G^*$ where P is the population data. Thus we fit

$$W^{*\prime} = XB$$

so

$$\hat{B} = (X'X)^{-1}X'W^{*\prime}$$
$$= (G^{*\prime}PP'G^*)^{-1}G^{*\prime} PW^{*\prime}.$$

The predicted factor wages for a new population vector $\bar{p}$ are

$$\bar{w} = \bar{x}B$$

where

$$\bar{x} = \bar{p}'G^*$$

and the predicted wage profiles are

$$\bar{y} = G^*\bar{w}.$$

Substituting, we get

$$\bar{y} = G^*\hat{B}'\bar{x}'$$
$$= G^*W^*P'G^*(G^*'P\ P'G^*)^{-1}G^*'\bar{p}$$
$$= GA^{-1}AWP'GA^{-1}(A^{-1}G'P\ P'GA^{-1})^{-1}A^{-1}G'\bar{p}$$
$$= GWP'G(G'PP'G)G'\bar{p}$$

which is independent of A, the normalization matrix.

References

Anderson, T.W. and Herman Rubin (1956), 'Statistical Inference in Factor Analysis' in *Proceedings of the Third Berkeley Symposium on Mathematical Statistics and Probability*, UC Press, Berkeley.

Berger, Mark C. (1984), 'The Effect of Cohort Size and the Earnings Growth of Young Workers', forthcoming in *Industrial and Labor Relations Review*.

Easterlin, R.A. (1977), 'What Will 1984 Be Like: Socioeconomic Implications of Recent Twists in Age Structure', *Demography*, 15, 4 (November), 397–432.

——, M.L. Wachter, and S.M. Wachter (1978), 'Demographic Influences on Economic Stability: the United States Experience', *Population and Development Review*, 4, 1 (March), 1–23.

Freeman, Richard B. (1979), 'The Effect of Demographic Factors on Age–Earnings Profiles in the US', *Journal of Human Resources*, 14, 3, 289–313.

—— (1976), *The Overeducated American*, Academic Press, New York.

Harmon, Harry H. (1967), *Modern Factor Analysis*, University of Chicago Press, Chicago.

Joresky, K.G. and D. Sorbom (1979), *Advances in Factor Analysis and Structural Equation Models*, Abt Associates, Cambridge, Mass.

Mincer, J. (1974), *Schooling Experience and Earnings* NBER.

Murphy, K., M. Plant, and F. Welch (1984), 'Wage Dynamics: A Technical Analytic Framework', forthcoming.

Smith, J.P. and F. Welch (1978), 'The Overeducated American? A Review Article' in *Proceedings of National Academy of Education*, 5.

Welch, F. (1979a), 'Effects of Cohort Size on Earnings: the Baby Boom Babies' Financial Bust', *Journal of Political Economy*, 87, 5 pt. 2 (October) S65–S97.

—— (1979b), 'Linear Synthesis of Skill Distributions', *Journal of Human Resources* 4, 3, (summer), 314–327.

—— and W. Gould (1976), 'An Experience Imputation or an Imputation Experience', mimeograph, RAND Corp.

Whittle, P. (1952), 'On Principal Components and Least Squares Methods of Factor Analysis', *Skandinavisk Aktuarietidskript*, 223–39.

3 The Effect of Cohort Size on Relative Wages in Japan

LINDA G. MARTIN and NAOHIRO OGAWA

The ageing of the Japanese population is occurring at an unprecedented rate, and there is a growing awareness in Japan that a variety of social and economic changes will be necessary to accommodate the ageing process. In business circles, there is concern about the implications of a slower-growing and older labour force. Government officials are concerned about the future viability of old-age pension schemes and the growing burden of medical services for the elderly. Overall, there is some evidence that these changes in the labour force and in the expenditures on social security programmes may lead to an economic slow-down in the long run (Ogawa, 1982).

In this chapter, we focus on one feature of Japanese labour markets, the seniority wage system, and investigate how it had changed in the last twenty years as the population has aged. In the first section we describe some of the institutional characteristics of Japanese employment and wage structure. In the second section we review the pattern of change of the past three decades in the age composition of the productive-age population and of employed persons. The third section examines the effect of age structure change on relative wages at both national and industry levels. The final section summarizes major findings.

Institutional Characteristics of Japanese Employment and Wage Structure

To facilitate the discussion that follows, we should first describe some of the fundamentals of Japanese employment and wage practices. The seniority

Earlier drafts of this chapter were presented at the Seventh World Congress of the International Economic Association, Madrid, 5–9 September 1983, and at the IUSSP/IIASA Seminar on Economic Consequences of Population Composition in Developed Countries, Laxenburg, Austria, 12–14 December 1983. The authors are grateful to Shoichi Kajiwara of the Ministry of Labour and Makoto Kondo of the Economic Planning Agency for their assistance in obtaining some of the data required for the present study. Thanks are also due to Yasuhiko Saito, Taichi Yamaguchi, Toshio Takashima, and Tomoko Sugihara of Nihon University and to the computer staff at the East–West Population Institute for their assistance in the data preparation and analysis.

wage system and lifetime employment are the two major institutional features of the Japanese labour market. However, the systems are by no means universal in Japan. Men working for small companies are less likely to be employed under their aegis. Furthermore, because Japanese women have usually retired upon marriage or upon giving birth, they have not been a part of these systems, which were originally instituted after World War I to cope with the scarcity and high turnover of skilled workers.

Under the seniority-based wage system, salary increases with the age of an employee, his duration of service, and his job responsibilities. Salaries include the basic monthly wage, earnings for overtime, cost-of-living allowances, and various duty and incentive allowances (Martin, 1982). In 1981, the basic monthly wage corresponded to 90 per cent of a male worker's average monthly earnings (Ministry of Labour, 1983*b*: 104). Besides these monthly earnings, bonuses are usually given twice a year. Although the size of the bonus is closely tied to monthly earnings, it varies considerably from year to year. In 1981, bonuses amounted to three-and-a-half months' wages for the average male worker.

Despite the renown accorded the Japanese seniority wage system, during the 1970s there were some years when the male age–earnings profile in Japan was very similar to that in the United States (Martin, 1982). One significant difference, however, is that the age–earnings profile was rising in the United States in the 1970s with the increase in the number of younger workers relative to older workers, whereas in Japan it was falling, at least in the early 1970s, with the ageing of the labour force, as will be discussed in detail later. Nevertheless, experience and length of service are rewarded in both countries. The Japanese are simply more explicit in linking age to wages.

Lifetime employment in Japan provides job stability to workers, who in turn exhibit a high level of loyalty to their employers. It should be noted that this feature of Japanese labour markets also is not unique to Japan. Sterling (1983) has found that similar proportions of male workers in Japan and the United States experience stable, long-term employment. Furthermore, an important aspect of lifetime employment in Japan, where there is no legislation setting a lower age limit for mandatory retirement, is that workers are required to retire at an age specified by the company. In 1981, average retirement age was 57.6 years, very low in comparison to other highly industrialized countries and in comparison to Japanese life expectancy (Ogawa and Suits, 1983). Although the age limit has been gradually rising in recent years, it has increased by only 2.1 years since 1965.

One of the main deterrents to the extension of retirement age is related to the practice of the seniority wage system. Under this wage system, the postponement of retirement age implies larger wage bills. In the recent past, however, due to the relative increase in aged workers and the relative decrease in young workers, many businesses have been gradually replacing the seniority-based wage system with an ability-oriented one (Ogawa and

Suits, 1983). In 1970, 27.9 per cent of the business enterprises with more than thirty employees reported that they had a system in which wages were tied to work requirements. In 1979, however, the percentage of businesses using this wage system increased to 45.1. Despite these recent changes, to a considerable extent the seniority wage system is still a source of employers' strong preferences for young workers.

Although some business enterprises, mainly larger ones, have established re-employment programmes and employment extension programmes for older workers (Furuya and Martin, 1981), these programmes offer employment opportunities only to selected employees after their reaching retirement age. Most older workers tend to be hired by small-scale businesses in such industries as trade and services. During the period 1970–80, the service industry had a net addition of 315,000 workers aged 60 or older, and the wholesale and retail trade industry gained 311,000, as opposed to an increase of only 104,000 in manufacturing (Statistics Bureau, 1970 and 1980). Generally work can be found only with reduced pay, prestige, and job stability. Thus, the ageing of the Japanese labour force, which we will discuss next, presents a particular challenge in view of the country's employment patterns and labour institutions.

Ageing of the Working-Age Population and the Labour Force

In a virtually closed population such as the Japanese one, transformation of the age structure is induced by changes in fertility and mortality. Following the post-war baby boom (1947–9), Japan experienced an unprecedented decline in fertility. Over the period 1947–57, the total fertility rate (TFR) fell by over half from 4.54 to 2.04 children per woman. There was little change until the first oil crisis of 1973, when it began to fall again, and by 1981 TFR was 1.74 (Ishikawa, 1983: 66). In addition, remarkable mortality improvements were recorded from the late 1940s to the mid-1960s. The expectation of life at birth for males increased from 50.06 in 1947 to 63.24 years in 1957 and for females from 53.96 to 67.60 years over the same period. In 1981, life expectancy in Japan was among the highest in the world: 73.79 for males and 79.13 for females (Institute of Population Problems, 1982: 25).

Primarily because of the rapid fertility decline, the shift in the age structure of the Japanese population has been increasingly pronounced in recent years. In Table 3.1 we have listed several demographic indices representing changes in the age composition of the Japanese population over the period 1950–80. These indices show that the proportion of the aged population relative to the productive-age population has been steadily increasing, while that of the young population has been decreasing. These changes can be seen in the index of aged dependency and the index of young dependency in the first two lines of the table. Until 1970 the substantial shrinkage of the young population resulted in lowering total dependency, as shown in the third line.

Table 3.1.   Selected demographic indices for Japan, 1950–80

	1950 (per cent)	1960	1970	1980
$\dfrac{65+^a}{15\text{-}64}$	8.27	8.92	10.24	13.49
$\dfrac{0\text{-}14^b}{15\text{-}64}$	59.26	46.78	34.69	34.89
$\dfrac{(0\text{-}14)\ +\ (65+)^c}{15\text{-}64}$	67.54	55.69	44.93	48.35
$\dfrac{15\text{-}24}{15\text{-}64}$	32.81	29.38	27.56	20.42
$\dfrac{55\text{-}64}{15\text{-}64}$	10.18	10.95	11.39	12.77

Source: Statistics Bureau, Prime Minister's Office, *Population Census of Japan*, various years.
[a] Index of aged dependency.
[b] Index of young dependency.
[c] Index of total dependency.

During the period 1970–80, however, the decline in the index of young dependency tapered off, and the increase in the relative size of the aged population started to play a dominant role in the determination of the level of total dependency. These changes in the relative proportion of the two age groups, old and young, have shifted the emphasis from the quantitative question of 'how many dependents' to the qualitative one of 'what kind of dependents' the working population has to support.

The composition of the working-age population has also been gradually affected, as the size of young cohorts entering has declined. The last two indices in Table 3.1 show the proportion of the working-age population (15–64) composed of the very youngest (15–24) and of the very oldest (55–64). Clearly, the former has declined and the latter increased in the post-war period.

Although labour force participation also has an effect on the age composition of the labour force, the above changes in the age composition of the Japanese working-age population are closely linked to those in the distribution of workers. Table 3.2 shows the distribution of employed persons by

Table 3.2.   Age distribution of Japanese employed persons, 1950–80

Age	1950 Thousands (per cent)	1960	1970	1980
Total	35,574 (100.0)	43,690 (100.0)	52,236 (100.0)	55,811 (100.0)
15–19	4,998 (14.0)	4,608 (10.5)	3,184 (6.1)	1,513 (2.7)
20–24	5,801 (16.3)	6,434 (14.7)	8,036 (15.4)	5,503 (9.9)
25–39	11,452 (32.2)	16,026 (36.7)	18,751 (35.9)	21,121 (37.8)
40–59	10,525 (29.6)	12,493 (29.6)	17,400 (33.3)	22,282 (39.9)
60+	2,798 (7.9)	3,680 (8.4)	4,864 (9.3)	5,392 (9.7)

Source: Statistics Bureau, Prime Minister's Office, *Population Census of Japan*, various years.

age over the period 1950–80. Because of both demographic change and increased school attendance, the youngest age group (15–19) shrank enormously in terms of its number and share over the period under review. It declined from 14.0 per cent in 1950 to only 2.7 per cent in 1980. The number of employed persons aged 20–4 decreased from 1950 to 1960, but increased in 1970 because of the post-war baby boom and then declined to 9.9 per cent in 1980. Thus at the beginning of the thirty-year period young workers accounted for over 30 per cent of the work-force, but at the end for only 13 per cent.

The main corps of the workers at ages 25–59 recorded steady growth in both numbers and percentage. Another age group that increased in numbers was the 60-and-over group. Despite a decline in participation, especially in the 1960s, as agriculture became less important in Japan's economy, this group of workers continued to increase. In contrast to a 70 per cent shrinkage of the age group 15–19, this oldest age group expanded by 93 per cent during the period 1950–80.

These age-structural shifts of the work-force have caused a continuous rise in the mean age of workers. For instance, the average age of a worker outside agriculture was 31.0 years in 1962, 33.5 in 1971, and 37.0 in 1981 (Ministry of Labour, *Basic Survey of Wage Structure*, various years). However, there have been differences in the pattern of increase in mean age across the various industries, as industry-specific employment opportunities have changed over time. Figure 3.1 presents changes in the mean age for selected industries for the period 1962–81. Among the nine non-agricultural industrial groupings in the Basic Survey of Wage Structure, the mining industry, which has been declining in economic importance and whose work-force shrank by 50 per cent in the last decade (Statstics Bureau, 1970 and 1980), has continually shown the highest mean age—43.0 in 1981. The rapidly growing wholesale and retail trade industry has exhibited the lowest average age throughout the period, with 33.4 years in 1981. Even so, the average age in this industry increased by 5.3 years from 1962 to 1981, an indication of the importance of changes in age distribution of labour supply apart from changes in the demand for labour. The only industry whose work-force has aged more than wholesale and retail trade is the manufacturing industry; average age increased from 30.1 in 1962 to 37.7 years old in 1981. Although manufacturing output has increased dramatically, growth has been capital-intensive, and relatively less hiring has taken place than in other growing industries. The work-force in manufacturing actually declined in size in the 1970s (Statistics Bureau, 1970 and 1980).

Age Structure Effects on Relative Wages

Given the significant ageing of the Japanese labour force that has taken place in the last twenty years, one might expect that the change in age

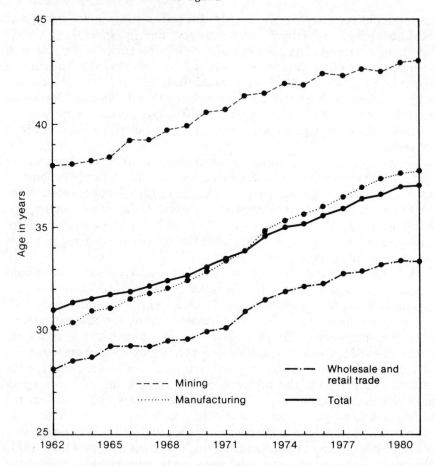

Figure 3.1.   Changes in the mean age of the work-force for selected industries, 1962–81

structure would have an effect on the pattern of wages by age of worker. If workers of different ages are not perfect substitutes for each other in production, that is, if older workers do jobs different from those of younger workers, then we would expect that a change in the relative supply of the two age groups of workers would have an effect on the relative wages of the groups. Results of analysis of cohort size effects on age–earnings profiles in the United States reported by Welch (1979), Freeman (1979), Berger (1983), and Welch and Plant in this volume confirm this hypothesis. In earlier work, Martin (1982) investigated changes in the Japanese age–earnings profile from 1962 to 1978. Her preliminary results also indicate a negative cohort size effect on wages. We now have three more years of data, as well as revised estimates of labour force size and wage data by industry, and will update and expand that analysis.[1]

The source of data for the analysis is the Basic Survey of Wage Structure (BSWS), which is conducted on an annual basis by the Ministry of Labour. Although it is nationwide in its coverage and the sample included 65,000 firms in 1981, this survey is limited in that it covers only firms with ten employees or more, thus excluding numerous small firms of the cottage-industry type. It should be noted also that BSWS does not collect information on the agriculture and government industries and that data on the service industry are not available for every year, so that industry has been excluded from our analysis.

Figures 3.2 and 3.3 depict the age-earnings profiles in selected years for males and females respectively. Both males and females are grouped into the following six age categories: 20–4, 25–9, 30–4, 35–9, 40–9, 50–9, and 60+. In these graphs, the age–earnings profile is represented by the ratio of average monthly earnings (excluding bonuses) for each age group to earnings of the

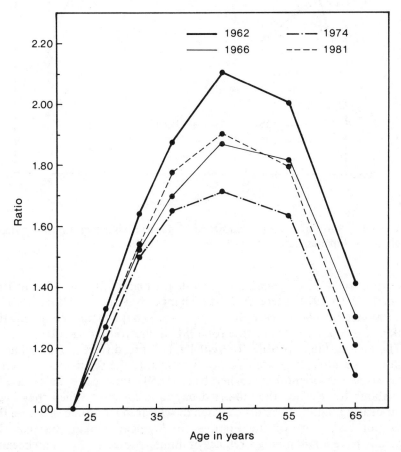

Figure 3.2. Ratio of average monthly earnings for each age group to earnings of 20–4 age group, Japanese males, 1962, 1966, 1974, 1981

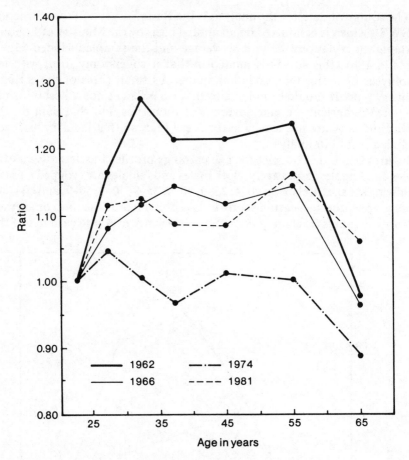

Figure 3.3. Ratio of average monthly earnings for each age group to earnings of 20–4 group, Japanese females, 1962, 1966, 1974, 1981

age group 20–4. The age–earnings profile for males fell from 1962 to 1973. From 1973 to 1974, there was little change, but from 1975 to 1981 the differentials in relative earnings among age groups expanded again, thus making the age–earnings profile for 1981 similar to that for 1966.

The age–earnings profile for females is quite different from that for males. Generally, there are two peaks reflecting the segmented careers of most women. As mentioned earlier, traditionally Japanese females have left the labour force when they married or, more recently, when they began child-bearing, and then returned when the children left home. Because they have not been part of the lifetime employment system, because they generally have not had long stretches of uninterrupted service, and because, even if they did, they were not rewarded as much for seniority as their male counterparts, the female age–earnings profile is much flatter (note the larger scale, as well as the shape). However, the pattern of change in the profile is similar to that for males. In the 1960s and early 1970s, the female profile fell, but in the last half of the 1970s increased. Another notable change in the female age–earnings profile has been in the age at which earnings are the highest: from the thirties in the 1960s to the late twenties in the early 1970s and to the fifties in the late 1970s.

Let us now examine the sources of these changes in the age–earnings pattern. Using data from 1962 to 1981, we have undertaken several regression analyses. The dependent variable we use is the wage ratio (WR) or the ratio of earnings of workers aged 40–9 to earnings of workers of 20–4. As explanatory variables we use (*a*) CYCLE, the deviation of the logarithm of real gross domestic product (GDP) from its trend (Economic Planning Agency, 1975, 1982, and 1983*a*), and (*b*) LABOR, the ratio of the labour force size for ages 40–9 to that for 20–4 (Ministry of Labour, *Annual Report on the Labour Force Survey*, various years).

The first explanatory variable is expected to reflect the influence of changes in the general economic situation on the age–earnings profile. It might be expected that because of employers' greater commitment to and investment in older workers and because of their desire to attract young workers in high-growth periods, there would be a negative relationship between the dependent variable and the economic growth variable. That is, young workers would do relatively well in boom periods, but older workers would not be so negatively affected as younger workers in slow-growth periods.

The variable LABOR is incorporated in our analysis to represent the effect of age structure changes on relative wages.[2] Although changes in the educational attainment of the age groups 20–4 and 40–9 might be another possible explanatory variable, it has not been included in the present study for two reasons. First of all, data on the educational attainment of these two age groups are not available for each year of the period under consideration. Secondly, there is fragmentary evidence that changes in the age–earnings profile occurred independently of changes in the educational attainment of these age groups (Martin, 1982).

Figure 3.4 displays the levels and trends of these key variables over the period 1962–81. The top and middle panels of Figure 3.4 show the changing patterns of the wage ratio (WR) and the labour force ratio (LABOR) for males and females respectively. For both sexes, the labour ratio increased thoroughout the period except around 1970 when the effect of the baby boom cohort on the 20–4 group in the denominator of the ratio became apparent. In general, until around 1974 the wage ratios and labour ratios moved in opposite directions. However, after 1974 all of these ratios increased. In contrast, as shown in the bottom panel of Figure 3.4, throughout the period under consideration the cycle variable moved in a direction opposite to the

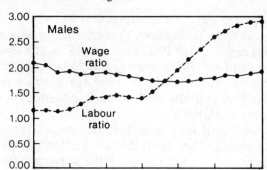

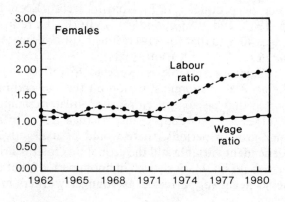

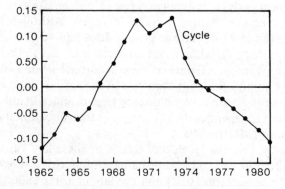

Figure 3.4. Movement of key variables, 1962–81

wage ratios. The high-growth period of the late 1960s and early 1970s coincided with the lowest values of the wage ratios.

The upper panel of Table 3.3 summarizes the results of the regression analysis of the natural logarithm of the wage ratio for males 40–9 relative to males 20–4, using the natural logarithm of the labour force ratio and the

Table 3.3. Results of regression analysis for males and females, ages 40–9 versus ages 20–4, 1962–81

Sex	Constant	Explanatory variables		$\bar{R}^2$
		LABOR	CYCLE	
Males	0.6490	– 0.0663 (0.0343)	—	0.1262
	0.6128	—	– 0.4453* (0.1126)	0.4351
	0.6623	– 0.0905* (0.0188)	– 0.5163* (0.0767)	0.7475
Females	0.1183	– 0.1151* (0.0376)	—	0.3057
	0.0808	—	– 0.2259 (0.1121)	0.1389
	0.1301	– 0.1514* (0.0259)	– 0.3411* (0.0694)	0.6962

Values in parentheses below each coefficient are standard errors.
*Significantly different from zero at the 5 per cent level.

business cycle indicator as explanatory variables separately and jointly. As Freeman (1979) has shown, the coefficient on the labour force ratio variable can be interpreted in terms of the elasticity of substitution between the two age groups of workers, with a large negative coefficient indicating less substitutability. When entered into a regression equation by itself, the

Table 3.4. Results of regression analysis for males, various age groups, 1962–81

Age groups	Constant	Explanatory variables		$\bar{R}^2$
		LABOR	CYCLE	
40–9/35–9	0.1487	– 0.1560* (0.0143)	– 0.0790* (0.0236)	0.8784
40–9/30–4	0.2376	– 0.1452* (0.0203)	– 0.2170* (0.0340)	0.8905
40–9/25–9	0.3911	– 0.0713* (0.0289)	– 0.3640* (0.0534)	0.7443
35–9/30–4	0.0981	– 0.0882* (0.0360)	– 0.1654* (0.0264)	0.8715
35–9/25–9	0.2870	– 0.0182 (0.0362)	– 0.2722* (0.0374)	0.7309
35–9/20–4	0.5398	– 0.0475* (0.0225)	– 0.3844* (0.0606)	0.6682
30–4/25–9	0.1836	– 0.0191 (0.0212)	– 0.0712* (0.0283)	0.1852
30–4/20–4	0.4406	– 0.0599* (0.0184)	– 0.2163* (0.0556)	0.4499
25–9/20–4	0.2597	– 0.0663* (0.0183)	– 0.1322* (0.0504)	0.4080

Values in parentheses below each coefficient are standard errors.
*Significantly different from zero at the 5 per cent level.

labour force ratio has a negative, but insignificant, effect on the total monthly earnings ratio. When combined with the cycle variable, however, the labour force ratio does have a significant negative effect. The cycle variable by itself explains slightly more than 40 per cent of the variation in the wage ratio.

The lower panel of Table 3.3 presents the regression results for females. Contrary to what is found for males, the labour force ratio by itself shows a significant negative effect upon the female wage ratio, whereas the cycle variable alone does not have a significant effect. But, as is the case with males, the equation with both variables shows significant negative effects for both.

The above regression results were based on the wage ratio between the two age groups 40–9 and 20–4. Tables 3.4 and 3.5 present the wage ratio regression results for other age-group combinations for males and females respectively. We present only the results for the equations in which both explanatory variables are entered. The results are fairly consistent. For males, there is a negative CYCLE effect for all age combinations, and a significant negative LABOR effect for all except 35–9/25–9 and 30–4/25–9. The implication is that these last pairs of age groups are more substitutable for one another than the other pairs. In general, the coefficients on LABOR are largest in absolute value for cases in which the age group 40–9 is in the numerator, indicating that this age group performs duties that are distinct from those of the other age groups. For females, four of the combinations

Table 3.5.   Results of regression analysis for females, various age groups, 1962–81

| Age groups | Constant | Explanatory variables | | $\bar{R}^2$ |
		LABOR	CYCLE	
40–9/35–9	– 0.0952	0.1711* (0.0346)	0.1999* (0.0401)	0.7777
40–9/30–4	– 0.0207	0.0219 (0.0312)	0.3633* (0.0476)	0.8197
40–9/25–9	0.0827	– 0.1300* (0.0355)	0.0067 (0.0562)	0.4073
35–9/30–4	– 0.0060	– 0.1078 (0.1342)	0.1760 (0.0958)	0.0810
35–9/25–9	– 0.0219	0.0221 (0.1209)	– 0.3289* (0.1174)	0.2446
35–9/20–4	– 0.0228	– 0.3097* (0.0632)	– 0.8178* (0.1202)	0.7068
30–4/25–9	– 0.0044	– 0.0355 (0.0634)	– 0.4565* (0.0772)	0.6365
30–4/20–4	– 0.0173	– 0.2618* (0.0443)	– 1.0143* (0.0959)	0.8590
25–9/20–4	0.0548	– 0.0917* (0.0271)	– 0.2805* (0.0576)	0.5352

Values in parentheses below each coefficient are standard errors.
*Significantly different from zero at the 5 per cent level.

show negative LABOR effects: 40-9/25-9, 35-9/20-4, 30-4/20-4, and 25-9/20-4. Five of the combinations have negative CYCLE effects, and these effects are especially large for the 35-9/20-4 and 30-4/20-4 combinations. For the 40-9/35-9 group there are positive coefficients for both LABOR and CYCLE. There is also a positive CYCLE coefficient for 40-9/30-4. We obtain similar results when we use the population ratio as an explanatory variable instead of LABOR, so it is not the case that higher wages are inducing greater participation of the 40-9 group relative to the 35-9 group. We speculate that these positive coefficients stem from the peculiarities of the female labour market, but do not have a precise explanation at hand.

Although the results are not shown in the tables, we should mention that for males the cycle variable alone has a significant negative effect on the wage ratio in all but one case (40-9/35-9). There is a negative coefficient for the labour ratio variable alone for the 40-9/35-9, 40-9/30-4, 35-9/30-4, and 25-9/20-4 combinations. For females, LABOR has a negative effect for the 40-9/25-9 case and a positive effect for 40-9/35-9 and 40-9/30-4. CYCLE has a positive effect for the last two combinations and a negative effect for 35-9/25-9, 35-9/20-4, 30-4/25-9, 30-4/20-4, and 25-9/20-4.

In general, the above results indicate that the cycle variable plays a more important role than the labour ratio in the determination of the wage ratio. This observation is confirmed if we look at the beta coefficients (coefficients standardized by the standard deviations of the dependent variable and the relevant independent variable) from the regression results in which both explanatory variables are entered. For example, for the male age group combination of 40-9 and 25-9, the beta coefficient on LABOR is -0.2882 and on CYCLE is -0.7965. So the change induced by a unit change in standard deviation units in CYCLE has a much larger effect on WR than does a unit change in LABOR, as estimated for the period 1962-81. Seven out of ten of the age group combinations for males and eight out of the ten female combinations show the same general result.

To identify sources within the economy of the negative age compositional effects on relative wages at the macro level, we have re-estimated the same equations on the basis of industry-specific time-series wage and economic growth data. Only the labour data used here are at the national level. The industries included in these regresssions are (a) mining, (b) construction, (c) manufacturing, (d) finance and insurance, (e) wholesale and retail trade, (f) transportation and communication, and (g) electricity, gas, and water supply. We have concentrated on the 40-9/20-4 combination, so the results shown in Table 3.6 are comparable to those for all industries that were presented in Table 3.3.

Let us first discuss industries in which there is a significant negative cohort effect on the wage ratio. These industries are manufacturing, wholesale and retail trade, transportation and communication, and electricity, gas, and

Table 3.6.   Industry-specific wage ratio (40–9/20–4) regression results for males and females, 1962–81

Industry/sex	Constant	Explanatory variables		$\bar{R}^2$
		LABOR	CYCLE	
Mining/males	0.3091	0.0518*	– 0.1083	0.1591
		(0.0244)	(0.1347)	
Mining/females	0.0413	– 0.0330	– 0.1293	– 0.0454
		(0.0417)	(0.1510)	
Construction/males	0.4155	0.0118	– 0.2763*	0.6892
		(0.0187)	(0.0433)	
Construction/females	– 0.0155	0.0236	– 0.2127*	0.4771
		(0.0352)	(0.0533)	
Manufacturing/males	0.6816	– 0.1400*	– 0.3484*	0.6547
		(0.0266)	(0.0830)	
Manufacturing/females	– 0.0085	– 0.0664*	– 0.1805*	0.3701
		(0.0269)	(0.0551)	
Finance/males	0.8548	0.0751*	– 0.2902*	0.3800
		(0.0294)	(0.1223)	
Finance/females	0.4779	– 0.1156	– 0.5110	0.3043
		(0.0641)	(0.1745)	
Wholesale/males	0.7881	– 0.1037*	– 0.4298*	0.8041
		(0.0170)	(0.0566)	
Wholesale/females	0.1831	– 0.1138*	– 0.1826*	0.4404
		(0.0307)	(0.0669)	
Transport/males	0.6071	– 0.1276*	– 0.3597*	0.7180
		(0.0238)	(0.0649)	
Transport/females	0.3176	– 0.0732*	– 0.0872	0.1600
		(0.0334)	(0.0597)	
Electricity/males	0.8150	– 0.0916*	– 0.3305*	0.6690
		(0.0209)	(0.0617)	
Electricity/females	0.5317	– 0.1354*	0.2320*	0.7113
		(0.0306)	(0.0591)	

Values in parentheses below each coefficient are standard errors.
*Significantly different from zero at the 5 per cent level.

water supply. In the manufacturing industry, the cohort size effect for males is larger than is the case of all industries. The coefficients for the other industries with significant negative effects for males are similar to the overall results. For females, the coefficients on the labour force ratio tend to be smaller than that for females in all industries.

These industry-specific regression results seem to suggest that especially for males the manufacturing industry is an important source of the negative sign for the coefficients on the cohort size variable at the aggregate national level. This result is not surprising, because the manufacturing industry employed over half the male workers included in our analysis for 1962 and 43.1 per cent of those in 1981. For the males in the mining and finance industries, there are positive cohort size effects, but because these industrial labour groups are relatively small their effects are masked at the aggregate level. As mentioned in the earlier discussion of mean ages of workers in the various industries, the mining industry is a declining, ageing industry whose employment has been halved in the 1970s. There has been very little change over the twenty-year period in its age–earnings profile, which has consistently been the flattest of all the industries' profiles. In contrast, growth of the finance industry has been surpassed by only manufacturing and wholesale and retail trade, and there has been a large increase in the finance industry's age–earnings profile, which has consistently been the steepest. The finance industry is considered a prestige industry for employment among new graduates and usually selects the pick of the crop for its new employees. Thus, in different ways both of these exceptional industries can be viewed as operating on the fringes of the labour market in Japan, and one might expect that they would not be affected by changes in the overall supply of labour. However, we do not have an explanation for why the aggregate labour ratio has a positive effect on the wage ratio for these specific industries. In future work, we plan to look further at differentials in age–earnings profiles by firm size, as well as by industry.

Conclusion

The Japanese population has undergone considerable change in its age composition in the post-war period. After the post-war baby boom from 1947 to 1949, fertility declined dramatically, and the ageing of the population that has already begun is expected to accelerate in the next few decades. In this chapter we have shown how these changes in age distribution have affected relative wages in Japan. We have found that age composition is an important factor, but not necessarily the most important one. The oil shocks and recessions of the 1970s coincided with the passage of the baby boom through the younger age groups of the work-force and with the overall ageing of the population, and thus economic factors tended to outweigh demographic factors in the analysis.

Even so, we continue to believe that age distribution has played an important role and will increase its role in wage determination as time goes by. It is not surprising that the Japanese baby boom has not had the impact of the American baby boom. There is a great difference—a duration of three years as against seventeen. The former can get lost in a business cycle, while the latter stands out. What will demand greater attention is the ageing of the Japanese population. Casual empiricism indicates the seriousness with which the Japanese view the problem. Surely the Japanese press devotes more inches of print to ageing issues than any in the world. The Economic Planning Agency (1983b) in its recent *Japan in the Year 2000* cites 'the arrival of the ageing society' as one of the three major trends in Japan's future. Several of the largest corporations have announced plans for encouraging early retirement to lower their wage bills, at the same time as the government is pushing the companies to raise their official age limits.

What may indeed be fortuitous is the coincidence of the growing importance of the tertiary industries with the ageing of the population. Employers in these industries seem to be willing to hire inexperienced workers, both young and old. Of the total number of newly hired employees in 1981, 21.4 per cent found their jobs in the service industry. Of newly hired employees aged 55 and over, 30.9 per cent found their jobs in services (Ministry of Labour, 1983*b*: 22), so even if workers must leave their 'lifetime jobs' in their late fifties, opportunities may be open to them elsewhere. Also, Japanese workers seem to be willing to make these switches. There is a strong desire to work to old age in Japan. As Ogawa and Suits (1983) found, workers under the age of 55 have a strong preference for the extension of their working lives even if it means the sacrifice of increasing wages or of a handsome retirement benefit. Thus we have probably seen only the beginning of the effect that the ageing of the populaton will undoubtedly have on the seniority wage and lifetime employment systems in Japan.

Endnotes

1. Unfortunately, we still do not have access to individual-level data, so we cannot carry out more sophisticted analysis of cohort size effects, such as has been done with United States data.
2. In some of our preliminary analysis we used the ratio of the population, rather than labour force, aged 40–9 to that aged 20–4. The results were virtually the same as those reported here. We also tried using the growth rate of GDP as our economic variable, but it exhibited large year-to-year fluctuations and did not contribute very much to the explanation of the change in WR.

References

Berger, Mark C. (1983), 'The Effect of Cohort Size on Earnings Growth: A Reconsideration of the Evidence', *Working Paper in Economics*, E–60–83, College of Business and Economics, University of Kentucky, Lexington, Kentucky.

Economic Planning Agency (1975), *Economic Analysis*, 57, Tokyo.

—— (1982), *1982 Annual Report on National Accounts*, Tokyo.

—— (1983*a*), *1983 Annual Report on National Accounts*, Tokyo.

—— (1983*b*), *Japan in the Year 2000: Preparing Japan for an Age of Internationalization, the Aging Society and Maturity*, English translation published by the *Japan Times*, Tokyo.

Freeman, Richard B. (1979), 'The Effect of Demographic Factors on Age–Earnings Profiles in the US', *Journal of Human Resources*, 14, 3, 289–318.

Furuya, Kenichi and Linda G. Martin (1981), 'Employment and Retirement of Older Workers in Japan', *NUPRI Research Paper Series*, 8, Nihon University Population Research Institute, Tokyo.

Institute of Population Problems (1982), 'The 35th Abridged Life Tables', *Institute of Population Problems Research Series*, 228, Tokyo.

Ishikawa, Akira (1983), 'Population Reproduction Rates for All Japan: 1981', *Journal of Population Problems*, 165, Tokyo, 64–74.

Martin, Linda G. (1982), 'Japanese Response to an Aging Labor Force', *Population Research and Policy Review*, 1, 1, 19–42.

Ministry of Labour (1983*a* and various years), *Annual Report on the Labour Force Survey*, Tokyo.

—— (1983*b*), *Yearbook of Labour Statistics 1981*, Tokyo.

—— (various years), *Basic Survey of Wage Structure*, Tokyo.

Ogawa, Naohiro (1982), 'Economic Implications of Japan's Aging Population: A Macro-economic Demographic Modelling Approach', *International Labour Review*, 121, 1, 17–33.

—— and Daniel B. Suits (1983), 'Retirement Policy and Japanese Workers: Some Results of an Opinion Survey', *International Labour Review*, 122, 6, forthcoming.

Statistics Bureau, Prime Minister's Office (various years), *Population Census of Japan*.

Sterling, William (1983), 'Patterns of Job Duration in Japan and the United States', manuscript, Department of Economics, Harvard University (April).

Welch, Finis (1979), 'Effects of Cohort Size on Earnings: The Baby Boom Babies' Financial Bust', *Journal of Political Economy*, 87, 5, (October).

4 British Labour Market Responses to Age Distribution Changes

JOHN ERMISCH

The potential importance of the numbers born into a given generation for its members' earnings and employment experience, particularly early in their working careers, has been demonstrated by the work of Easterlin, Freeman, Wachter, and Welch for the United States. Somewhat less is known about how generation size has affected its members' labour market experience in other countries. The analysis which follows begins by examining how relative wages among age groups in the labour force would need to respond to changes in the size of different age groups in order to maintain full employment of all workers. It is shown how the degree of complementarity (in Hicks's sense) between the various groups of workers determines the nature of this response. In particular, the complementarity/substitutability between women and young male workers is important because the supply of each relative to other labour fluctuated over the post-war period in Britain. The empirical analysis focuses on three groups of workers: young men (aged under 21), older men, and women. The proportion of young men in the labour force fluctuated because of earlier fluctuations in the birth-rate and because of a change in the minimum school-leaving age, while women's share of the labour force changed primarily because of changes in labour force participation rates. Relative earnings among these groups did not generally move in the expected direction, and the British labour market was persistently out of equilibrium. During the 1950s and 1960s there was an excess demand for young male workers. As a consequence, their growing numbers during 1955–65 were easily absorbed into employment, while their relative earnings rose. It also appears that this excess demand spilled over into the demand for women workers, particularly part-timers, and this may have played an important part in the sharp rise in their labour force participation rates during 1961–6. Non-market forces continued to dominate wage determination, and by the 1970s an excess supply of young male workers emerged, despite a sharp decline in their relative numbers between 1965 and 1973. The emergence of excess supply may be at least in part attributable to the rapid growth in the supply of a substitute for young men in production —women. Growth in the number of young men relative to older men and women since 1973 was accompanied by a rise in their earnings relative to older men and a fall relative to women. The result has been a rise in their unemployment rate relative to older men and a fall relative to women. The burden of adjustment to the growing number of labour market entrants in the 1970s (because of the baby boom sixteen years earlier) has therefore fallen on their ability to find a job rather than on their relative earnings. After the excess demand for young workers, which characterized the 1960s disappeared, changes in generation size in Britain had their main effect on young people's unemployment experience relative to others.

Some Labour Market Relationships

An important aspect of the impact of changes in the age distribution on the labour market is the effect of the relative numbers of workers of different ages on their relative pay. If age groups are not close substitutes for one another, and labour markets are to clear, then changes in relative wages in response to changes in relative numbers are necessary. An important concept for the analysis of this response is Hicks's *elasticity of complementarity* between any two production inputs, which measures the effect on the price of one input of a change in the quantity of another input, holding marginal cost and the quantities of other inputs constant. It is intimately related to but not identical with the more traditional *elasticity of substitution*, which is measured more often. The latter registers the effect on the quantity of an input employed of changes in the price of another input, holding output and other input prices constant. Use of measures of the latter and the relationship between the two concepts can sometimes provide an insight into the change in relative wages needed to maintain full employment when the age distribution of the labour force changes.[1]

It is helpful first to illustrate the case of only two inputs, let us call them young and older workers. For simplicity, assume that the production function is of the constant elasticity of substitution (CES) class. Then the relationship between relative wages (w_1/w_2) and relative numbers in employment (N_1/N_2) is given by:

$$ln(w_1/w_2) = ln(a/(1-a)) - (1/s)ln(N_1/N_2) - ((b-q)/s)t,$$
$$s > 0, \ 0 < a < 1, \quad (1)$$

where s is the elasticity of substitution between young and older workers, and a measures the inherent intensity of production in the use of young workers (type 1). The last term of equation (1) measures the bias in 'technical change' over time (t), where technical change refers both to changes in the production process and changes in the composition of production. In this context, the elasticity of complementarity is $1/s$, and since $s > 0$, an increase in the number of young workers relative to older workers must reduce the relative wage of young workers in order to maintain full employment of all workers. When there are only two inputs, they must be substitutes in the production of a given output, but they must also be complements in the production of a variable output. In Hicks's terminology, they are *p-substitutes* and *q-complements.* In general, when their elasticity of complementarity is positive, two inputs are *q*-complements, and they are *q-substitutes* when their elasticity of complementarity is negative. Thus if two groups of workers are *q*-substitutes, then the wages of one of these two groups relative to those of a third group would fall with an increase in the supply of the other of these two groups, other supplies constant. This can be seen in the case of three inputs, say young men, older men, and women, when the logarithmic differential of one of the wage ratios is written:

$$dln(w_1/w_2) = k_1(C_{11} - C_{21})dln(N_1) + k_2(C_{12} - C_{22})dln(N_2)$$
$$+ k_3(C_{13} - C_{23})dln(N_3) \quad (2)$$

where C_{ij} is the elasticity of complementarity between inputs i and j, k_j is the share of input j in total costs, and $C_{ii} < 0$. From (2), the effect of an increase in type 3 workers, holding the numbers of types 1 and 2 workers constant, on the wage ratio (w_1/w_2) is $k_3(C_{13} - C_{23})$. It will be negative if types 1 and 3 workers (say young men and women) are *q*-substitutes (i.e., $C_{13} < 0$), since in this case of three inputs only one pair may be *q*-substitutes, and then they must also be *p*-substitutes. In other words, under these fairly plausible assumptions a rise in the supply of women workers relative to others would lower the wages of young men relative to those of older men, and an increase in the relative supply of young men would have a similar depressing effect on the wages of women relative to older men. Even if all inputs are *q*-complements for one another, the effects would be qualitatively similar if young men and women are less complementary in production than older men and women; that is, $C_{13} < C_{23}$. It is also clear from equation (2) that if two groups of workers are *q*-substitutes, then an increase in the supply of one, holding the other constant, reduces its wages relative to the other less than if they were *q*-complements. (Note that the effect on the relative wage w_i/w_j is $k_i(C_{ii} - C_{ij})$, and when i and j are *q*-complements $(C_{ii} - C_{ij}) < C_{ii}$, but when they are *q*-substitutes $(C_{ii} - C_{ij}) > C_{ii}$.)

Therefore, when the demographic composition of the labour force is changing, all relative wage ratios generally must change to assure full employment. Wage adjustment may not, however, occur, or it may be insufficient. The implications of this are most easily seen in the two-factor case. Let L_i represent the supply of labour type and $n_i = N_i/L_i$, which is the 'employment rate' (i.e., the complement of the unemployment rate). Equation (1) can then be rewritten as

$$ln(n_1/n_2) = -s.ln(1 - a)/a) - s.ln(w_1/w_2) + ln(L_2/L_1) - (b - q)t. \quad (3)$$

It is clear from (3) that if the wage ratio were fixed, then increases in the supply of type 1 workers relative to type 2 would lower the employment rate of type 1 workers relative to that of type 2 workers, raising the relative unemployment rate of type 1 workers. Lack of adjustment in relative wages would be reflected in changes in relative unemployment rates and (not considered in the illustration in equation (3)) changes in labour force participation rates.

Finally, a bias in technical change ($b \neq q$) would affect the change in relative wages or relative employment rates of two groups or workers. Neutral technical change corresponds to $b = q$ in equations (1) and (3).

Age Distribution Changes and the British Labour Market

The major influence on the age distribution of the British labour force has been the fluctuation in fertility during this century, particularly since the 1920s. Entry into the labour force around the age of sixteen has been common, and to illustrate the initial impact of fertility on labour force composition Figure 4.1 shows births lagged sixteen years. The age-related information on earnings and employment in Britain has, until recently, only made the rough division between men aged under 21, men aged 21 and over, women aged under 18, and women aged 18 and over. The earnings data are also restricted to manual occupations, mainly in production industries.[2] Thus the focus of the empirical analysis is on the earnings of young people relative to older men and women. In that the earnings data are for manual occupations this may not be an inappropriate focus, since the age–earnings profile is unlikely to be very steep after one's early twenties: the 'learning phase' is short in these occupations. In any case, evidence from the 1970s, when more detailed age, occupation, and industrial earnings data are available, suggests that the changes in relative earnings among age and sex

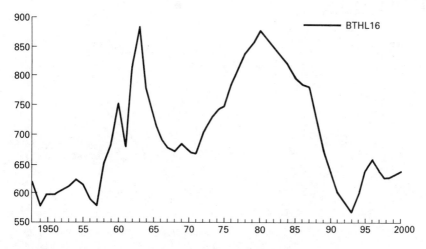

Figure 4.1. Births lagged sixteen years, England and Wales

groups in manual occupations are broadly indicative of changes in relative earnings more generally.

Earnings of females aged under 18 have remained a roughly constant proportion of the earnings of women aged 18 and over, so it was assumed that these two groups were close enough substitutes to make it proper to treat 'women' as one group of workers.[3] Two other groups were distinguished, men aged 21 and over and younger men. Thus, for simplicity, the focus of the analysis will be on the relative earnings and employment experience among these three broad demographic groups.

The supply of women workers relative to men expanded rapidly during the post-war period from just under 31 per cent of the labour force in 1951 to almost 40 per cent in 1981. Over 60 per cent of this growth was concentrated in two relatively short periods, 1961–6 and 1971–5. This is the important background against which changes in the relative supply of young workers took place.

From 1947 to late 1972 the minimum school-leaving age in Britain was 15, and then it was raised to 16. Taking males of at least the minimum school-leaving age but less than 21 to be young men 'of working age', Figure 4.2 shows that between the mid-1950s and the mid-1960s the supply of young men of working age expanded dramatically relative to the number of all men of working age (15 or 16 to 64). The relative supply of young men then fell rapidly during the second half of the 1960s, after which it made a quantum fall because of the raising of the minimum school-leaving age. During the 1970s, the relative supply of young men of working age expanded rapidly again because of the baby boom of 1955–65 shown in Figure 4.1. There was, of course, an upward trend in participation in post-compulsory education

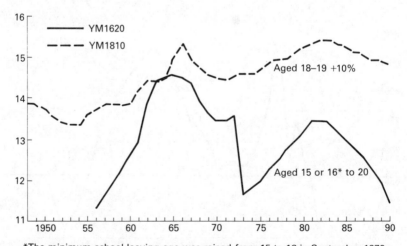

*The minimum school leaving age was raised from 15 to 16 in September 1972.

Figure 4.2. Young men of working age relative to all men of working age

among young men of these ages, but this would only slightly dampen these fluctuations in relative supply. Moreover, some of this change in partici- pation appears to be related to labour market conditions (see Pissarides, 1981), so adjusting the figures in Figure 4.2 for educational participation would to some extent confuse labour market responses to age distribution changes with the changes themselves.

The expected effect of these changes in relative supply on relative hourly earnings depends upon the respective elasticities of complementarity. The increase in the supplies of both young men and women relative to older men during 1955–65 would be expected to have reduced the earnings of each relative to older men, with the increase in the relative supply of one reinforc- ing the fall in the relative earnings of the other if young men and women were *q*-substitutes, or if they were less complementary with one another than either of them were with older men. Yet Figure 4.3 shows that women's hourly earnings only fell slightly relative to older men (the earnings of women in part-time jobs moved similarly to those of full-timers), and that young men's hourly earnings rose relative to older men and to women. At the same time, the unemployment rates of young men and women remained low.

Some of the increase in young men's relative earnings is spurious, reflect- ing changes in the age composition of the employees under the age of 21. Recent age-specific earnings data indicate a fairly steep age-earnings gradient among men under 21. During 1952–72 the average age of men aged under 21 in employment was rising, thereby tending to raise the average age

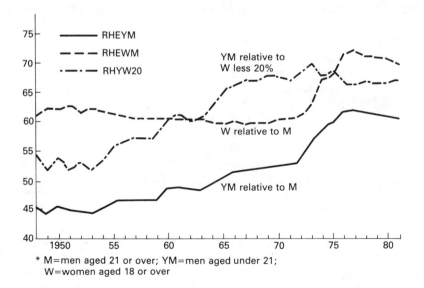

* M=men aged 21 or over; YM=men aged under 21;
  W=women aged 18 or over

Figure 4.3. Relative hourly earnings (full-time workers in manual occupations)

of male employees aged under 21. Attempts to control for these age-compositional changes suggest that the rise in young men's relative.hourly earnings is less steep than Figure 4.3 indicates, but it does not disappear. Furthermore, the steep increase in young men's relative earnings during the first half of the 1970s also remains, despite the strong effect of the raising of the minimum school-leaving age on the average age of young employees. (See Wells, 1983, 16–24).

It is possible that relative supply and relative earnings could move in the same direction if young men and older men are *q*-substitutes, but they must be strong *q*-substitutes (such that $k_1(C_{11} - C_{21}) > 0$ in equation (2)). This could also occur when women are increasing relative to older men, if older men and women are *q*-substitutes (in which case $k_3(C_{13} - C_{23}) > 0$ in equation (2)). But these strong substitution conditions appear unlikely to prevail. Relative earnings changes during 1959–65 in conjunction with the low unemployment rate of young men in this period suggest that either there are strong biases in 'technical change' or that non-market factors dominate wage determination, leading to sustained labour market disequilibrium.

If technical progress or capital accumulation produce larger efficiency gains among older male workers (e.g. $q > b$ in equation (1)), then it is possible that the relative wages of young men could rise despite the increase in their relative supply. Econometric analyses of the youth labour market do not, however, generally support this proposition.[4] As will be explained further below, an excess demand for young male workers during 1955–65 appears the more likely alternative.

During the latter 1960s and the first half of the 1970s the composition of the labour force shifted strongly in favour of women, and there was a sharp

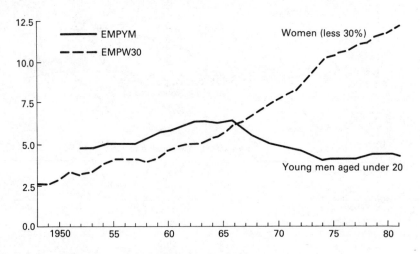

Figure 4.4.   Shares of total employment (per cent)

decline in the supply of young male workers because of age distribution changes in the late 1960s and the raising of the minimum school-leaving age in late 1972 (see Figure 4.2). The sharp rise in young men's earnings relative to older men during 1972-7 (Figure 4.3) may be consistent with the fall in their relative supply, and the latter could also help explain the dramatic rise in women's earnings relative to older men during 1972-7, if young men and women are q-substitutes. Nevertheless, the large rise in women's earnings relative to older men's during 1970-7 is also a product of the introduction of the Equal Pay Act over the first half of the 1970s (see Greenhalgh, 1980), and there was a large rise in the young men's unemployment rate relative to older men's (see Figure 4.5). The latter development is not consistent with a shortage of young men. Rather it suggests a labour market out of equilibrium with relative wages being set in large part by forces other than the labour market's.

The arguments for the predominance of non-market factors in wage determination are strong for the 1970s. Over the post-war period to 1970 collective bargaining agreements tended to reduce the age at which adult wage rates were payable, but there was a marked acceleration in this trend during the first half of the 1970s. It appears that this acceleration was a consequence of lowering the age of majority from 21 to 18, and that this increased the relative pay of boys aged 16-17 as well as that of young men aged 18-20 (see Wells, 1983, 22-3). In addition, the Equal Pay Act raised the earnings of women relative to men, and incomes policies were also operating to compress wage differentials during 1973-4. Thus collective bargaining arrangements, legislative changes, and macroeconomic policies appear to have been important in setting relative wages independently of labour market forces.

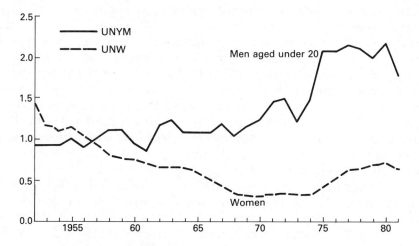

Figure 4.5. Relative unemployment rates

Changing Disequilibrium in the British Labour Market

With relative earnings not fully responsive to changes in relative supplies, the British labour market was always in a state of disequilibrium. In such a market there are mainly quantity adjustments to changes in relative supplies and in the more or less exogenous relative wage levels. Figure 4.4 indicates how the composition of employment changed over the post-war period. Young men's share of total employment rose until the mid-1960s, and then it fell until 1974. This relative employment growth occurred in spite of a rise in their relative earnings between 1955 and 1966. Even though their relative supply was growing (Figure 4.2), there was no upward trend in their unemployment rate relative to older men's until the 1970s (see Figure 4.5). Although it did rise relative to the unemployment rate of women, it did not exceed 3 per cent before 1967.[5] The ability to absorb into employment the large cohorts of young men entering the labour market during 1955–65 in the face of their rising earnings relative to older men and to women strongly suggests that there was excess demand for young workers during this period, and this is supported by econometric analysis which indicates that there was excess demand for young workers until about 1969 (see Merrilees and Wilson, 1979, and Wells, 1983). Since this econometric analysis indicates that women are *p*-substitutes for young men, this excess demand would spill over into the demand for women workers, and this may help explain the rapid rise in women's labour force participation rates during the first half of the 1960s and also the fall in their unemployment rate relative to men.

The second half of the 1960s saw a fall in the relative supply of young men, which would have tended to raise the value of their relative wage consistent with equilibrium, but there was also a rise in the supply of women workers relative to others. If young men and women are *q*-substitutes, this rise in relative supply would have moderated the rise in young men's equilibrium-relative wage. In this sense, the increase in the relative supply of women may have been partly responsible for the emergence of an excess supply of young men after 1969 noted above. It may also be a result of the reduction in the ages at which adult rates were paid after 1969, but there in addition appears to have been a rise in training costs during the second half of the 1960s, and there may also have been a structural break in the composition of labour demand which increasingly favoured women in the second half of the 1960s (see Wells, 1983, 27–30). The latter may indeed have been a product of the growing use of women's labour, particularly in part-time jobs, during the first half of the 1960s, which made employers more aware of the advantages of employing women in part-time jobs (see Ermisch, 1983, 143–5). A structural change in labour demand may also have arisen because the composition of employment was increasingly shifting in favour of the service industries. Total employment reached its apex in 1966, and after that employment in the production industries fell while service employment rose.

In contrast to the earlier period, it is possible to identify the demand function for young workers in the period since 1969, and from it the effect of the unresponsiveness of relative wages to relative labour supplies on relative employment and unemployment rates can be assessed. Since 1973 the supply of young men has been expanding relative to older men (Figure 4.2), and relative to women (particularly since 1977). During this same period, young men's hourly earnings fell relative to women's and rose until 1977 relative to older men's (Figure 4.3). As a consequence, the young men's unemployment rate has risen relative to older men's, and it has fallen since 1974 relative to women's (not shown). Recent econometric analysis suggests that the rise in the young men's unemployment rate relative to older men's primarily reflects the rise in the relative unemployment rate of young men aged under 18, and that this rise was in large part a consequence of the rise in their relative earnings.[6] This suggests that it is the relative wages of young men aged under 18 which have been moving most out of line with market-clearing relative wages, creating an excess supply of young men under the age of 18. The econometric analysis also indicate that older men and women are *p*-substitutes for young men (employment elasticities with respect to relative wages of -2.9 and -1.45 respectively). These results are consistent with young men and women being *q*-substitutes, although they are also consistent with all three groups being *q*-complements for one another. Although the relative supply of young workers declines over the remainder of the 1980s, adjustment toward equilibrium in the labour market still probably requires a fall in young men's earnings relative to older men, and, if young men and women are *q*-substitutes, a reduction in women's earnings relative to older men's. The decline in young men's earnings relative to older men's since 1977 appears to have reduced their relative unemployment rate (see Figures 4.3 and 4.5). As the decade progresses, however, the downward pressure on young men's and women's relative earnings should abate.

Analysis of the British labour market indicates that recognition of the disequilibrium state of the labour market is important in assessing the implications of age distribution changes for relative earnings and unemployment. It also underlines the fact that relative wages among demographic groups are affected by the complementarity relationships between groups and the supplies of all groups. In particular, the evidence for substitutability between women and young men suggests that the growth in the supply of women workers and changes in their relative earnings may be closely related to changes in the supply, relative earnings, and employment experience of young male workers.

Endnotes

1. More prescisely, the discussion uses the definition of the elasticity of complementarity introduced by Sato and Koizumi (1973), which is the inverse of Hicks's (1970) original definition.
2. The industries covered are all manufacturing industries; mining and quarrying (except coal-

mining); construction; gas, electricity, and water; transport and communication (except railways and sea transport); certain miscellaneous services; and public administration. With the exception of the data in Figure 4.1, the data referred to in this paper have recently been collected in a consistent form in the data appendix of Wells (1983).

3. Consistent aggregation requires that the marginal rate of substitution between young and older women (which equals their wage ratio) be independent of the quantities of other inputs employed. A sufficient condition is that young and older women be strong q-substitutes such that $C_{ii} = C_{ij} = C_{jj}$.

4. A trend was never statistically significant in the labour demand functions for young men estimated by Wells (1983). Although Hutchinson *et al.* did find such a trend, their estimation covered a period where, as argued below, there was an excess demand for young male workers, making it doubtful that they identified a demand function.

5. These unemployment rates are based on *registered* unemployment. Until recently, women have not had an incentive to register, because they could opt out of national insurance payments in return for losing their eligibility to unemployment benefit. Because of rule changes, there has been an upward trend in their propensity to register during the latter 1970s, thereby tending to overstate the real rise in the women's unemployment rate.

6. Wells's (1983) 'best' equation for the demand for young men aged under 18 is:

$$\Delta ln(N_y/N) = 0.01 - 2.93 \quad \Delta ln(W_y/W_{om}) - 1.45 \quad \Delta ln(W_y/W_f) - 0.04 \text{ ROSLA}$$
$$\quad\quad\quad\quad (0.09)\,(5.4) \quad\quad\quad (2.7) \quad\quad\quad\quad (1.3)$$
$$\bar{R}^2 = 0.89 \; DW = 2.04 \text{ (absolute value of } t\text{-statistic in parentheses)}$$

where N_y is employment of young men aged under 18; N is total employment; W_y is young men's earnings, W_{om} is older men's earnings, and W_f is women's earnings; ROSLA is a dummy variable equal to 1 in 1973, 0 elsewhere, to reflect the change in the minimum school-leaving age.

References

Ermisch, J.F. (1983), *The Political Economy of Demographic Change*, Heinemann Educational Books, London.

Greenhalgh, C. (1980), 'Male–Female Wage Differentials in Great Britain: Is Marriage an Equal Opportunity?', *The Economic Journal*, 90 (December), 751-75.

Hicks, J. (1970), 'Elasticity of Substitution again: Substitutes and Complements', *Oxford Economic Papers*, 22 (November), 289-96.

Hutchinson, G., N. Barr, and A. Drobny (1979), 'A Sequential Approach to the Dynamic Specification of the Demand for Young Male Labour in Great Britain', Department of Economics Working Paper, 60, Queen Mary College, London University.

Merrilees, W. and R. Wilson (1979), *Disequilibrium in the Labour Market for Young People in Great Britain*, Manpower Research Group Discussion Paper, 10, Warwick University.

Pissarides, C. (1981), 'Staying on at School in England and Wales', *Economica*, 48 (November), 345-64.

Sato, R. and T. Koizumi (1973), 'On the Elasticities of Substitution and Complementarity', *Oxford Economic Papers*, 25 (March), 44-56.

Wells, W. (1983), *The Relative Pay and Employment of Young People*, Department of Employment Research Paper, 42 (December).

Part 2

Fertility, Age Distribution, and Intergenerational Relations

Introduction: Intergenerational Relations

W. BRIAN ARTHUR

The three chapters in this section—on overlapping-generations models, social security policy analysis, and the microeconomics of fertility in a growth-theoretic setting—together span much of the current research interest in population economics.

Willis's chapter, Chapter 6, is perhaps the most comprehensive statement of the overlapping-generations model to date. Recall that overlapping-generations models were first set up by Samuelson in 1958 in part to investigate the problem of intergenerational support: cohorts at retired, non-working ages have consumption needs but have no direct 'endowments'—no labour—to exchange with younger, productive cohorts to fulfil these needs. Direct trading between cohorts is therefore not possible. Samuelson showed that contrivances such as fiat money could act as an intermediary: cohorts could trade part of their product for 'money' when young and productive, and use these 'savings' when old to exchange for the product of a new generation. Providing the exchange intermediary is recognized by society as a store of wealth, and expectations of its value continue to be fulfilled, such transfers between cohorts can go on indefinitely with everyone better off over their life cycle. In posing a simple question—how productive endowments and consumption needs might be matched over the life cycle—Samuelson unlocked a wealth of insights: into much of the *raison d'être* of money, the family, the banking system, and other social institutions; into the determination of the interest rate; and into the role of economic expectations and of transfer relationships between the generations. The overlapping-generations model has been much studied in the thirty or so years of its existence.

Willis develops a Diamond-style framework for the overlapping-generations model that is at once flexible and general. The framework accounts for cohort transfers that take place both through the market and outside the market: within the family, for example. A full demographic age dimension permits age-specification of labour participation, consumption need, and demographic behaviour. The primary intermediary of cohort exchange—or store of value—is ownership of the capital of competitive firms. In this system capital and labour together produce output and both grow eventually in a steady-state Solow equilibrium at the population growth rate. Aggregate life-cycle saving and corporate needs for expansion of capital are equilibrated in a savings-investment market. Following the work of Gale and Kim, Willis shows that such a system can strike a steady-state equilibrium either at an interest rate that differs from the population growth rate with aggregate credit balances at zero, or alternatively (if devices like fiat money are allowed) at an interest rate equal to the population growth rate with non-zero credit balances. He classifies these equilibria, shows the economic and demographic conditions under which each type will emerge, and examines whether they can be upheld by a private banking system. The model is general enough to allow fertility and transfer behaviour to be made endogenous, and to permit comparative static analysis of the effects of changes in societal and familial transfer arrangements, fertility behaviour, human capital acquisition, and economic production possibilities. This enlarged framework, instructive in itself, will undoubtedly prove itself useful in other studies.

In Chapter 5, Keyfitz also takes up the question of transfers between cohorts—social security transfers this time—in the context not of an abstract theoretical model but rather of the actual US economy. In this real-world economy the population is not in steady-state growth, however: cohorts swell and contract, in no consistent time-pattern. A pure pay-as-you-go system like that of the US then performs badly in terms of cohort fairness. Small retired cohorts lucky enough to be followed by larger working ones tend to be well supported; large retired cohorts followed by small working ones tend to be poorly supported. This latter will increasingly be the case in most of the developed countries in the future. Pay-as-you-go may then become politically less feasible over time as well as financially less supportable.

Keyfitz's chapter suggests three ways to redress partially this cohort inequity problem. The present system guarantees constant benefits to each individual, which favours smaller cohorts. A system of constant *contributions* from each individual, on the other hand, would favour larger cohorts. An average of these would impart greater equity. Alternatively, each cohort might take care of itself directly by building up its own fund backed by the holding of capital stock. Alternatively again, each cohort might contribute a fixed amount in its working years. In this Lapkoff scheme people in large cohorts pay in less and receive less, people in smaller cohorts pay in more but receive more. Once again cohort equity is assured. Keyfitz assesses each of these schemes for rates of return and for economic and political feasibility. He concludes that a combination of the three schemes would be both workable and expedient.

In Chapter 7 Cigno combines the new microeconomic theory of fertility with neo-classical growth theory. Making population endogenous with a Solow growth model is not new: indeed, Solow's original article allowed population growth to be determined by economic circumstances, and there has been no shortage of similar models since. But these earlier studies represent population growth simply as a function of the capital–labour ratio. Cigno, by contrast, represents fertility as determined by family income, parental preferences, and implicit 'child prices'. This allows a fully endogenous dynamic system where population growth drives the supply side of the economy and economic circumstances in turn determine population growth. Steady states can be analysed. The richer substitution possibilities of this model lead to some surprising results. Family allowances, Cigno finds, increase income, consumption, and the number of children per family—but permanently reduce the amount spent on each child.

5 Some Demographic Properties of Transfer Schemes: How to Achieve Equity Between the Generations

NATHAN KEYFITZ

When population and the economy are growing rapidly no one need be much concerned about equity between the generations. Our descendants will be more numerous than we, and they will also be richer, and for these reasons combined they will have no trouble supporting us after our retirement; we could even have a higher standard of living in retirement than we had while working, and all at acceptable cost to the individual worker paying the bill. It is when the population settles into equilibrium, and the prospects for the economy are 1 or 2 per cent growth rather than 4 or 5, that support of the old becomes expensive enough for the public to make intergenerational comparisons of costs and benefits. One comparison is between the amounts that are paid by the baby boom generation, now supporting the small generation that preceded it, and the large amount that its smaller successor will have to pay. The difference is great enough to throw doubt on whether pensions will actually be paid in the years after 2015.

The purpose of this article is to show three ways in which equity can be secured. None of them is without some inconvenience, and hope must lie in a partial application of each, in a combination that can provide an acceptable approach to equity.

We could move towards equity by holding constant over time the individual contribution rather than the benefit. Instead of collecting enough taxes from each generation to pay a fixed pension to the previous one in its old age, the system would collect the same amount from all and divide the total collected among the pensioners in place. That confers an advantage on the small generation rather than the large. Averaging this fixed contribution with the fixed pension would provide a measure of equity.

A second way is to charge a tax sufficient that average costs over the long term are covered and to build up a reserve in times like the present when a large cohort is paying for a small one, to be spent over the years from 2015 onward when a small cohort will be paying for a large one. If, as has been pointed out many times, all goods are perishable, so that there is no durable repository of value, then no reserve can be carried, and each generation must pay whatever it currently costs to maintain the previous one. Such an argument overlooks the existence of capital, of which durable productiveness over time is the very definition. We do of course need to worry about the limits to the amount of capital that the economy can effectively use, and investment considerations make it unlikely that equity would be reached by this means alone.

The third device is to think of the unit for social security purposes not as the individual but as the cohort. If we consider each cohort paying $1 billion for the support of the previous generation, then in a sense there is perfect equity. The large generation would as individuals pay smaller premiums and receive smaller benefits than the smaller generation, and the equity would be bought at the price of pensions for some too small to live on. Hence again this procedure can be recommended only in part, but it is a useful adjunct to the other two approaches.

Before taking up these three approaches in detail we consider the logic of transfer schemes. In particular we investigate who it is that will pay the pensions of those blanketed in at the start of pay-as-you-go security schemes: the money has to come from somewhere. If the scheme were liquidated we would know who paid: it would be the last contributors, who received no benefits. They would be paying for ancestors who died long before they were born. In fact social security schemes are not intended to be liquidated, but the slowing of growth is equivalent to a partial liquidation, and such slowing seems unavoidable.

Transfer schemes include a simple gift from one person to another, a chain letter, inheritance of wealth from one generation to another, support of parents by their children, unemployment insurance, and (largest of all in money transferred) old-age security. We will show some of the inequities to which pure transfer schemes can lead when money is passed on immediately, so that no reserve is held, and how these inequities can be mitigated by delay in passing on the funds, that is, by a (full or partial) reserve. They can also be mitigated by allowing the contributions and pensions to vary suitably. While the considerations of this chapter apply to many kinds of transfer, it is to social security that the argument is principally directed and the conclusions applied.

Transfer Chains

Think of persons A, B, and C, and suppose that a unit of money is transferred from A to B and a unit from B to C. We have one gainer, one loser, and one person whose position is unchanged. This is aside from the cost of making the transfers, which here, as in more elaborate cases, we will assume to be negligible. That assumption is not unrealistic when the work is done by modern computer methods; less than 1 per cent of the US social security programme is spent on administration.

One may wonder what there is to say about arrangements for merely passing money around, for at first they seem overall to be no-gain, no-loss, and completely uninteresting. Yet from the properties of these pure exchange schemes we can explain some of the most critical features of social security programmes. For instance, suppose that A receives a unit from B, B a unit from C, C from D, and so on through a chain twenty-six persons long. If the unit is the generation, then the net effect is that Z, at the end of the chain six or seven centuries later, has contributed to A. Something like this is needed to understand how people in a later century will contribute to the support of those old people present at the start of social security in 1940. The initial beneficiaries receive much more than they pay, and the scheme generates no income, so we are challenged to find exactly who is covering the extra benefits to those initial payees. We do not claim that the question is an easy one, but on the whole it can be said that the extra benefits obtained while the scheme is expanding are covered by those contributing subsequently when the scheme is stationary or contracting.

Only in a first approximation is it true that the transfers are economically neutral. If the contributors and the beneficiaries differ systematically in how they spend the money, then different parts of the economy will be stimulated or depressed by the transfer. This is a deeper subject than that of this paper, and no further reference will be made to it. We will consider only the first round of effects of the transfers, admitting that the neglected economic effects, the reverberations of those transfers, are undoubtedly important, but at least for now abstracting from them.

Suppose that there are a number of individuals in each of the categories A, B, and C, and that everyone pays out one dollar. Let there be two Bs, who divide A's dollar between them, and three Cs, who divide the two dollars from the Bs among them. Now the As and the Bs have a net loss, and the Cs are the gainers. In any such finite or closed chain the gains offset the losses. But if the chain is indefinitely prolonged, so that there are four Ds, five Es and so on, with everyone still paying out one dollar, then everyone loses.

Just as everyone loses in this situation, so everyone gains if the money is passed the other way, with the two Bs transferring to A, the three Cs transferring to the Bs, and so forth. As long as the chain continues each member of it receives more than he or she pays out; only if it is somehow broken and the transfer game ended is there a loss, and that loss is confined to the last members of the chain. The gains here steadily diminish, and if the participants are successive generations of a reproducing population the gains will depend on the ratio of the numbers of persons in those generations. With positive growth every generation obtains a positive return. If there are g_n persons in the nth generation and g_{n+1} in the $n + 1$th, then each member of the nth generation increases its holding in the ratio g_{n+1}/g_n. The ideal chain letter is one in which the series is in a constant ratio $g_{n+1}/g_n = R$, for example. If $R = 4$ each participant gets back the 4th power of 4; if $R = 10$

the 10th power of 10. Caldwell (1982) shows how many features of social life, including reproductive practices, can be explained by the direction and amount of wealth flows. The present analysis is confined to one specific part of the total flow.

If the chain is increasing everyone gains; if it decreases everyone loses. For an infinite chain this statement is unqualified; for a finite chain the last members are an exception. We will have a special interest in the transition from an increasing to a decreasing chain.

Quasi-Interest

Whenever transfers take finite time they may be thought of as carrying quasi-interest. B gives a dollar to A and thirty years later receives two dollars from C; he is justified in thinking of the increase as interest on the money that he laid out thirty years earlier. He doubled his money, true, but the doubling took so long that it amounts to only a little more than 2.3 per cent interest per annum.

The use of the rate of interest to measure how well any individual or group has done takes proper account of time and seems the most suitable of all the infinite ways of making comparisons between transfer schemes. If there is a series of payments $p_1, p_2, \ldots$ at times $t_1, t_2, \ldots$ and a series of benefits $B_1, B_2, \ldots$ at times $T_1, T_2, \ldots$ then the rate r that equalizes the discounted payments with the discounted benefits will be the effective rate of interest. (Whether we discount to the birth of the scheme or to some other date makes no difference.) Thus r is the solution to the equation

$$p_1 e^{-rt_1} + p_2 e^{-rt_2} + \ldots = B_1 e^{-rT_1} + B_2 e^{-rT_2} + \ldots$$

where the zero point on the time-scale is arbitrary.

The equation can be solved in many ways, of which a functional iteration seems the easiest to programme. If d is an arbitrary quantity more or less equal to the difference between the mean time of contribution and of benefit and r is a provisional rate of interest, an improved rate will be r^*, where

$$r^* = \frac{1}{d} ln \left\{ e^{rd} \left[\frac{B_1 e^{-rT_1} + B_2 e^{-rT_2} + \ldots}{p_1 e^{-rt_1} + p_2 e^{-rt_2} + \ldots} \right] \right\}.$$

The formula may be verified by noting that if $r^* = r$ it reduced identically to the equation to be solved. Convergence to more decimals than could possibly be of use rarely requires more than ten iterations.

Demographic Properties of Transfer Chains

Such a method can be applied to any transfer scheme in which we can make estimates of the sizes of the groups between which the transfers will take place. In our case it will be the number of persons of working age and the

Table 5.1.   Implicit percentage rate of return on social security payments for successive birth cohorts

	Fraction of 1979 birth-rates		
	0.50	1.00	1.50
1960–5	0.89	1.05	1.17
1980–5	− 0.55	0.49	1.12
2000–5	− 1.84	− 0.12	1.01
2020–5	− 1.93	− 0.22	1.16
2040–5	− 1.54	− 0.21	1.13

Three levels of births; US data, fixed pensions.

number of persons of retired age. We will see how the value of *r* will evolve in the future if the projected population turns out to be realized, and also what various departures in the rates of birth, death, and migration from those regarded as the most probable will do to the value of *r*.

The centre column of Table 5.1 shows the return to the several cohorts over time. Persons born in 1960–5 obtain a positive interest of 1.05 per cent on their contributions; these are the people who will be contributing between 1980 and 2025. Other cohorts up to the end of the century will likewise have positive returns, though they will be smaller; cohorts born in the twenty-first century will suffer negative interest, as we see continuing down their centre column in Table 5.1. Other columns of Table 5.1 show the effect of higher or lower birth rates.

Effect of Deaths

In contrast to the decisive effect of variations in fertility, mortality makes relatively little difference. The cohort of the years 2000–5 would draw − 0.04 per cent with half the mortality of 1979, and − 0.20 per cent with 50 per cent greater mortality than that of 1979.

Labour Force Participation

Beyond considerations of the effect of birth, death, and immigration as described at greater length in Keyfitz (1985), we may apply restrictions that occur in real social security schemes and see what difference these restrictions make to the rate of quasi-interest. For instance, the labour force participation rates have been changing, with those for men in Western countries showing declining rates at all ages, and in particular at ages in the fifties and sixties. A falling labour force participation rate means a diminution in the contributions to the social security programme, and if the individuals are above the age at which drawing is permitted they will at the same time increase the number of beneficiaries. Thus the financial condition

Table 5.2. Applying labour force participation rates: implicit percentage rate of return on social security payments for successive birth cohorts

	Fraction of 1979 birth-rates		
	0.50	1.00	1.50
1960–5	0.00	0.57	0.48
1980–5	– 1.73	0.36	1.86
2000–5	– 2.95	– 0.77	0.78
2020–5	– 2.94	– 1.11	0.34
2040–5	– 2.53	– 1.10	0.32

Three levels of births; US data, fixed pensions.

of the scheme suffers in two ways. Only the change in contributors is here taken into account, and Table 5.2 shows the striking fall in the rate of quasi-interest obtained when participation rates are entered into the calculation. The effect of falling male rates has in the past been offset by rising female rates, but sooner or later all the women who want to be in the labour force will have entered and there will be no further offset of any subsequent male decline.

Tables 5.1 and 5.2 used a defined and fixed benefit. It was as though one dollar was paid each year to each person over 65 and the tax on the existing working population was adjusted to provide exactly the sum needed for this. We saw how this is advantageous to the large cohort.

Defined Benefits versus Defined Contributions

The other way of doing the calculation is to suppose that each person of working age makes a unit annual payment and that the payments are divided among those entitled to benefit in that year (Table 5.3). This produces a different result in that the large cohort can then be at a disadvantage; its members pay out a unit even though the old people of the time are few, and when it comes to collect it will have small pensions because the numerous

Table 5.3. Implicit percentage rate of return on social security payments for successive birth cohorts

	Fraction of 1979 birth-rates		
	0.50	1.00	1.50
1960–5	– 1.57	– 0.14	0.91
1980–5	– 2.14	– 0.21	1.22
2000–5	– 1.69	– 0.21	1.14
2020–5	– 1.32	– 0.21	1.12
2040–5	– 1.03	– 0.20	1.11

Three levels of births; US data, fixed contribution.

pensioners must share a fixed amount from each of a small cohort. But Table 5.3 shows that the intercohort variation is generally small.

The small variation among cohorts in Table 5.3 is in part an artefact of the population projection on which the calculation is based. Variation among cohorts for the contributors of the next generation is set by the 1980 age distribution with which we start; there is no corresponding way of ascertaining variation among numbers of contributors born later than 1980. Like other projections, this one implicitly recognizes birth variation in the form of a baby boom only for the past. We do well if we can guess the trend for the future, without hoping to anticipate variations about the trend, and all the present calculations assume rates fixed at the 1979 level.

Only in a stable population, with no fluctuations in cohort size, but steady increase or decrease, would the two ways of making the calculation (fixed benefit and fixed contribution) give the same result. It can be argued that the two formulations straddle the ideal, which is an equal return in quasi-interest to the outlay in all generations, and that an average of the defined contribution and defined benefit may come close to giving this level rate of return, the same quasi-interest to small and large cohorts.

The point is applicable to legislative action to take account of the baby boom. When the premiums and benefits do not correspond at any given moment, Congress can modify either the one or the other. If on an *ad hoc* basis it adjusts contributions consistently over a period of time it favours the large cohorts; if it modifies benefits it favours the small cohorts. My reading of changes currently being made is that they include some of both kinds of adjustment, and clearly Congress has in mind the equity problem with which this chapter is concerned. But an unfunded scheme, in which there is no explicit recognition of cohorts, attains equity only very roughly.

A Partial Reserve Scheme

An alternative approach to the equity problem is the maintenance of a partial reserve. This would avoid inequities that could cause abandonment of social security, with results similar to the ending of a chain letter. Today's

Table 5.4.   Estimated persons of pension and of contributing age, US 1980–2060, with fertility of late 1970s and slowly declining mortality

	Total population (thousands)	Persons aged 65 + (thousands)	Persons aged 20–64 (thousands)	Persons 65 + /20–64 (ratio)
1980	226,506	25,545	128,157	0.199
2000	264,136	32,595	159,752	0.204
2020	285,697	44,866	172,268	0.260
2040	288,161	55,943	165,482	0.338
2060	280,280	53,879	163,887	0.329

workers, contributors to social security, have good reason to question whether they will themselves ever draw social security. The members of the baby boom especially, aware that the heavy costs they will impose from about 2015 will fall on a small cohort of workers, cannot but doubt whether that small cohort succeeding them will submit to the high taxes that would be required. Table 5.4 shows that the ratio of drawing ages to contributing ages 0.199 in 1980, rises to 0.338 by 2030, when the baby boom qualifies for pension, an increase of nearly 70 per cent. The tax, now 13 per cent (not 19.9 per cent, because a higher proportion of the wage is taxed than is replaced by the benefit), would have to increase by about 70 per cent, 22 per cent of the covered wage, if all non-demographic elements in the calculation remain the same.

Despite current social security taxes, which look high to many, it may be said that the large cohorts are not paying their way, for their taxes are just sufficient to cover the pensions of the preceding rather small generation of retirees, who will increase slowly or not at all during the remainder of the century as those born in the 1930s retire (Table 5.4).

Some modesty is required in presenting such forecasts because of that unknown factor, future fertility. If the birth-rate is 25 per cent higher than in the late 1970s, which would not put it very much above replacement level, the increase by 2040 would be only 32 per cent; if births are 25 per cent lower, which is about the level for West Germany, we would have a 125 per cent rise over the present (Table 5.5).

Whatever formal legislation and government accounting say, there is a sense in which each generation derives its moral claim from its own payments. The bond between the generations notwithstanding, if one pays less it is setting an example of inequity to the generation following that it may in due course come to regret.

An ordinary funded pension as actuarially calculated is population-independent and hence meets the condition of equity between the generations. None of the troubling questions now confronting social security can arise for it. Of course other problems would arise, and we cannot contemplate full funding, if only because the transitional participants would have to

Table 5.5. Estimated persons of pension age as a fraction of those of contributing age US 1980–2060

	Fertility relative to that of late 1970s	
	25% below	25% above
1980	0.199	0.199
2000	0.204	0.204
2020	0.290	0.236
2040	0.449	0.264
2060	0.434	0.265

pay on both schemes. We seek to know the minimum funding that would secure the desired equity between the generations.

Partial funding is distinctly different from an actuarial reserve scheme. In the partial funding here proposed, aimed at a level premium, one stays with pay-as-you-go, but raises the contribution (by an amount that will turn out to be some 25 per cent over the 1980 level; the level premium would be lower than pay-as-you-go after about 2020). The partial reserve would be allowed to rise (and later fall) with fluctuations in the size of contributing and drawing populations. The increase of about a quarter in the contribution over the present would produce a reserve at one time equal to ten years of benefits.

Formal Conditions for Partial Funding

The formulas are easily set down in terms of $f(a, t)$, the density of population at age a and time t; thus $f(a, t)da$ is the number of individuals between age a and $a + da$ at time t. Calling the unknown uniform annual contribution p, supposed the same for everyone and at all times considered, we have the total contributions accumulated up to time T and discounted at interest δ as equal to

$$c = p \int_0^T \int_\alpha^\beta f(a, t)dae^{-\delta t}dt, \tag{1}$$

where α is the age of starting work and β the age of retirement. The total paid out, likewise discounted at interest δ, is

$$b = \int_0^T \int_\beta^\omega f(a, t)dae^{-\delta t}dt, \tag{2}$$

so the reserve at time T, $V(T)$, must be the difference (1) – (2). We can now set p such that the reserve after 100 years is 0:

$$V(100) = c - b = 0. \tag{3}$$

Estimates for mid-1980 in the United States are 25,545,000 persons aged 65 and over, against 128,517,000 aged 20–64 at last birthday. For purposes of this discussion we are taking it that the former are pensioners and the latter the contributors who pay those pensions. In fact these were 23,336,000 OASDI beneficiaries on the retirement programme in 1980 and 97,608,000 contributors, but any closeness of these figures to the demographic counts arises through offsetting: thus among the beneficiaries were many persons aged 62–4, and these, along with the unemployed of all ages, were not contributors. Once again, our object in the present calculations is not to account for the present fund, nor to project its finances into the future, but only to measure the purely demographic factors that will come into play.

Calculation of Partial Funding Premium

For mid-1980 the ratio of 65 and over to 20–64, counting both sexes and disregarding alike employment status and pension status, was 25,545 : 128,517 or 0.199. There was approximately one older person or each five persons of working age. That would seem to make the required tax rate about 20 per cent, but in fact it was 13 per cent, divided between employer and employee, again largely because the fraction of salary replaced on retirement was less than 100 per cent, and the fraction taxed was much closer to 100 per cent.

First we think of a projection of the population with present fertility rates if money carries no interest and we wish to accumulate a fund that will just be exhausted at the end of 100 years. The required rate is 0.282 (Table 5.6); a tax of 0.282 of whatever part of the wage is to be replaced, disregarding unemployment and suchlike, would permit all generations for the next 100 years to pay the same premium and receive the same benefit. Note that this abstracts from inflation as well as from expansion of the economy. In a rough application of this result one can say that an increase in the ratio 0.282 : 0.199 = 1.4 would do it; we would need to raise the annual contribution by about 40 per cent from 1980 onward in order to be able to provide equity among the generations.

Table 5.6 incidentally shows that the problem is a long-term one. For equity over the next 25 years the tax would only have to go up in the ratio 0.203 : 0.199, or practically not at all, to build a reserve that would provide equity but be exhausted at the end of the 25 years.

We can improve the calculation by crediting the interest drawn by the resultant reserve. If the interest was 2 per cent then the tax need only be 0.251 for equity over 100 years; if it is 4 per cent, only 0.228. Four percent may be high for the real rate of interest averaged over a number of decades; two per cent would seem conservative, and if so the immediate rise in the tax rate would be given by 0.251 : 0.199 or about 26 per cent. A very rough

Table 5.6. Effect of time horizon and rate of interest on premium required for equal treatment of generations (fertility of late 1970s)

Length of time from 1980 to:		Rate of interest		
	Years	0%	2%	4%
2005	25	0.203	0.203	0.203
2030	50	0.234	0.223	0.215
2055	75	0.266	0.242	0.225
2080	100	0.282	0.251	0.228
2105	125	0.291	0.255	0.229

confirmation of this is found in the OASDI calculation of the cost rate for 1982–2006 as 11.37 per cent of taxable income, against an average cost rate of 14.36 per cent for the average of 1982–2056, also 26 per cent higher. (There are many offsetting divergences in the two calculations.)

Fluctuating Reserves

We may track out the amount of reserve and see how much it changes over the course of the century. Table 5.7 shows the ratio of reserve to benefits with rate of interest at 2 per cent, and Table 5.8 shows the ratio at 0 and 0.04. Evidently one needs less reserve if the rate of interest is high, but one can sum up the tables by saying that at the peak, about the year 2015, the needed reserve would be between about eight and twelve years' benefits. The fund accumulates most rapidly in the first decade of the twenty-first century, and that is when the temptation to expand benefits or put the money to other purposes will be strongest.

Bearing in mind that it was its political attractiveness that brought pay-as-you-go social security in the first place, we have to fear its unpopularity as the scheme matures and becomes more expensive. One can easily imagine a pressure to curtail, even abandon, social security in its present form at some

Table 5.7. Change in reserve during five-year period centred on given data, with interest at 2 per cent

Period	Average annual change over five-year period (thousands)	Cumulative reserve as of end of period (thousands)	Ratio of reserve to annual benefit
1978–82	6,684	33,420	1.31
1983–7	6,815	71,007	2.52
1988–92	6,344	110,194	3.61
1993–7	6,061	152,087	4.70
1998–02	7,467	205,418	6.30
2003–7	8,961	271,828	8.25
2008–12	8,278	341,806	9.78
2013–17	4,153	398,520	10.12
2018–22	– 1,665	432,109	9.63
2023–7	– 8,662	434,245	8.51
2028–32	– 14,291	408,457	7.30
2033–7	– 15,649	373,169	6.53
2038–42	– 14,444	340,196	6.08
2043–7	– 12,849	311,728	5.74
2048–52	– 12,763	280,696	5.21
2053–7	– 13,126	244,585	4.54
2058–62	– 13,491	202,851	3.76
2063–7	– 13,316	157,604	2.94
2068–72	– 12,998	109,187	2.05
2073–7	– 12,687	57,235	1.09
2078–82	– 12,651	0	0.00

Unit = $1 benefit per person 65 + . Tax rate = 0.2508 of unit.

Table 5.8. Effect of rate of interest on reserve (accumulated reserve as fraction of benefit payment)

	Rate of interest	
	0.0%	0.04%
1980	2.08	0.73
2000	8.56	4.00
2020	10.77	7.62
2040	5.73	5.39
2060	2.97	3.84
2080	0.0	0.0

time in the next quarter-century. It is to anticipate and prevent this that the calculations of how to make the scheme bear less heavily on certain generations are devised. The durability of the scheme would be increased by its holding a substantial reserve.

Growth Rates and Interest Rates

Populations of industrial countries are setting down towards a stationary state, and little benefit to social security can be hoped for from an infinitely expanding chain of people. The main hope of pay-as-you-go is in the expansion of the economy. If the economy were to grow indefinitely at 3 per cent per annum, then pay-as-you-go is no dearer and no cheaper than funding that provides interest at 3 per cent.

Judging from the past a real interest rate of 3 per cent seems not unreasonable; what about the growth rate? A survey of seventeen established economists, asking the opinion of each on growth over the next sixty years in developed countries, gave the following results: −0.5 per cent; 0.5; 0.5; 0.75; 1.0; 1.0; 1.0; 1.2; 1.2; 1.5; 1.5; 2; 2; 2; 2; 2.5; 3; 3; or an arithmetic average of 1.5 per cent, a median of 1.2 per cent. Only for very brief periods has the real rate of interest been as low as 1.2 or 1.5 per cent. On this and other grounds (King and Zeitz, 1983), it seems safe to take it that over the long term interest rates will be higher than economic growth. The intuitions on which this is based seem more trustworthy than those models in which interest and growth rates are equal.

Equity without Reserves

Shelley Lapkoff (1983) of Berkeley has shown how equity in rates of return may be secured without any reserve. Her device is to have large cohorts pay smaller premiums and secure smaller benefits, and small cohorts pay larger premiums and obtain larger benefits. Suppose in fact that we divide both contributors and beneficiaries by the cohort number, say as it stands at age 20. That makes all cohorts artificially equal; if the projection is with fixed death rates and migration, it is as though we were dealing with a stationary population. In a stationary population with one person (or one million) in each cohort under pay-as-you-go, all would pay the same contribution and draw the same benefit. Lapkoff's idea is simple: make the cohort rather than the person the unit, then translate to a per person basis by dividing by the cohort size.

Putting the matter on a per person basis and having a stationary population projected with fixed rates is unnecessarily restrictive. One could go on to multiply the successive cohorts by a geometric series and still have the same equality between the generations. The benefit would be steadily increasing over time without disturbing equality. Once again the cohort would share the contributions and the benefit, so that for each individual everything would be inversely proportional to the number of persons in the cohort to which he or she belonged. Of course the rate of increase could not be chosen arbitrarily, but would have to conform to the actual population as it evolved over time.

No exceptional administrative difficulty would arise in implementing this. People of the same age would contribute and draw alike; the employer would use the information on the age of the employee in setting up the contribution, and the social security administration would do likewise in setting the benefit.

The complaint would be not on equity but on the inadequacy of benefits for members of large cohorts. To correct this the large cohort could have a funded supplement.

Conclusion

The tendency of pay-as-you-go to favour early participants can be understood in terms of a chain of transfers. The early generous pensions must be paid for by someone unless expansion continues to infinity; it looks as though a large instalment on that payment will be made starting about thirty-five years from now. The political advantage that made pay-as-you-go attractive in the first place could operate in reverse about the year 2020: there could be a political gain in (partial or complete) repudiation of the scheme on the grounds that the baby boom had not paid its full dues.

One way to avoid this would be to keep adjusting the scheme by legislative action so that it tended towards fixed contribution from all cohorts rather than fixed benefit. More practical would be an intermediate arrangement, or an averaging of fixed contribution and fixed benefit.

Another way would be to build a partial reserve, by setting a contribution rate about 25 per cent greater than now paid; that contribution rate would hold for 100 years if 2 per cent annual real interest could be drawn on the reserve. The reserve would reach its peak about 2020 and then be equal to about ten years' benefit; it would run down to zero at the end of 100 years.

A third means of securing equality would be to regard each cohort as the unit, rather than each person. The totals of the cohorts would be the same in respect of both contributions and benefits; if there are a persons in the average cohort and n in the given cohort, a person in the given cohort would pay a/n of the average contribution and obtain a/n of the average benefit.

Each of these is unworkable in its pure form. For example, a reserve of ten times the annual contribution, even temporarily, probably could not be satisfactorily invested. It is up to the authorities to devise some combination of the above three devices that will be acceptable in the present, equitable in the future, and in accord with the needs of the economy.

References

Caldwell, John C. (1982), *Theory of Fertility Decline*, Academic Press, New York.

Hurd, Michael D. and John B. Shoven (1983), 'The Distribution Impact of Social Security', Working Paper No. 1155, National Bureau of Economic Research, Cambridge, Mass.

Keyfitz, Nathan (1985), 'The Demographics of Unfunded Pensions', *European Journal of Population*, 1, 5–30.

King, Timothy and Robin Zeitz (1983), 'Taking Thought for the Morrow: Prospects and Policies for Aging Populations', draft manuscript.

Lapkoff, Shelley (1983), 'Pay-as-you-go Retirement Systems in Nonstable Populations', paper presented at the annual meeting of the Population Association of America.

6 Life Cycles, Institutions, and Population Growth: A Theory of the Equilibrium Interest Rate in an Overlapping Generations Model

ROBERT J. WILLIS

In neo-classical growth theory, the rate of interest plays a crucial role in determining the balance a society achieves between the welfare of current and future generations. Unfortunately, conventional growth theory has tended to ignore the family, which is the social institution that bears the greatest responsibility in determining the size and resource endowment of future generations through its decisions concerning reproduction and the allocation and distribution of its resources to its members. In this chapter I present a theoretical framework in which microeconomic models of individual and family life-cycle economic and demographic behaviour can be integrated into a dynamic general equilibrium model of the determination of the equilibrium rate of interest in a competitive economy. Only a partial degree of integration is actually achieved in this chapter, because key variables such as marriage, fertility, and intrafamily transfers are treated as exogenous, whereas they would be treated as endogenous within a complete model. Thus the focus of this discussion is chiefly on the consequences of population growth and family behaviour for the equilibrium interest rate.

Samuleson's (1958) overlapping-generations (OG) model provides a natural starting-point for such a framework. At the most basic level, the OG model may be viewed as the marriage of the two major social accounting schemes, national income and wealth accounting and formal demography. The fruitfulness of this marriage is twofold. First, the theoretical variables associated with modern microeconomic life-cycle theories of individual and

This is a revised and shortened version of a paper with a similar title which was presented at an IUSSP/IIASA workshop in Laxenburg, Austria, 12–14 December 1983. Research for the paper was supported by a grant from the Center for Population Research, NICHD, and a fellowship from the Hoover Institution. It was written while the author was on the faculty of SUNY at Stony Brook. I would like to thank many people for their helpful comments on the earlier version of this paper, especially B. Arthur, A. Cigno, R. Lee, S. Rosen, and W. Sanderson.

household behaviour (such as the life cycle consumption theory as developed by Fisher, 1930, Friedman, 1957), and Modigliani and Brumberg, 1954 correspond much more closely to the age-structured accounting magnitudes associated with OG model than to conventional national income-accounting magnitudes, which suppress age structure. A second important virtue of the OG model as a social accounting scheme is that it directly incorporates the constraints on the age distribution in any given period which are implied by the past history of fertility and mortality in the population. Moreover, it is easy to introduce measures of life cycle demographic behaviour such as age-specific fertility, nuptiality, and mortality schedules into the model and use standard results from formal demography to relate these life cycle measures to the aggregate rate of population growth and the cross-sectional age distribution (see Coale, 1972).

The theoretical framework presented in this chapter brings together and synthesizes several strands of a burgeoning literature in which the OG model has been applied (and sometimes misapplied) to a wide range of problems in many areas including capital theory, monetary theory, public finance, labour economics, and economic demography. The basic framework is a discrete-time version of a Samuelson (1958)–Diamond (1965) overlapping-generations model in which individuals are born in a given period t and are assumed to live for $n + 1$ periods from birth at age zero to death at age n in period $t + n$. The rate of population growth is related to an age-specific fertility schedule, and age-specific mortality is assumed to be zero until the end of age n. Throughout the chapter, attention is confined to steady states in which the rate of population growth is constant.

The economy is divided into a production sector made up of competitive firms which use physical capital and labour to produce output and an individual sector. Individuals are assumed to supply labour according to a life cycle profile of labour (measured in efficiency units) whose level and shape is first taken as given and later treated as endogenously determined by investment in human capital. Each individual is assumed to choose his or her life cycle consumption profile by maximizing an intertemporal utility function subject to a lifetime wealth constraint which is determined by present value of that individual's life cycle labour income plus (or minus) the present value of life cycle intrafamily transfer receipts plus (or minus) the present value of lifetime tax payments and transfer receipts from the government.

The term *individual sector* rather than the more conventional term *household sector* is employed because the individual is used as the unit of analysis for most of the discussion. In this approach, the family in which the individual resides is treated as an attribute of the individual, and its economic impact on the individual is captured by the age-specific transfers received by the individual from other family members and the age-specific transfers he or she makes to other family members. The way in which results from this approach may be translated into the more conventional household approach is illustrated toward the end of the chapter by a simple example in which individuals, depending on their age, either reside in the family of origin into which they are born or in a family of procreation formed by marriage in which they bear their own children.

The model is specified in the next section. In the following sections the properties of a stationary competitive equilibrium in an economy with a constant rate of growth and unchanging technology are investigated, using a version of the OG model originated by Gale (1973) and extended by Kim (1981). This model emphasizes the relationship between the competitive determination of aggregate income and consumption, on the one hand, and the net supply of lending by the individual sector and demand for borrowing by the production sector, on the other hand.

The subsequent section sets up the model by relating the age-specific asset or credit position of representative individuals of each age in a given period to the individual's history of saving and dissaving, which is determined by life cycle income and consumption paths and the market rate of interest. The aggregate net supply of credit by the individual sector in a given period is equal to the sum of the age-specific credit positions multiplied by the number of individuals of each age, while the net demand for credit by the production sector is equal to the size of the aggregate capital stock that it is optimal for firms to hold in the next period. Following Gale (1973), it is shown that a stationary competitive equilibrium may either be 'balanced' or 'golden-rule'. A balanced equilibrium corresponds to a situation in which the aggregate supply and demand of credit are equal and the rate of interest is not necessarily equal to the rate of population growth, whereas a golden-rule equilibrium occurs when the rate of interest is equal to the rate of population growth and the aggregate supply and demand for credit are not necessarily equal.

Five possible types of competitive equilibrium are identified in the following section, and the properties of each type are discussed briefly with respect to its efficiency and the nature of the institutions needed to support it. For example, it is noted that all equilibria in which the interest rate is equal to or greater than the rate of growth are Pareto-efficient and that Samuelson's (1958) well-known monetary equilibrium corresponds to a golden-rule equilibrium within which the aggregate supply of credit exceeds aggregate demand and there is a 'biological interest rate' equal to the rate of population growth.

Next, the determination of the rate of interest corresponding to each equilibrium type is represented by a point in a simple supply-and-demand diagram. It is argued that certain equilibrium types satisfying Gale's (1973) conditions will not be supported in a market economy. A pleasant outcome of this argument is the conclusion that comparative static analysis of the determinants of the equilibrium interest rate can be conducted within a very simple supply-and-demand framework in which the aggregate supply curve of credit is perfectly elastic at the biological interest rate over some initial range and then begins to rise.

The remaining two sections of the paper are devoted to comparative static analysis. In the first, some accounting measures are developed which show how the aggregate supply of credit is related to the age structure of the population and the age patterns of consumption, labour income, and inter-generational transfers through families and the government. For example, it is shown that the effect of variations in life cycle pattern of labour income on the aggregate supply of credit in a golden-rule state can be expressed as the product of the present value of lifetime labour income multiplied by the mean age at which individuals in the population receive labour income. The 'mean age of producing', in turn, depends on both the age distribution of the population and on the shape of the individual life cycle profile of labour income. At a given rate of growth, the aggregate supply of credit will tend to be smaller and the equilibrium interest rate higher as the mean age of producing is larger.

The final section provides some examples of comparative static applications of the model. In one example, it is shown how a technological improvement which increases the rate of return to investment in education tends to reduce the aggregate supply of credit and raise the rate of interest by increasing the mean age of producing. In another example, the family rather than the individual is used as the unit of analysis in order to examine the consequences of variations in parental expenditures on child-rearing and other intergenerational transfers within the family (such as bequests or old-age support) on the supply of credit and the equilibrium interest rate. It is shown that the larger are net parental transfers per child and the later the age at which parents bear children, the larger is the aggregate supply of credit and the lower is the equilibrium interest rate. As a final example, the relationship between the results of this analysis and earlier results by Arthur and McNicoll (1978) and Lee (1980) concerning the effects of variations in the rate of population growth on per capita economic welfare is examined. In the conclusion some ways in which the framework outlined in this chapter might be extended are briefly discussed.

The Model

Diamond's (1965) model, extended to many generations, provides the basic model for this chapter. Each individual lives $n + 1$ periods of equal length with $n \geq 1$ indexed by $i = 0, \ldots, n$. Individuals are regarded as a male–female pair who marry at age m_0 and reproduce according to an age-specific fertility schedule, b_i, until the end of the childbearing period at age m_1. Thus, $b = \sum_{m_0}^{m_1} b_i$ is the gross reproduction rate (i.e., the number of girls per mother). For simplicity, mortality is assumed to be zero prior to the end of the $(n + 1)$th period. Hence b is also the net reproduction rate.

Nuptiality and fertility are assumed to remain constant across generations, implying that the population grows at a constant rate of g per cent per period, where g satisfies the identity $\sum_{m_0}^{m_1} \dfrac{b_i}{(1 + g)^i} = 1$ and also implies a stable geometric age distribution $\psi(i) = (1 + g)^{-i} \sum_{i=0}^{n} (1 + g)^{-i}$. The population of the generation of age i in period t, denoted by $P(i, t)$, is $P(i, 0)(1 + g)^t$ for given $P(i, 0) > 0$ and $g > -1$ and for $t = \ldots, -1, 0, 1, \ldots$

There is one consumption good and one capital good in the economy. Both are produced by the same production technology, which can be expressed by a real valued function of capital and labour input, denoted $F(K(t), L(t))$, where $F(\cdot, \cdot)$ is assumed to be homogeneous of degree one.

Individuals have life cycle endowments of labour $\ell = (\ell_0, \ldots, \ell_n)$ where $\ell_i \geqslant 0$ and $\ell \neq 0$. The age-specific endowments, $\ell_i \, (i = 0, \ldots, n)$, are interpreted as measuring labour supply in efficiency units, reflecting life cycle variation in both hours of work and productivity per hour due to variation in physical and mental maturity, health, investment in human capital, and labour supply decisions as well as the state of technology. Initially ℓ is treated as parametric and later it will be assumed to depend on human capital investment and technology. Throughout the chapter, work–leisure choices will be ignored.

In most of this study, the analysis will be limited to stationary programmes in which fertility behaviour and, hence, the rate of population growth is treated as exogenous. A *stationary programme* is a programme in which each individual in every generation has the same life cycle consumption profile, $c = (c_0; \ldots, c_n)$, and in which the rate of population growth g and capital–labour ratio, $k = (K(t)/L(t))$, is constant in each period.

Each individual has a utility function over his/her lifetime consumption denoted by $u(c) = (c_0, \ldots, c_n)$, which is assumed to be twice continuously differentiable, strictly increasing and strictly quasi-concave. As in much of the previous literature on optimal population growth (for example Arthur and McNicoll, 1978, Samuelson, 1975), this invidualistic utility function will be the primary object of the behavioural and welfare analysis of the discussion. However, I wish to interpret the analysis as a sub-problem which emphasizes the consequences of population growth within a broader framework in which fertility is determined endogenously by parents who care about the number and welfare of their children.

This interpretation can be made rigorous by assuming that the demand for children is based on the preferences of altruistic parents who care about the lifetime utility of their children in addition to the utility they receive from their own life cycle consumption. (See, for example, Becker, 1983, Razin and Ben Zion, 1975, Willis, 1985.) In the following analysis I shall treat the individual rather than the household as the optimizing agent and assume that a new-born individual seeks to maximize $u(c_0, \ldots, c_n)$. This individualistic metaphor is justified by our treatment of fertility as exogenous and by the fact that the parental altruism hypothesis implies that parents will choose the same consumption path for a dependent child as the child would choose for itself if it were capable of exercising independent choice. Conversely, the results of the analysis can be translated back into the more natural household framework and may be interpreted as the outcome of optimal household decisions conditional on fertility behaviour. This is done informally in some of the discussion later in the chapter.

For any given population growth rate $g > -1$ there exists a feasible consumption profile c^* which maximizes $u(c)$ among all feasible consumption profiles c. The programme with c^* is called a *golden-rule* programme. Under assumptions made above and to be made below, a golden-rule programme always uniquely exists, and is denoted by $c^*(g) = c(g)$. Also define $v^*(g) = u(c^*(g))$.

Let $K(t)$, $L(t)$, and $C(t)$ respectively denote aggregate capital and labour inputs and aggregate consumption in period t. Then

$$F(K(t), L(t)) = C(t) + K(t+1) = C(t) + I(t) + (1-\delta)K(t) \qquad (1)$$

in any feasible programme where δ is the depreciation rate with $0 \leqslant \delta \leqslant 1$ and $I(t) = K(t+1) - (1-\delta)K(t)$ is net investment in period t. Note that $F(\ )$ is a gross output function; its relationship to conventional production functions is explained shortly. Also

$$C(t) = \sum_{i=0}^{n} P(i, t)c_i = P(0, 0)(1+g)^t \sum_{i=0}^{n} \frac{c_i(t)}{(1+g)^i} \qquad (2)$$

and

$$L(t) = \sum_{i=0}^{n} P(i, t)\ell_i = P(0, 0)(1+g)^t \sum_{i=0}^{n} \frac{\ell_i(t)}{(1+g)^i}. \qquad (3)$$

Dividing (3) by $L(t)$ and defining $\tilde{c}(t) = (C(t)/L(t))$, $k(t) = K(t)/L(t)$, and $f(k) = F(k, 1)$

$$\tilde{c}(t) = f(k(t)) - (1+g)k(t+1) \qquad (4)$$

where $\tilde{c}(t)$ and $k(t)$ are consumption and capital per unit of labour in period t.

It is assumed that $f(0) = 0$; f is twice continuously differentiable;

$f'(k) > 0$ for $k \geqslant 0$; $f''(k) < 0$ for $k \geqslant 0$;
and $\lim_{k \to 0} f'(k) > 1 + g > \lim_{k \to \infty} f'(k)$.

It is important to note that f is a gross output function and not the production function. The relation between f and the gross production function f_G and the net production function f_N used, respectively, by Deardorff (1976) and Samuelson (1975) is

$$f(k) = f_G(k) + (1 + \delta)k = f_N(k) + k \tag{5}$$

One may think of f as a measure of 'full GNP' per unit labour defined as the sum of the current output of consumption and investment goods given by $f_G(k)$ plus the output of a 'storage technology', $(1-\delta)k$, which transforms current capital into future capital.

Assume further that there exist perfectly competitive models for capital and labour, so that the interest rate and the wage rate are determined competitively by

$$\begin{aligned} 1 + r(t) &= f'(k(t)) \\ w(t) &= f(k(t)) - k(t)f'(k(t)). \end{aligned} \tag{6}$$

Concentrating on stationary programmes in which $k(t)$ and $c(t) = (c_0(t),$ $\ldots, c_n(t))$ remain constant for all t and all generations, (7) can be rewritten as

$$\begin{aligned} 1 + r(k) &= f'(k) \\ w(k) &= f(k) - kf'(k). \end{aligned} \tag{7}$$

It is convenient to normalize the aggregate magnitudes by dividing both sides of (2) and (3) by the number of new-borns in period t, $P(0, 0)(1 + g)^t$, in order to rewrite (1) as the *social budget constraint* per new-born in period t as

$$\begin{aligned} \sum_{i=0}^{n} \frac{c_i(t)}{(1 + g)^i} &= [f(k(t)) - (1 + g)k(t + 1)] \sum_{i=0}^{n} \frac{\ell_i}{(1 + g)^i} \\ &= w \sum_{i=0}^{n} \frac{\ell_i}{(1 + g)^i} + (g - r)k(r) \sum_{i=0}^{n} \frac{\ell_i}{(1 + g)^i}. \end{aligned} \tag{8}$$

Since age-specific magnitudes such as age-specific consumption and labour productivity remain constant over time in a stationary programme, cross-sectional and longitudinal life cycle profiles are identical. In a golden-rule programme with $r = g$, note that the second line of (8) implies that the present value of lifetime labour income for each individual is equal to the present value of his/her lifetime consumption when c and ℓ are given a longitudinal interpretation. Also note in this case that aggregate consumption in the cross section is equal to aggregate labour income.

Competitive Equilibrium

Typically, the optimal life cycle consumption path $c(r) = (c_0(r), \ldots, c_n(r))$ will diverge from the life cycle path of labour earnings, $w(r)\ell = w(r)(\ell_0, \ldots,$

ℓ_n). In practice, societies employ both market and non-market institutions to bridge the gap between consumption and labour income over the life cycles of its individual members. The primary non-market institutions are the family and the government. The family makes intergenerational transfers (both in money and in kind) in the form of parental expenditures on children, bequests, and, in some societies, transfers from working-age children to their elderly parents. Many government tax, transfer, and expenditure programmes also generate either explicit or implicit government transfers. Prominent examples, of course, are social security and public schooling.

Let $\tau = (\tau_0, \ldots, \tau_n)$ be the profile of non-market intergenerational transfers from all sources given or received by a representative individual over his/her life cycle where $t = (\tau_0^+, \ldots, \tau_n^+)$ and $t = (\bar{\tau}_0, \ldots, \bar{\tau}_n)$, respectively, denote the age-specific profiles of net receipts and net payments or intergenerational transfers. Specifically, $\tau_i^+ = \tau_i$ if $\tau_i > 0$ and $\tau_i^+ = 0$ otherwise, while $\tau_i^- = |\tau_i|$ if $\tau_i < 0$ and $\tau_i^- = 0$ otherwise for $i = 0, \ldots, n$. The sum of age-specific transfers across all individuals in a given period t is 0, that is,

$$\sum_{i=0}^{n} \frac{\tau_i}{(1+g)^i} = \sum_{i=0}^{n} \frac{\tau_i^+}{(1+g)^i} - \sum_{i=0}^{n} \frac{\tau_i^-}{(1+g)^i} = 0. \tag{9}$$

Also let $y = (y_0, \ldots, y_n)$ be the net, post-transfer income of a typical individual where $y_i = w_i + \tau_i$, $(i = 0, \ldots, n)$.

In addition to financing investment in physical capital, private savings, together with borrowing and lending in private credit markets, offer a second way in which deviations between life cycle savings and labour income can be bridged. We now consider the stationary dynamic equilibrium of a competitive economy in which the population growth rate g and the life cycle pattern of non-market intergenerational transfers, τ, are exogenous constants. The economy is divided into an *individual sector* consisting of individuals of all ages $i = 0, \ldots, n$ and a *production sector* made up of firms.

Following Gale (1973), the aggregate credit of the individual sector may be derived in the following way. Let an individual's savings during his ith period of life be defined as

$$s_i = y_i - c_i = w\ell_i + \tau_i - c_i, \quad i = 0, \ldots, n. \tag{10}$$

His credit position at the beginning of his ith period of life, denoted by a_i, is defined to be

$$a_{i+1} = s_i + a_i(1 + r), \quad i = 1, \ldots, n \tag{11}$$

where it is assumed that he begins life with no assets and that any bequests he makes are already incorporated into τ_n so that $a_0 = a_{n+1} = 0$.[1]

Given w and r, the typical individual's problem is to choose $(c_0, \ldots, c_n)$ so as to maximize $u(c)$ subject to the individual's lifetime wealth, $W(r)$, where

$$W(r) = \sum_{i=0}^{n} \frac{w\ell_i + \tau_i}{(1+r)^i} = \sum_{i=0}^{n} \frac{c_i}{(1+r)^i} = 0 \tag{12}$$

and the non-negativity constraint $c_i \geq 0$. Given $w > 0$ and $r > -1$, the solution denoted by $c(w, r)$, $s(w, r)$, and $a(w, r)$ uniquely exists and is called an individually optimal (IO) consumption programme. In light of (7), only (w, r) pairs which are generated by the same ks are considered, and the market programme is simply written as $c(r)$, $s(r)$, and $a(r)$.

Using (8), (9), and (10), define the aggregate savings of the individual sector as

$$\tilde{S}_I = P(0, 0)(1+g)^t \sum_{i=0}^{n} \frac{s_i(r)}{(1+g)^i}$$

$$= P(0, 0)(1+g)^t \left[\sum_{i=0}^{n} \frac{w\ell_i - c_i}{(1+g)^i} \sum_{i=0}^{n} \frac{\tau_i}{(1+g)^i} \right] = K(r, t; g)(g-r) \tag{13}$$

and, using (11), also define the aggregate credit of the individual sector as

$$\tilde{A}_I(r, t; g) = P(0, 0)(1+g)^t \sum_{i=0}^{n} \frac{a_{i+1}(r)}{(1+g)^i}. \tag{14}$$

Multiplying (11) by the population of age i, summing over i, and using $a_{n+1} = 0$, we obtain

$$\sum_{i=0}^{n} \frac{a_{i+1}}{(1+g)^i} = \sum_{i=0}^{n} \frac{w\ell_i + \tau_i + c_i}{(1+g)^i} - \left(\frac{1+r}{1+g}\right) \sum_{i=0}^{n} \frac{a_{i+1}}{(1+g)^i}$$

From this expression and from (8) and (14), it follows that

$$\frac{g-r}{1+g} \tilde{A}_I(r, t; g) = \tilde{S}_I(r, t; g) = w(r)L(t) - C(r, t; g) = K(r, t)(g-r) \tag{15}$$

Given g and $r > -1$, (15) is always satisfied in the uniquely determined IO programme.

The aggregate savings and aggregate credit of the production sector are respectively defined by

$$\tilde{S}_p(r, t; g) = (1+r)K(t) - K(r, t+1) = K(r, t)(r-g) \tag{16}$$

and

$$\tilde{A}_p(r, t; g) = -K(r, t+1; g) = -(1+g)K(r, t). \tag{17}$$

The aggregate savings of the production sector are defined as the amount it pays for the present period's capital minus the amount it receives for the next period's production. Its aggregate credit is the amount that it owes at the end of the period for next period's capital; it is always negative. It is immediate that

$$\frac{g-r}{1+g} \tilde{A}_p(r, t; g) = \tilde{S}_p(r, t; g) \tag{18}$$

Now define the aggregate savings and aggregate credit of the whole economy by

$$\tilde{S}(r, t; g) = \tilde{S}_1(r, t; g) + \tilde{S}_p(r, t; g) \tag{19}$$

and

$$\tilde{A}(r, t; g) = \tilde{A}_1(r, t; g) + \tilde{A}_p(r, t; g) \tag{20}$$

Combining the equations from (13) to (20) shows that the aggregate credit balance satisfies the relationship

$$(g - r)\tilde{A}(r, t; g) = \tilde{S}(r, t; g) = 0. \tag{21}$$

A stationary competitive equilibrium given $g > -1$ is a triple $(r, k(r), w(r))$ which satisfies the economy's social budget constraint (8) or, equivalently, satisfies (21).

Since all magnitudes in a given period t are proportional to the size of the population in a stationary equilibrium, it is convenient to eliminate calendar time by summarizing the basic results of this section in normalized form by letting $A(r; g) \doteq \tilde{A}(g; g)/P(0, 0)(1 + g)^t$ be the normalized aggregate credit balance where $P(0, 0)(1 + g)^t$ is the population of new-borns in period t. This normalization also permits a number of relevant magnitudes to be expressed in terms of per capita lifetime present values (such as present value of life-time earnings).

Thus, from (20) the normalized aggregate credit balance is

$$A(r; g) = A_1(r; g) + A_p(r; g) \tag{22}$$

where, from (14), the normalized individual sector credit balance is

$$A_1(r; g) = \sum_{i=0}^{n} \frac{a_i}{(1 + g)^i} \tag{23}$$

and from (17) the normalized production sector credit balance is

$$A_p(r; g) = -(1 + g)k(r) \sum_{i=0}^{n} \frac{\ell_i}{(1 + g)^i} = -\hat{k} \tag{24}$$

where $\hat{k}$ is the normalized value of next period's capital stock, $K(r, t + 1)$. Finally, from (21), a competitive equilibrium must satisfy the relation

$$A(r; g)(r - g) = 0. \tag{25}$$

Balanced and Golden Rule Equilibria

According to (25), the product of the (normalized) aggregate credit balance $A(r; g)$ and the difference between the interest rate and population growth rate $(r - g)$ must be zero in a stationary competitive equilibrium. Five distinct types of equilibria which satisfy this condition are illustrated by the non-blank cells in the three-by-three table in Table 6.1 formed by the possible negative, zero, and positive values of $A(r; g)$ and $r - g$, respectively. Much of this chapter is concerned with the economic significance of each type of equilibrium and analysis of how population growth, technology, preferences, and non-market intergenerational transfers through families and government influence the type of equilibrium that will occur in a given economy.

Using Gale's (1973) terminology, we can distinguish between *balanced* and *golden-rule* equilibria. Balanced equilibria correspond to the three cells in the middle column in Table 6.1 and golden-rule equilibria correspond to the three cells in its middle row. The centre cell corresponds to an equilibrium that is both balanced and golden-rule. In this section I describe each of the five types of equilibria and comment briefly on their economic significance, beginning with the balanced equilibria.

If $A(r; g) = 0$ with r not necessarily equal to g, the equilibrium is called balanced. It corresponds to a situation in which the rate of interest adjusts to equate the aggregate supply of lending and demand for borrowing. Aggregate lending is provided by members of age groups who wish to save and aggregate borrowing consists of the sum of the demand for 'consumption loans' by members of other age groups and the demand for 'investment loans' by firms.

The credit market balance from which this equilibrium gets its name can be explained intuitively by assuming that the credit market consists of a costless private banking system. Each bank makes loans to individuals and firms and accepts deposits and withdrawals from savings accounts held by individuals and firms. Banks charge the competitive interest rate on loans and pay the same interest rate on savings accounts. In steady state, the banking system is in a cash-flow equilibrium each period in the sense that revenues

Table 6.1.   Classification of types of competitive equilibria

	Sign of aggregate credit balance		
Sign of $(r - g)$	Positive	Zero	Negative
Positive		Efficient balanced	
Zero	Samuelson golden-rule	Balanced and golden-rule	Classical golden-rule
Negative		Inefficient balanced	

from repayment of principal and interest on past loans are just sufficient to support the volume of new loans being demanded.

The system is also in a balance sheet equilibrium. That is, its net worth is zero because the value of its liabilities (i.e., the value of savings accounts) is just equal to the value of its assets (i.e., the value of outstanding loans). Note that the banking system's balance sheet mirrors that of the private economy. That is, the aggregate assets of the individual sector, given by the value of individual savings accounts, is just equal to the aggregate liability of individual sector debt from outstanding consumption loans plus the aggregate liabilities of the production sector, given by the amount firms borrow to finance their next period's capital stock, $K(t +)$. Note that the net aggregate demand for wealth by the individual sector (i.e., the value of savings accounts minus debt from consumption loans) is just equal to the (normalized) real capital stock in a balanced equilibrium: that is, assuming $r \neq g$, the normalized versions of (15) and (17) imply that $A_i(r; g) = -A_p(r; g) = \hat{k}$, where $\hat{k}$ is the normalized value of next period's capital stock.

It is important to note that the equilibrium interest rate may be either larger or smaller than the population growth rate in a balanced equilibrium. Starrett (1972) has shown that a competitive equilibrium is Pareto-efficient if $r \geq g$ and is Pareto-inefficient if $r < g$. Specifically, given the consumption programme corresponding to a stationary competitive equilibrium in which $r \geq g$, it is not possible to find a feasible alternative programme in which the lifetime utility of some individual living at time t is increased which does not reduce the utility of some other individual living at time t or some subsequent period. Conversely, if $r < g$, it is possible to find such an alternative programme. Accordingly, I will refer to these two cases, respectively, as *efficient* and *inefficient* balanced equilibria.

Even if the aggregate credit balance is not zero, (25) will be satisfied if $r = g$. In this case, the equilibrium is *golden-rule* because $c(g) = c^*(g)$. Under the assumptions on production technology and the utility function, a golden-rule equilibrium always exists, given $g > -1$, and it yields the highest possible level of per capita welfare from own consumption, $u(c^*(g) = v^*(g)$, among all stationary programmes for a given g.

Gale distinguishes two types of golden-rule equilbria, depending on the sign of the aggregate credit balance. If $A(g; g) > 0$, the equilibrium is referred to as *Samuelson*. As is well known, $A(g; g) > 0$ is a necessary and sufficient condition for the existence of a Samuelsonian monetary equilibrium with a 'biological' interest rate determined by the rate of population growth (Samuelson, 1958). In this case the supply of savings exceeds the equilibrium investment demand, or, equivalently, desired wealth-holding by individuals exceeds the size of the equilibrium capital stock, so that a nominal asset such as fiat money or government debt is required to maintain equilibrium in credit markets at $r = g$. In equilibrium, the aggregate credit balance is equal to the sum of the credit balance of the private banking system (which is zero) and the value of the stock of money.

If $A(g; g)$ is negative, in Gale's terminology the corresponding golden-rule equilibrium is *classical*. In this case, there is excess demand for borrowing and a negative excess demand for wealth when $r = g$. I argue in the next section that a classical equilibrium cannot be supported by private market institutions.

A final possibility is that a competitive equilibrium satisfying (25) is both balanced and golden-rule because the aggregate credit balance is zero and the interest is equal to the population growth rate. Assuming that there are no non-market intergenerational transfers, Kim and Willis (1982) have shown that this equilibrium occurs when the rate of population growth is equal to an optimal population growth rate defined by Samuelson (1975) as that rate of growth which maximises per capita welfare. That is, let $r = g^*$ and $A(g^*; g) = 0$ where g^* is Samuelson's optimal rate of population growth. Then $v(g^*)$ is the maximum value of $v(g)$ for all $g > -1$. Samuelson called this case the 'goldenest of golden rules' (GGR).

Determination of the Equilibrium Rate of Interest

The determination of the rate of interest in a stationary competitive equilibrium can be illustrated by the simple supply-and-demand diagram in Figure 6.1 in which the interest rate is measured on the vertical axis and $\hat{k}(r)$, the normalized value of next period's aggregate capital stock $K(r, t+)$, is measured on the horizontal axis. The rate of population growth corresponds to the height of the horizontal line *ge*. The curve SS traces out the (normalized) individual sector aggregate credit balance $A_I(r; g)$ as a function of r, holding g constant. It represents the amount of credit the individual sector is willing

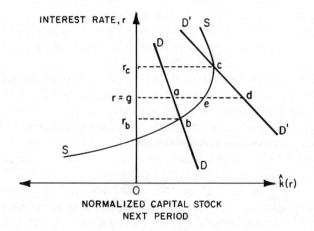

Figure 6.1. Aggregate supply and demand for credit

to supply at any given rate of interest (that is, the aggregate value of individual savings accounts and holdings of nominal assets such as fiat money minus the value of consumer debt). The curves DD and D'D' plot the absolute value of the (normalized) aggregate credit balance of the production sector $-A_p(r; g)$ as a function of r, holding g constant, corresponding, respectively, to situations in which capital is relatively less or more important in production. They represent the willingness of firms to incur debt in order to finance next period's capital and are derived from the demand for capital implied by the state of production technology.[2]

According to the discussion in the previous section, the competitive equilibrium in a given economy (an economy with a given rate of population growth, preferences, technology, and non-market intergenerational transfers) might be either balanced or golden-rule, depending on whether or not appropriate institutions exist to support the golden-rule equilibrium. For example, suppose that the demand for capital is relatively small, so that DD is the relevant demand curve. Two possible equilibria are marked at points a and b in Figure 6.1. Point b, given by the intersection of SS and DD, is an inefficient balanced equilibrium in which $r = r_b > g$ and the aggregate credit balance is zero. Point a, given by the intersection of DD and ge, is a Samuelson golden-rule equilibrium with the biological interest $r = g$. In this equilibrium, the demand for capital is given by the distance ga and the value of the nominal asset (for example, fiat money) is given by the distance ae. If capital is more important, so that the demand curve is D'D', the two possible equilibria are the efficient balanced equilibrium at point c in which $r = r_c > g$ or the classical golden-rule equilibrium at point d with $r = g$. The fifth possible type of equilibrium (both balanced and golden-rule) would occur if the demand curve intersected SS at point e.

In this section, I argue that Samuelson golden-rule or efficient balanced equilibria are the only equilibrium types that are truly consistent with stationary competitive equilibrium. Specifically, I first argue that private incentives to find a stable store of value will tend to eliminate the possibility of an inefficient balanced equilibrium (such as point b) and then show that private markets will not support a classical golden-rule equilibrium (such as point d). This implies that the supply curve of lending from the individual sector is perfectly elastic at $r = g$ over the range ge and then follows the rising or backward-bending segment of the SS curve, eS, for which $r \geq g$. The equilibrium rate of interest will be equal to the rate of population growth if the demand curve intersects the elastic portion of this supply curve, and will exceed the rate of population growth otherwise.[3]

Of all these equilibrium types, the Samuelson equilibrium has attracted by far the most attention, primarily because, as Wallace (1980) suggests, it appears to be the only competitive model which explains the demand for pure fiat money (which he defines as a durable commodity that is inconvertible and intrinsically worthless), and also because it illustrates the role of 'rational expectations' in a particularly pure form.

In a monetary equilibrium, the elderly in each period exchange fiat money for goods supplied by the young in order to provide for all or part of their old-age consumption. The young are willing to make this exchange because they expect money to have purchasing power in the future. In particular, as Samuelson (1958) showed, in a model without physical capital, if the purchasing power of money is expected to rise at the same rate as the rate of population growth, there will be a stationary equilibrium in which the quantity of goods supplied by each young 'saver' will permit each elderly person to fulfil the *ex ante* optimal life cycle consumption plan $c(g) = c^*(g)$, corresponding to the biological interest rate $r = g$ by selling the quantity of money accumulated during earlier periods of life. In this equilibrium, expectations are 'rational' in the sense that the market-clearing price of money in each period is just equal to the expected price. When physical capital is introduced, the argument is essentially unchanged except that the elderly fulfil their optimal consumption plan by drawing down both their savings accounts and their money holdings where, as shown earlier, the net value of individual sector savings accounts is equal to the optimal capital stock corresponding to the biological interest rate. Given expectations of the type just described together with the existence of a durable commodity (such as paper money or gold) that can serve as a store of value, an inefficient balanced equilibrium is not possible because, at the margin, individuals would prefer to hold money with its biological rate of return rather than physical capital with a lower rate of return.[4]

Samuelson (1958) viewed fiat money as a 'social contrivance' through which the young make intergenerational transfers to the old. That is, in each period the young provide real goods and services to the old in exchange for intrinsically worthless pieces of paper. The aggregate value of this transfer is equal to the purchasing power of the stock of money as illustrated by the distance *ae* in Figure 6.1. In contrast, a classical golden-rule equilibrium implies that net intergenerational transfers through the market are in the opposite direction. For example, in the classical equilibrium at point *d* in Figure 6.1 aggregate transfers from the older to the younger generation are equal to the distance *ed*.

I shall now show that private market institutions will not support a classical golden-rule equilibrium or, equivalently, that the direction of intergenerational transfers through the market cannot be from the older to the younger generation. Consequently, the only possible equilibrium when the demand for capital is given by D'D' in Figure 6.1 is the efficient balanced equilibrium at point *c*.

The argument is as follows. Recall from (12) that the individually optimal (IO) consumption programme $c(r)$ is chosen so as to maximize $u(c_0, \ldots, c_n)$ subject to the wealth constraint.

$$W(r) = \sum_{i=0}^{n} \frac{w(r)\ell_i + \tau_i}{(1+r)^i} = \sum_{i=0}^{n} \frac{c_i(r)}{(1+r)^i}$$

where $W(r)$, the present value of lifetime income of a representative individual, is equal to the present value of his/her lifetime consumption. Recall that in a golden-rule equilibrium with $1 + r = 1 + g = f'(k(g))$ and $W(r) = W(g)$ and the optimal consumption programme $c(g)$ this equation also satisfies the social budget constraint in (8).

As shown earlier, however, the negative aggregate credit balance in a classical golden-rule equilibrium corresponds to a positive net worth for the banking system. Assuming that the owners of banks in any given period are themselves members of the economy, this implies that the value of bank ownership shares constitutes a positive component of individual wealth. Thus if the aggregate credit balance is negative, the lifetime wealth of a representative individual will exceed $W(g)$, as defined above; consequently, the IO consumption programme will have a present value which exceeds the present value of $c(g)$. Because aggregate consumption under the $c(g)$ programme is just equal to the aggregate output minus the amount of investment required to maintain the capital–labour ratio at $k(g)$, this higher consumption programme is not feasible in a stationary competitive equilibrium with $r = g$.

Intuitively, the explanation for this result is that the maintenance of a classical equilibrium requires that individuals be willing to make implicit transfers to members of the younger generation by extending loans to them which will never be paid back. Since there is no reason for them to be willing to do so, the supply of lending will be smaller than the amount required to maintain the golden-rule equilibrium and the market-clearing interest rate will be higher than the rate of population growth, as illustrated by the efficient balanced equilibrium at point c in Figure 6.1.

Structural and Institutional Determinants of the Supply of Capital

The rest of this chapter emphasizes the comparative static implications of variations in factors that determine the equilibrium interest rate by affecting the position of the supply-and-demand curves for loans in Figure 6.1. The position of the demand curve is determined by the state of production technology embodied in the production function $f(k)$. The position of the supply curve involves a more complex interaction among a number of factors which may be divided into *structural* and *institutional* factors.

The structural factors include the nature of individual preferences for life cycle consumption $u(c)$, which influence the life cycle consumption profile c, and 'human capital technology' (for example a human capital production function) which influences the life cycle labour productivity schedule ℓ. The institutional determinants of the supply of capital concern the role of society's non-market institutions, especially the family and the government. Family fertility decisions determine the rate of population growth, and the family's allocation of resources among its members is an important component of the life cycle profile of non-market intergenerational transfers τ. Similarly, the government's influence on the supply of capital operates through the effects of taxes and transfers (including in-kind transfers) on τ.

In this section, I derive a relationship between the sign and magnitude of the aggregate credit balance of the individual sector in a golden-rule state, on the one hand, and the life cycle patterns of consumption, labour productivity, and public and private non-market intergenerational transfers on the other. This relationship provides a simple device for analysing how variations in the underlying structural and institutional determinants shift the supply curve of capital SS in Figure 6.1 when $r = g$.

As a first step, it is useful to derive an alternative expression for the aggregate credit balance of the individual sector. From (11), recall that the credit position of an individual of age i is

$$
\begin{aligned}
a_{i+1} &= s_i(r) + (1 + r)a_i \\
&= s_i(r) + (1 + r)s_{i-1}(r) + \ldots + (1 + r)^i s_i(r); \, i = 0, \ldots n
\end{aligned}
\tag{26}
$$

where $s^i(r) = y_i(r) - c_i(r)$; $y_i(r) = w(r)\ell_i + \tau_i$ and $a_0 = a_{n+1} = 0$. Define the normalized aggregate credit balance of the individual sector as

$$
A_1(r; g) = \frac{\tilde{A}_1(r, t; g)}{P(0, 0)(1 + g)^t} = \sum_{i=0}^{n} \frac{a_{i+1}}{(1 + g)^i}
\tag{27}
$$

where $P(0, 0)(1 + g)^t$ is the number of new-borns in period t and, hence, $A_1(r; t; g)$ is the aggregate credit balance of the individual sector per new born. Transferring the second line of (26) into (27), we obtain

$$
A_1(r; g) = \sum_{i=0}^{n} \frac{s_i(r) \sum_{j=0}^{n-i} \left(\dfrac{1+r}{1+g}\right)^j}{(1 + g)^i}.
\tag{28}
$$

The magnitude and direction of non-market intergenerational transfers can be expressed in a similar formula. Recall from (9) that the life cycle profile of intergenerational transfers τ is decomposed into an age profile of net transfers from an individual to others, denoted by τ^+, and a profile of the individual's net receipts from others denoted by τ^- where $\tau_i^+ = \tau_i$ if $\tau_i > 0$ and zero otherwise and $\tau_i^- = |\tau_i|$ if $\tau_i < 0$ and zero otherwise so that $\tau_i = t_i^+ + t_i^-$. In a given period, (9) states that the τ_i sum to zero in the aggregate.

Let T_{i+1} be the current value at the end of period t of the stream of non-market transfers an individual of age i has made to others since his birth in period $t - i$ where

$$T_{i+1} = -[\tau_i + (1+r)\tau_{i-1} + \ldots + (1+r)^i t_0]$$

$$= (1+r)^i \left\{ \sum_{j=0}^{i} \frac{t_j^- - t_j^+}{(1+r)^j} \right\} = (1+r)^i [V_i^-(r) - V_i^+(r)] \qquad (29)$$

where $V_i^+(r) = \sum_{i=0}^{n} \frac{\tau_i^+}{(1+r)^i}$ and $V_i^-(r) = \sum_{i=0}^{n} \frac{\tau_i^-}{(1+r)^i}$ are, respectively, the present values, evaluated at birth, of the non-market transfers received by the individual from others and the transfers made by the individual to others through age i. If $T_i > 0$, the individual has made a positive net transfer to others up to the current point in his lifetime and, if $T_i < 0$, he has received a net transfer from others. If $r = g$, note that (9) implies that by the end of life the present value of the amount an individual gives to others over his entire lifetime is equal to the amount he receives from others. That is,

$$V_n^+(g) = V_n^-(g) = V(g) \qquad (30)$$

Let $T_N(r; g)$ denote normalized aggregate net intergenerational wealth transfer in a given period. It is defined as the sum of the net wealth transfers received from others by individuals of each age (i.e., T_i) multiplied by the number of people of each age relative to the number of new-borns. Thus, using (29),

$$T_N(r; g) = \sum_{i=0}^{n} \frac{T_{i+1}}{(1+g)^i} = \sum_{i=0}^{n} \frac{[V_n^+(r) - V_n^-(r)](1+r)^i}{(1+g)^i}$$

$$= \sum_{i=0}^{n} \frac{(\tau_i^- - \tau_i^+) \sum_{j=1}^{n} \left(\frac{1+r}{1+g}\right)^j}{(1+g)^i}. \qquad (31)$$

If $T_N(r; g)$ is positive, the population alive in period t, in the aggregate, has made a positive wealth transfer to others. Since current period transfers sum to zero, it follows that the 'others' to whom the current population has made positive net transfers were members of the population in past periods who were, on average, born earlier than members of the current population. Thus if $T_N(r; g) > 0$ we shall say that the direction of intergenerational transfers is from the younger to the older generation. Conversely, if $T_N(r; g) < 0$ the direction of transfers is from the older to the younger generation.

It is useful to distinguish between private and public intergenerational transfers. Let $\tau = \tau_F + \tau_G$ where $\tau_F = \tau_F^+ - \tau_F^-$ and $\tau_G = \tau_G^+ - \tau_G^-$ denote, respectively, the age profiles of net transfers via the family and government. Then,

$$T_N(r; g) = T_F(r; g) + T_G(r; g) \qquad (32)$$

where $T_F(r; g)$ and $T_G(r; g)$ are, respectively, the normalized net intergenerational wealth transfers through families and the government.

In a golden-rule state with $r = g$, the formulas for the aggregate credit balance of the individual sector in (28) and aggregate non-market intergenerational transfers in (31) can be expressed as functions of a summary statistic of the cross-sectional distributions of age-specific consumption, earnings, and intergenerational transfers called the mean age of consuming, mean age of producing, and so on. Specifically, let x be an individual form of behaviour such as fertility or consumption which varies over the life cycle, and define the mean age of x as

$$\mu_x = \sum_{i=0}^{n} \frac{ix_i}{(1+g)^i} \Big/ \sum_{i=0}^{n} \frac{x_i}{(1+g)^i}. \tag{33}$$

If $x_i = 1$ for all $i = 0, \ldots, $ n, μ_x is the cross-sectional mean age of the individuals in the population in any period t corresponding to the stable age distribution implied by the constant population growth rate g. The higher g is, the lower is the mean age of the population. If x_i is, say, age-specific consumption (i.e., $x_i = c_i$), μ_c, the mean age of consuming, is a measure of the mean age of the population which weights each age group by its consumption. Similarly, denote μ_ℓ as the mean age of producing (i.e., $x_i = \ell_i$). Finally, let μ_F+ and μ_F-, respectively, be the mean ages of private transfer receipts and payments and μ_G+ and μ_G-, respectively, be the mean ages of public transfer receipts and payments.

In a golden-rule state, normalized aggregate non-market intergenerational transfers are equal to the difference between the mean ages of transfer receipts and transfer payments multiplied by the present value of the transfer receipts (or payments) that an individual will receive (or make) during his entire lifetime. Specifically, private and public intergenerational transfers are given, respectively, by

$$T_F(g; g) = V_F(g)[\mu_F+ - \mu_F-] \tag{34}$$

and

$$T_G(g; g) = V_G(g)[\mu_G+ - \mu_G-] \tag{35}$$

where $V_F(g)$ and $V_G(g)$, respectively, denote the present value of lifetime private and public transfer receipts (or payments).

The proof is as follows. Set $r = g$ in (31) and write the result as

$$T_N(g; g) = (n+1) \sum_{i=0}^{n} \frac{(\tau^- - \tau^+)}{(1+g)^i} - \sum_{i=0}^{n} \frac{i(\tau^- - \tau^+)}{(1+g)^i}.$$

(9) implies that the term multiplied by $(n+1)$ is zero. Multiplying and dividing the remaining term by $V(g) = \Sigma \, \tau^+ /(1+g)^i$ and applying the formula for mean ages in (33) for $x_i = \tau^-, \tau^+$ gives

$$T_N(g; g) = V(g)[\mu_N + - \mu_N -] \tag{36}$$

Given $\tau = \tau_F + \tau_G$ and (32), the expressions in (34) and (35) follow immediately.

According to (34)–(36), the direction of non-market intergenerational transfers depends on the sign of the difference between the mean age of transfer receipts and transfer payments. In a social security programme, for example, the average age of beneficiaries is higher than the average age of taxpayers. Thus, $\mu_G + > \mu_G -$ and $T_G(g; g)$ is positive, confirming the intuitively obvious fact that a social security programme involves a net wealth transfer from the younger to the older generation. As another obvious example, the fact that parents are older than their children implies that the mean age of transfer receipts by young children from their parents is lower than the mean age of transfer payments that parents make to their own young children (i.e., $\mu_F + < \mu_F -$), thus $T_F(g; g)$ is negative, which indicates that parental expenditure on child-rearing represent a net wealth transfer from the older to the younger generation.

It is important to stress, however, that the direction of aggregate private and public intergenerational transfers depends on transfers (both monetary and in kind) from all sources. For instance, government programmes, such as public schooling, which benefit the young tend to offset the effect of social security programmes in determining the sign of $T_G(g; g)$. Similarly, old-age support received by parents from their grown children may offset the wealth transfer implicit in parental child-rearing expenditure.

We are now in a position to present the main result of this section. Setting $r = g$ in (28) and using the definitions of the mean ages of consuming and producing (i.e., μ_c and μ_t) from (33) we may express the normalized aggregate credit balance of the individual sector in a golden-rule state as

$$A_I(g; g) = W(g)[\mu_c(c(g); (g) - \mu_t(g)] - [T_F(g; g) + T_G(g; g)] \tag{37}$$

where $W(g)$ is the representative individual's wealth at birth, as defined in (12) when $r = g$ and $T_F(g; g)$ and $T_G(g; g)$ are given by (34) and (35).

To derive the expression in (37), set $r = g$ in (28) and write the result as

$$A_I(g; g) = \sum_{i=0}^{n} \frac{s_i(g)(n + 1 - i)}{(1 + g)^i} = (n + 1) \sum_{i=0}^{n} \frac{s_i(g)}{(1 + g)^i} - \sum_{i=0}^{n} \frac{i s_i(g)}{(1 + g)^i}$$

The term multiplied by $(n + 1)$ in the second line of this expression is zero by the social budget constraint in (8) when $r = g$. The expression in (37) is then obtained with the following steps applied to the remaining terms. Substitute $s_i = w\ell_i - c_i + \tau_i$ and use (34)–(36) to express the terms involving τ_i as $- [T_F(g; g) + T_G(g; g)]$; then multiply and divide the remaining terms involving c_i and ℓ_i by $W(g)$ and use the definition of μ_x in (33) for $x_i = (c_i(g), \ell_i)$ to obtain the rest of the expression.

As shown earlier, $A_I(g; g)$ is equal to the (normalized) net supply of credit by the individual sector when the interest rate is equal to the rate of population growth. The formula for $A_I(g; g)$ in (37) shows how the position of the supply curve SS at $r = g$ in Figure 6.2 is related to the structural and institutional factors mentioned at the beginning of this section. Shifts in SS caused by given variations in these factors can be analysed very simply through the use of the formula. Variations in structural factors which determine the life cycle patterns of consumption and labour productivity operate through the term $W(g)[\mu_c(c(g); g) - \mu_\ell(g)]$ and variations in institutional factors involving non-market intergenerational transfers operate through the term $- [T_F(g; g) + T_G(g; g)]$.

Recall that the (normalized) aggregate credit balance $A(r; g)$ is the sum of the individual and production sector credit balances $A_I(r; g)$ and $A_p(r; g)$, where the value of $- A_p(g; g)$ can be expressed as

$$- A_p(g; g) = W(g)(1 + g) \frac{k(g)}{\tilde{c}(g)} \qquad (38)$$

by multiplying and dividing the expression for $A_p(g; g)$ in (24) by the wage, $w(g) = f(k(g)) - f'(k(g))k(g)$, and noting from the definition of $\tilde{c}$ in (4) that $\tilde{c}(g) = w(g)$. Using (37) and (38), the normalized aggregate credit balance of the whole economy in a golden-rule state may be written as

$$A(g; g) = W(g)[\mu_c(c(g); g) - \mu_\ell(g)]$$
$$- \left[T_F(g; g) + T_G(g; g) - \frac{k(g)}{\tilde{c}(g)} \right]. \qquad (39)$$

In the previous section I argued that the equilibrium interest rate will equal the rate of population growth if the aggregate credit balance corresponding to the golden-rule programme is non-negative (that is, the equilibrium is either Samuelson or both golden-rule and balanced) and that the interest rate will exceed the growth rate if the golden-rule programme yields a negative aggregate credit balance.

It follows that the equilibrium rate of interest will be greater than or equal to the rate of population growth as $A_I(r; g)$ is less than or equal to $- A_p(r; g)$. Using (37) and (38), this proposition may be expressed formally as

$$r \geqslant g \text{ as } [\mu_c(c(g); g) - \mu_\ell(g)] - [T_F(g; g) + T_G(g; g)] \leqslant \frac{k(g)}{\tilde{c}(g)}. \qquad (40)$$

Assuming that the strong inequalities hold in (39), the rate of interest will tend to be higher the lower the mean age of consuming (μ_c), the higher the mean age of producing (μ_ℓ), the lower the mean age of family and government transfer receipts $(\mu_F + \text{ and } \mu_G +)$, and the higher the mean age of family and government transfer payments $(\mu_F - \text{ and } \mu_G -)$ because each of these variations results in a leftward shift of the SS curve in Figure 6.1.

Some applications of comparative static analysis are given in the next section.

Comparative Static Applications

The formula for $A_i(g; g)$ in (37) summarizes the effects on the aggregate supply of credit of life cycle consumption and labour productivity profiles, the life cycle pattern of non-market intergenerational transfers through the family and government, and the age structure of the population associated with a given rate of population growth. The effects of variations in several of these factors are examined in this section and the effect of variations in the rate of population growth is considered briefly at the end of the section.

(a) Diagrammatic Illustration of Determinants of the Supply of Credit

I shall begin by abstracting from the role of the family and government by considering a hypothetical pure market economy in which there are no non-market intergenerational transfers (i.e., $T_F(g; g) + T_G(g; g) \equiv 0$). In this economy, new-borns must rush to the bank in order to obtain the money

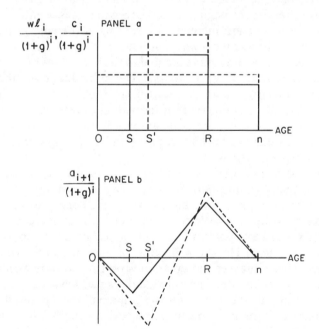

Figure 6.2. Age-specific consumption and labour income weighted by the age distribution (panel (*a*)) and age-specific credit position weighted by the age distribution (panel (*b*)) corresponding to two levels of schooling with $g = 0$

needed to finance their childhood consumption by borrowing against their future earnings capacity, and, later in life, they must accumulate sufficient savings to provide for their retirement consumption.

The determination of the sign and magnitude of $A_i(g; g)$ in this pure market economy is illustrated in Figure 6.2 for two stylized examples corresponding, respectively, to the sets of solid and dotted lines. In both examples, it is assumed that $g = 0$, which implies that the discount rate is $(1 + r) = (1 + g) = 1$ and that there are equal numbers of individuals of each age in the population in each period. For now consider only the solid lines in Figure 6.2.

The figure can be viewed from either a longitudinal or a cross-sectional perspective. First consider the former perspective. Panel (*a*) depicts the discounted life cycle labour income and consumption path of a typical individual from birth to death (i.e., $w\ell_i/(1 + r)^i$ and $c_i/(1 + r)^i$ for $i = 0, \ldots, n$, and panel (*b*) illustrates the individual's corresponding discounted credit position at the end of each age (i.e., $a_{i+1}/(1 + r)^i$ for $i = 0, \ldots, n$ where $a_{n+1} = a_0 = 0$). Since the interest rate is zero, note that the figure also depicts the undiscounted life cycle profiles of labour income, consumption, and credit position.

The individual is assumed to have zero labour productivity from birth until leaving school at the beginning of age S when he/she enters the labour force and earns a constant income until retiring at the end of age R, after which his/her labour income is zero until death at age n. The area under the (discounted) labour income curve is equal to the individual's lifetime wealth evaluated at birth (i.e., $W(g) = W(0)$). The individual's optimal lifetime consumption path $c(g) = (c_0(g), \ldots, c_n(g)$) is chosen so as to maximize $u(c)$ subject to $W(0)$. It is assumed that the individual's preferences are such that he/she chooses to consume the same amount in each period from birth to death. From the wealth constraint, the area under the (discounted) life cycle consumption path is also $W(0)$.

As illustrated in panel (*b*), at the beginning of life the individual must borrow to finance consumption, thereby going increasingly into debt until labour force entry at age S. At this point, he/she begins to repay the debt with the excess of income over consumption until, at some point in mid-career, he/she will have paid off the childhood borrowing so that his/her credit position is zero. He/she will, however, continue to save for retirement, which causes his/her net credit position to become positive in the latter stages of working life. The individual reaches a peak asset position at the retirement age R and then uses the principal and interest from these assets to finance retirement consumption, exhausting his/her assets upon death at the end of age n.[5]

So far, Figure 6.2 has been interpreted from the longitudinal perspective of a single representative individual. Now consider a cross-sectional perspective emphasizing the relationship between the age structure of the population and the operation of markets for credit and nominal assets. In this perspective, the labour income, consumption, and credit balance profiles in the two panels in Figure 6.2 represent the age-specific values of these variables for typical members of the population of each age, weighted by the number of people of that age relative to the number of new-borns.

In panel (a), the equality of the areas under the labour income and consumption curves is required to satisfy the social budget constraint in (8); that is, $\Sigma \cdot c_i/(1 + g)^i = \Sigma \, w\ell_i/(1 + g)^i$ when $r = g$. Give the uniform age distribution implied by $g = 0$ and the rectangular shapes of the labour income and consumption profiles, the mean ages of producing and consuming are simply $\mu_\ell(0) = \Sigma i\ell_i/\Sigma\ell_i = S + (R - S)/2$ and $\mu_c(0; 0) = \Sigma i c_i/\Sigma c_i = n/2$, respectively. The normalized aggregate credit balance of the individual sector, $A_1(0; 0)$, is the sum of the negative credit balance of the younger portion of the population and the positive credit balance of the older portion given, respectively, by the triangular areas above the below the horizontal axis in panel (b) in Figure 6.2. Applying the formula in (37), $A_1(0; 0) = W(0)[\mu_c(0; 0) - \mu_\ell(0)] = W(0)[n/2 - S - (R - S)/2]$.

As drawn in the case represented by solid lines in Figure 6.2, the mean age of consuming exceeds the mean age of producing, so that $A_1(0; 0)$ is positive. This implies that the value of savings accounts plus any nominal assets held by the older portion of the population exceeds the value of the outstanding debt of the young given by the value of their outstanding consumption loans. Thus, the individual sector has a positive aggregate demand for wealth, or, equivalently, a positive supply of net lending in the golden-rule programme. The equilibrium interest rate will equal or exceed zero depending on whether the aggregate demand for borrowing by the production sector is less than or greater than the aggregate supply of credit.

(b) Variations in Technology and Investment in Human Capital

To this point, this life cycle labour productivity profile ℓ has been treated as exogenous. I now wish to consider how a labour-augmenting technological improvement which increases the return to investment in schooling influences the aggregate supply of credit and the equilibrium interest rate by treating ℓ as endogenously determined by optimal investment in human capital.

Let age-specific productivity depend on schooling choice and the state of technology. Specifically, assume that the number of efficiency units of labour supplied by an individual of age i is $\ell_i = \ell_i(S, \alpha)$, where S is years of schooling and α is an index of technology such that $\ell_i > 0$ during the working phase of the life cycle, $i = S, \ldots, R$, and $\ell_i = 0$ otherwise. Also assume that the effect of schooling on efficiency units of labour is positive, but diminishing (that is, $\frac{\partial \ell_i}{\partial S} > 0$ and $\frac{\partial^2 \ell_i}{\partial S^2} < 0$) and that improved technology increases efficiency of labour (that is, $\dfrac{\partial \ell_i}{\partial \alpha} > 0$) for $i = S, \ldots, R$. Given α and the rate of interest, S is chosen so as to maximize the present value of lifetime labour income where the only cost of schooling is assumed to be the opportunity cost of foregone labour income. Thus, the schooling function

$$S = S(r, \alpha) \tag{41}$$

is the solution to the maximum problem

$$\max W \left(\frac{r}{S} \right) = \sum_{i=S}^{R} \frac{w(r)\ell_i(S, \alpha)}{(1+r)^i} \tag{42}$$

Clearly, the optimal level of schooling is a decreasing function of the interest rate so that $\dfrac{\partial S}{\partial r} < 0$. The effect of a technological improvement on schooling choice depends on whether an increase in α increases the marginal benefits from schooling by more or less than the marginal opportunity cost of schooling. For example, if $\ell^i(S, \alpha) = \alpha \ell_i(S)$ it is easy to show that the optimal schooling level is independent of α because the marginal costs and marginal benefits of schooling increase by the same proportion.

Since schooling levels are higher in more technologically advanced societies, it seems reasonable to assume that improvements in technology increase the marginal rate of return to educational investment (i.e., $\dfrac{\partial \ln \ell_i}{\partial \alpha} > 0$) so that $\dfrac{\partial S}{\partial \alpha} > 0$. This, together with the assumption that improved technology increases the number of efficiency units of age-specific labour at a given level of schooling (i.e., $\dfrac{\partial \ell_i}{\partial \alpha} > 0$) implies that lifetime labour earnings are an increasing function of α (i.e., $\dfrac{\partial W(r, \alpha)}{\partial \alpha} > 0$). Note that a change in α can be expressed as a labour-augmenting (i.e., Harrod-neutral) shift in aggregate production technology since $F(K(t), L(t), \alpha) = F(K(t), \beta(\alpha)L(t))$ where $\beta(\alpha) = \sum_{i=S(r,\alpha)}^{n} \dfrac{\ell_i(S(r, \alpha), \alpha)}{(1+g)^i}$ is the aggregate supply of efficiency units of labour per new-born, given the state of technology and optimal schooling choices.

Diagrammatically, the effect of improved technology in the golden-rule programme with $r = g = 0$ is illustrated by comparing the situations depicted by the solid and dotted lines in Figure 6.2. These correspond, respectively, to the steady-state programmes before and after the improvement. Relative to the initial bench-mark case, the level of schooling has increased from S to S' and lifetime wealth, given by the area under the dotted income curve in panel (*a*), has also increased. Because of the increase in wealth, the optimal consumption path is also higher. Assuming that $u(c)$ is homothetic, the higher level of wealth simply results in a proportionally higher level of consumption at each age, as is indicated by the dotted consumption path in panel (*a*).

Clearly, the effect of increased schooling in this example is to increase the mean age of producing while the mean age of consuming remains unchanged. Hence the aggregate credit balance of the individual sector is lower than in the bench-mark case. This is indicated in panel (*b*) by the increase in the normalized aggregate debt of the younger portion of the population and decrease in the normalized aggregate assets of the older portion given, respectively, by the areas of the dotted triangles below and above the horizontal axis in panel (*b*). Intuitively, this effect is the result of the increased period of 'dependency' during the beginning of life, when individuals must borrow to finance their consumption due to delayed labour force entry caused by the increase in schooling.

As drawn, $A_I(0; 0) < 0$ after the technology change. This implies that the supply of net lending has shifted to the left and is positioned in the second quadrant at the point where $r = g = 0$. Since the demand for borrowing from the production sector must be non-negative, it follows that the rate of interest must exceed zero and be higher than the initial rate of interest, assuming that a competitive balanced equilibrium exists.[6]

(c) Intergenerational Transfers by the Family

By definition, any viable society must bear and nurture the young until, at a minimum, the young are capable of surviving to reproduce and nurture the young of the next generation. Needless to say, the 'cradle to grave' pure market economy which was used above as an expository device provides an inadequate institutional basis for reproduction and nurture. Rather, in all societies these are the primary tasks of the family.

So far, I have adhered strictly to the use of the individual as a unit of analysis. To a considerable extent, this obscures the role of family decision-making concerning reproduction and nurture and the relationship of these decisions to the pattern of intrafamily transfers at the micro level and to the aggregate supply of credit at the macro level. In this section, I present a highly simplified example to illustrate how to integrate the family into our model by considering the individual life cycle in relation to the family of origin into which the individual is born and resides as a child and in relation to the family (or families) of procreation which he or she forms by marriage.

Assume that each individual lives in his/her family of origin from birth until completing school and entering the labour force at the end of age S. At some later age, the individual (i.e., male–female pair) marries and forms a family of procreation. For simplicity, assume that the pair bears *b* children (of a given sex) simultaneoùsly when they are at age $i = \mu_b$. Letting j index the age of their children, the parents are of age $i = \mu_b + j$ when the children are of age j. From the parents' point of view, the degree of generational overlap is from $i = \mu_b, \ldots, n$, and from the child's point of view it is from $j = 0, \ldots, n - \mu_b$. In this simple case, the rate of population growth is given by the relation $b = (1 + g)^{\mu b}$ where μb is the mean age of child-bearing.

In order to calculate $T_F(g; g)$ it is most convenient to disaggregate the transfers by categories. For purposes of the illustrative example in this section, I shall distinguish three categories: (1) child-rearing expenses; (2) transfers by adult children to their parents (such as old-age support), and (3) transfers by parents to their adult children (such as bequests).

Assume that a child attending school consumes more than it produces. During this period of dependency, also assume that its parent provides for the child's consumption and that any of the child's earnings accrue to the parent. The present value of the parent's child-bearing expenditures per child are

$$E(r) = \sum_{i=0}^{S} \frac{(c_i - w\ell_i)}{(1 + r)^i} \qquad (43)$$

The values of S and c_i in (43) will be equal to the corresponding values of $S(r, \alpha)$ and $c_i(r)$ for $i = 0, \ldots, S$ in the individually optimal programme if it is assumed that the parent operates as a perfect 'agent' for the child by choosing the level of schooling investment that maximizes the child's life-time wealth and by allocating consumption in conformity to the child's preferences, $u(c)$. In this case, the magnitude of $E(r)$ is determined entirely by structural factors, that is, by the child's preferences and by the nature of its human capital production function, given the state of technology. Obviously, there are other possible assumptions about parental behaviour (for example, the parent might attempt to reduce the costs of the child by limiting the child's schooling and reducing its consumption below the IO levels). For simplicity, I shall assume that the parent carries out the IO programme on the child's behalf while the child is a dependent.

After completing schooling and entering the labour force, the child may make transfers to its parents, especially when the parent is old. From the parent's point of view, these transfer receipts may be viewed as returns on his/her prior investment in rearing the child. Let the present value of these payments, evaluated at the birth of the child, be given by $R(r)$. Alternatively, the parent may wish to make a net wealth transfer to his/her children which exceeds the amount transferred to them through the child-bearing expenditure. The parent may do so by giving them a bequest (through transfers either at the time of death or while living). Let the present value of the bequest, evaluated at the birth of the child, be $B(r)$.

From the parent's point of view, the net cost of a child is

$$Q(r) = E(r) - R(r) + B(r) \qquad (44)$$

and the total expenditure on children is $bQ(r)$. Note that $Q(r)$ depends on both the structural factors which determine $E(r)$ and on the degree of parental altruism which determines the amount of wealth the parent wishes to transfer to each child. Note that $Q(r)$ may be viewed as a measure of 'child quality' in the sense of Willis (1973) or Becker and Lewis (1973) while $E(r)$ is a measure of child quality in the sense of DeTray (1973).

Recall from (36) that $T_F(g; g) = V_F(g)[\mu_F + - \mu_F -]$ where $\mu_F +$ is the mean age of receiving transfers from others in the family, $\mu_F -$ is the mean age of giving transfers to others in the family, and $V_F(g) = V_F^+(g) = V_F^-(g)$ is the present value of transfer receipts or transfer payments over the lifetime of an individual. In steady state, note that any transfer received early in life by an individual from his/her own parent will be correspond μ_b years later to a transfer payment of that amount to each of his/her own b children. Similarly, any transfer payment made by an individual to the parent early in life will correspond μ_b years later to a transfer receipt of that amount from each child. For any given type of intrafamily transfer, it follows that $[\mu_F + - \mu_F -] = \mu_b$ if the transfer receipt occurs first and that $[v_F + - v_F -] = v_b$ if the transfer payment occurs first.

It follows immediately that the normalized net wealth transfer from the older to the younger generation within families in a golden-rule state is equal to the net cost per child multiplied by the mean age of child-bearing; that is

$$- T_F(g; g) = Q(g)\mu_b = [E(g) - R(g) + B(g) + B(g)]\mu_b \qquad (45)$$

Recall from (37) that the normalized aggregate supply of credit in the golden-rule state is greater the larger is $- T_F(g; g)$. Hence, for given technology and preferences, (45) implies that the supply of credit is larger and the equilibrium rate of interest is lower, the greater is net parental expenditure per child $Q(g)$ and the later is the mean age of child-bearing, μ_b.

The effects of intrafamily transfers on the supply of credit can be illustrated with an example similar to that depicted in Figure 6.2. Assume that individuals spend the first quarter of life in school, the next half at work, and the last quarter in retirement. Their income is a constant y while they are working and their consumption is constant throughout life at $c = y/2$. Each individual has one child, so that the rate of growth is $g = 0$ and the mean age of consuming and mean age of producing are both equal to $n/2$.

In the absence of intrafamily transfers, the aggregate supply of credit is zero at $r = g = 0$ because the aggregate debt of the younger half of the population is exactly equal to the aggregate credit of the older half. Now suppose that parents provide for their children's consumption while they are in school but that there are no other intrafamily transfers, so that $R(g) = B(g) = 0$ and $Q(g) = E(g) = (y/2)S$. Also assume, initially, that parents bear their one child upon leaving school at age $\mu_b = S$. In this case, individuals begin working life without debt and devote all their income to their own consumption plus their child's consumption until they reach age μ_b + S = 2S when their children leave home. At this point, they still have zero assets and they begin saving for retirement at the rate $y - c = y/2$, reaching a peak asset position of $(y/2)$S at retirement. Thereafter, they run down their assets by using the savings at the rate $y/2$ per year until their death at age n. The normalized aggregate credit balance of the individual sector, given by summing the age-specific credit positions across all ages, is $A_I(0; 0) = (y/2)$S.

Now suppose that the child-bearing is delayed by S years after school-leaving, so that μ_b = 2S. In this case, new workers begin saving $y - c = y/2$ per year until they begin having children. At this point, they have accumulated assets whose value is $S(y/2)$. Once their child is born, no further saving takes place until children leave home and the parents are of retirement age. Retired parents finance retirement consumption out of the assets accumulated prior to child-bearing. Summing the age-specific credit positions of the whole population, it is easy to see that $A_I(0; 0)$ has risen from $(y/2)$S to $(y/2)$S + $(y/2)$S^2 as a result of the delay in child-bearing.

(d) Intergenerational Transfers and the Welfare Effects of Population Growth

Arthur and McNicoll (1978) analysed the effect on per capita welfare of a small increase in the rate of population growth using a continuous-time version of the overlapping-generations model specified earlier in this chapter. Specifically, they compared the level of per capita welfare in two golden-rule states associated with an initial growth rate g and a slightly higher rate $g + \Delta g$ by taking the total derivative of the social budget constraint in (8) and solving for the (equivalent of the) elasticity of the present value of lifetime consumption with respect to the rate of population growth. The expression they obtain is proportional to the expression for $A(g; g)$ in (39) if $T_F(g; g) = T_G(g; g) = 0$. Lee (1980) generalized the Arthur–McNicoll analysis by showing that the same kind of expression holds when this derivative is evaluated around any initial consumption profile c and capital–labour ratio k.

Their results can be related to mine by defining $T(r; g)$ as the normalized *social* intergenerational transfer of wealth from all sources as

$$T(r; g) \equiv T_F(r; g) + T_G(r; g) + A(r; g). \qquad (46)$$

In a golden-rule state with $r = g$, and $A(g; g)$ not necessarily equal to zero,

$$T(g; g) = W(g)[\mu_c(c(g); g) - \mu_\ell(g)] - (1 + g)\frac{k(g)}{\tilde{c}(g)} \qquad (47)$$

where (47) is obtained by adding $T_F(g; g) + T_G(g; g)$ to both sides of (39). Alternatively, in an efficient balanced equilibrium with $r \geqslant g$, $A(r; g) = 0$

and the formula for T(r; g) is given by (31).

The expressions in (46) and (47) illustrates a point made by Samuelson (1958) when he noted that families, the government, and asset markets are the three principal types of social institution through which intergenerational transfers take place. However, intergenerational transfers only involve non-market institutions if the equilibrium interest rate exceeds the rate of population growth, since A(r; g) = 0.

The relationship between T(r; g) and variations in the rate of population growth can be derived by following Lee (1980). Let $\theta\bar{c}$ = $c(r)$, where θ is a scalar which measures the uniform percentage amount by which the life cycle consumption path can be increased or must be decreased to satisfy the social budget constraint when the rate of population growth is increased by a small amount and $c(r)$, $k(r)$, and r, are treated as constraints. The logarithmic derivative of θ with respect to $(1 + g)$, denoted by $\tilde{\theta}$, measures the elasticity of lifetime wealth W(r) of each individual with respect to a change in the population growth rate.

This derivative is obtained by substituting $\theta\bar{c}$ = $c(r)$ into the social budget constraint in (8) and using the implicit function theorem to obtain

$$\tilde{\theta}(r) = \frac{d\log \theta}{d\log (1 + g)} = [\mu_c(c(r); g) - \mu_\ell(g)] - \frac{(1 + g)k(r)}{\tilde{c}(r)}. \tag{48}$$

It follows from (47) and (48) that $\tilde{\theta}(r) = \tilde{\theta}(g) = $ T(g; g)/W(g) in a golden-rule state with r = g. Thus, the sign of $\tilde{\theta}(g)$ is positive if the direction of social intergenerational transfers is from the younger to the older generation and negative if it is in the opposite direction.

Conclusion

Since the approach and findings of this chapter were summarized in considerable detail in the introduction to the chapter, I will conclude with some brief remarks on possible extensions of the framework outlined herein. One obvious extension is to incorporate an explicit model of family fertility behaviour into the framework in order to analyse the causes and consequences of population growth within a single unified model. Some progress along these lines has been made by Ben Zion and Razin (1975), Becker (1983), Willis (1985), and others in altruistic models which assume that parents care about the number and welfare of their children. Although these models restrict the lifetime to two or three periods, their major results tend to carry over to the $n + 1$ period discrete-time model employed in this discussion or to continuous-time OG models. Conversely, however, the extension of models of endogenous fertility to multi-period discrete-time or continuous-time models may yield interesting new insights, as is suggested by the effect of variations in the timing of life cycle fertility on the supply of credit which was shown in this chapter.

Two other important extensions of the framework involve consideration of the nature of economic–demographic interactions in non-stationary situations and relaxation of the assumption that all individuals are identical. The former extension would permit a closer examination of truly dynamic problems such as the effect of baby booms and busts on the economy, and the latter would allow for the analysis of the determinants of the distribution of income within and across generations (see Becker and Tomes, 1984,) for an excellent paper dealing with this latter set of issues).

Although additional theoretical refinement would be welcome and interesting, I believe that the most important area for additional work is to attempt to use theories of the type presented here as the basis for the formulation and empirical testing of hypotheses about economic–demographic interactions.

Endnotes

1. For completeness, individual asset balances should include the value of individual ownership shares in firms. However, competition implies that pure profits are zero in stationary equilibrium, so the value of equity holdings is also zero. Hence, for notational simplicity I have omitted share ownership from the definition of the a_i terms.

2. I have drawn SS as a backward-bending supply curve and have assumed that demand curves such as D'D' always cut SS from below when it is negatively sloped to ensure that a balanced equilibrium exists and is unique. Other shapes are possible. For example, the problem that Samuelson (1975) encountered in finding a value of g^* corresponding to a minimum rather than a maximum of $v(g)$ would be represented in Figure 6.1 by a situation in which SS cuts D'D' from above (see Deardorff, 1976, Samuelson, 1976).

3. If the level of fertility and the direction and magnitude of intergenerational transfers within families are determined endogenously by 'altruistic' parents who derive utility from the number and welfare of their children, Willis (1985) shows that privately optimal family decisions will lead to a Pareto-efficient competitive equilibrium in which the rate of interest exceeds the rate of population growth. Such an equilibrium is an efficient balanced equilibrium like the one at point c in Figure 6.1. An implication of this result is that the demand for fiat money will always be zero and, consequently, that the large literature which has emerged concerning the role of money in overlapping-generations models since it was first proposed by Samuelson (1958) may be of little practical value in explaining the determination of the real rate of interest. Also see Tobin (1980) for additional reasons for doubting the practical value of the OG model as a basis for a theory of money.

4. It must be conceded, however, that the case in favour of a monetary equilibrium is not entirely secure. For example, Cass, Okuno, and Zilcha (1979) have shown that there exists a continuum of partially monetized equilibria associated with alternative rational expectations concerning the sequence of current and future expected prices of money in which the real interest rate ranges between the biological rate in the 'fully monetized' Samuelson equilibrium and the lower rate associated with the inefficient balanced equilibrium. In these partially monetized equilibria, allocations are neither stationary nor Pareto-optimal.

5. Note that the minimum and maximum credit positions occur, respectively, at ages S and R when $r = 0$. If $r > 0$, the two extremes occur at somewhat later ages and if $r < 0$, at somewhat earlier ages.

6. Note, however, that a balanced equilibrium would not exist if the supply curve of credit from the individual sector was negatively sloped (or not sufficiently positively sloped) for interest rates greater than zero and, therefore, never intersected the demand curve for credit by the production sector. Moreover, as was shown earlier, a classical golden-rule equilibrium cannot exist. Hence, it is possible that no equilibrium exists in this case. It is beyond the scope of this chapter to determine conditions for existence of balanced equilibrium; for our purposes, existence will be

assumed (see Kim, 1983).

Intuitively, however, it can be argued that existence is more likely the more elastic are the relevant behavioural relations in the model. Specifically, the demand for credit is more elastic the greater is the elasticity of substitution between capital and labour in production and the supply of credit is more elastic the greater is the intertemporal elasticity of substitution in consumption and the greater the elasticity of human capital investment with respect to the rate of interest. The latter two elasticities influence, respectively, the degree to which an increase in the interest rate shifts consumption to later ages, which increases μ_c, and the degree to which life cycle labour productivity is shifted to earlier ages by a reduction in optimal investment in schooling, which reduces μ_l. If both these elasticities are zero, the supply of credit decreases as the interest rate increases because of the increased cost of debt service by the young and the increased age at which individuals achieve a zero credit position. For sufficiently high elasticities, the induced changes in the age structure of consumption and labour productivity will offset the debt service effect and the supply curve of credit will be positively sloped.

References

Arthur, W. Brian and Geoffrey McNicoll (1978), 'Samuelson, Population and Intergenerational Transfers, *International Economic Review* 19 (February), 241–6.

Becker, Gary S (1983), 'Some Notes on Population Growth and Economic Growth', mimeo, University of Chicago.

——and H. Gregg Lewis (1973), 'On the Interaction between the Quantity and Quality of Children', *Journal of Political Economy*, 82 (March/April), S279–S288.

——and Nigel Tomes (1984), 'Human Capital and the Rise and Fall of Families', Working Paper No. 84–10 (October), Economic Research Center, NORC.

Cass, David, Masahiro Okuno, and Itzak Zilcha (1979), 'The Role of Money in Supporting the Pareto Optimality of Competitive Equilibrium in Consumption–Loan Type Models', *Journal of Economic Theory*, 20 (February), 41–80.

Coale, Ansley J. (1972), *The Growth and Structure of Human Populations*, Princeton University Press, Princeton.

Deardorff, Allan V. (1976), 'The Growth Rate of Population: Comment', *International Economic Review*, 17, 510–15.

DeTray, Dennis N. (1973), 'Child Quality and the Demand for Children', *Journal of Political Economy*, Supplement (March/April).

Diamond, Peter A. (1965), 'National Debt in a Neoclassical Growth Model', *American Economic Review*, 55, 1126–50.

Friedman, Milton, (1957), *A Theory of the Consumption Function*, Princeton University Press, Princeton.

Fisher, Irving (1930), *The Theory of Interest*, Yale University Press, New Haven.

Gale, David (1973), 'Pure Exchange Equilibrium of Dynamic Economic Models', *Journal of Economic Theory*, 6, 12–36.

Kim, Oliver (1981), 'The Overlapping Generations Model: Equilibrium, Optimality and Institutional Requirements', Ph.D. dissertation, State University of New York at Stony Brook.

——(1983), 'Balanced Equilibrium in a Consumption Loans Model', *Journal of Economic Theory*.

——and Robert J. Willis (1982), 'The Growth of Population in Overlapping Generations Models', unpublished manuscript, SUNY at Stony Brook.

Lee, Ronald D (1980), 'Age Structure, Intergenerational Transfers, Consumption and Economic Growth', *Revue Economique* (November).

Modigliani, Franco and Richard Brumberg (1954), 'Utility Analysis and the Consumption Function: An Interpretation of Cross-Section Data' in Kenneth K. Kurihara (ed.), *Post-Keynesian Economics*, Rutgers University Press, New Brunswick, 388–436.

Rasin, Assaf and Uri Ben Zion (1975), 'An Intergenerational Model of Population Growth', *American Economic Review*, 65 (December), 923–33.

Samuelson, Paul A. (1958), 'An Exact Consumption Loan Model of Interest With or Without the Social Contrivance of Money', *Journal of Political Economy*, 66, 467–82.

——(1975), 'The Optimum Growth Rate for Population', *International Economic Review*, 16, 531–8.

——(1976), 'The Optimum Growth Rate for Population: Agreement and Evaluations, *International Economic Review* (June), 516–25.

Starrett, David (1972), 'On Golden Rules, the "Biological Rate of Interest", and Competitive Inefficiency', *Journal of Political Economy*, 80, 276–91.

Tobin, James (1980), 'Discussion' in *Models of Monetary Economics*, J. Karaken and N. Wallace (eds.), Federal Reserve Bank of Minneapolis, Minneapolis (1980), 83–90.

Wallace, Neil (1980), 'The Overlapping Generations Model of Fiat Money' in *Models of Monetary Economics*, J. Karaken and N. Wallace (eds.), Federal Reserve Bank of Minneapolis, Minneapolis, 49–82.

Willis, Robert J. (1973), 'A New Approach to the Economic Theory of Fertility Behavior', *Journal of Political Economy*, 81, supplement (March/April), S14–S64.

——(1985), 'Externalities and Population', unpublished paper, Population Growth and Economic Development Working Group, Committee on Population Growth, National Research Council.

7 Macroeconomic Consequences of the 'New Home Economics'

ALESSANDRO CIGNO

In contrast with the standard approach to the analysis of consumer behaviour, where the demographic structure of the consumption unit is either ignored or put out of sight by the application of adult-equivalence scales, the central focus of the so-called 'new home economics' is precisely the determination of that structure and the allocation of family resources among family members—usually grouped into two categories, adults and children. Some progress has been made, since Becker's seminal contribution,[1] in the theoretical and empirical analysis of models of the individual family, but relatively little has been done to investigate the macroeconomic implications of such models.[2] The present chapter is intended as a small contribution to our understanding of those implications within the context of a simple growth model.

The Household Sector

Let us assume that the behaviour of the household sector, including its reproductive behaviour, may be described as the result of the utility-maximizing decisions of an aggregate family unit. For the purposes of this discussion it is not necessary to specify how the utilities of individual family members are aggregated into a family preference function, but, since children have no say on whether or not to be born, it seems natural to suppose that family decisions reflect adult preferences and, perhaps, parental perceptions of children's tastes.

Following a well-established tradition of the new home economics literature (see Becker, 1981, chs. 5 and 7), I shall suppose that these decisions are made in two stages: at any instant, the current family income Y is first allocated between current expenditure and savings, then current expenditure is allocated between adult consumption and child-related expenditures. More specifically, it will be assumed that the fraction of income saved is, in the aggregate, a positive constant σ and that current expenditure is allocated

I am grateful to B. Arthur, A. Graziani, R. Lee, and R. Willis for useful comments. Any remaining errors or shortcomings are my own.

so as to maximize some function of consumption per adult a, voluntary expenditure per child c, and number of children[3] per adult n,

$$u = u(a, c, n), \tag{1}$$

subject to the current expenditure constraint

$$a + (b + c)n = (1 - \sigma)y, \tag{2}$$

where y is income per adult and b is the 'price' of a birth, that is, the sum total of all costs that must necessarily be incurred (by law or custom) to bring a child into the world.

This specification of the family choice problem needs to be justified, because the current and future a, c, n, y, and σ ought to be simultaneously determined so as to maximize some intergenerational utility function. We may, however, think of the current $u(\ )$ as having been derived by backward programming, and of the current y and σ as reflecting optimal future choices of a, c, and n, given the family's initial assets.

The specification of current expenditure implies that the adult consumption good, the child consumption good, and the good in terms of which we measure the cost of a birth are all produced by the same technology. It also implies that, although b is a constant, the opportunity cost of a child in terms of adult consumption is a variable,

$$z \equiv b + c. \tag{3}$$

This is consistent with the new home economics idea that the 'quality' of children (subsumed, in the present model, into the relationship between u and c) depends on the amounts of parental time and other goods expended on each child (see Becker and Lewis, 1973, Willis, 1973). But, thanks to the implicit assumption of a common technology, we are spared the problem of having to allocate adult time between child-raising and income-raising activities. Assuming that the family labour capacity is proportional to the number of adults, we can then write

$$Y = yL \tag{4}$$

and

$$Y = Kr + Lw, \tag{5}$$

where K is the stock of capital, r its rental price, and w the wage rate.

If the number of children were exogenous, or effectively constrained by some physiological ceiling, the family choice problem would be reduced to the choice of two items of expenditure, a and c, subject to a linear budget constraint. In this case n would act as the exogenously given 'price' of c in terms of a, and it would be easy to derive the effects of any exogenous change in this or any other parameter. Such a situation is more readily associated with developing than with developed societies.

If, however, the number of children is freely chosen, subject only to the family budget (that is, parents do not wish that they could have more children than nature permits), then matters are considerably more complicated, because c and n enter the expenditure equation multiplicatively. The conditions for an interior optimum, in this case, are

$$\frac{u_c}{u_a} = n, \tag{6}$$

$$\frac{u_n}{u_a} = z, \tag{7}$$

and

$$a + zn = (1 - \sigma)y, \tag{8}$$

where (6) and (7) equate the marginal rates of substitution of adult consumption for, respectively, child consumption and number of children to the respective marginal costs, both of which are endogenous, while (8) is a non-linear budget constraint.

The consequences of this complication become apparent when we try to establish the sign of the effects of changes in the exogenous variables on a, c, and n: in addition to the usual problem of demand analysis, that such changes may have substitution and income effects of opposite sign, and that, with more than two variables, there may be relations of complementarity as well as substitutability between pairs of them, we also have the problem that the income and substitution effects (other than the direct-substitution effects on c and n) depend crucially on the term

$$u_{nc} - u_c = -\frac{u_c}{n}\left(1 - \frac{n}{u_c}u_{cn}\right), \tag{9}$$

which can be negative or positive, according to the degree of substitutability between expenditure per child and number of children. But, rather than making arbitrary assumptions about the form of $u(\ )$, as is often done in order to obtain firm predictions, it seems more sensible to wait and see which preference structure is required for the existence of a sustainable equilibrium.

A Simple Growth Model

In order to complete the picture we now need an aggregate production function, with or without some provision for endogenous technical progress. Manna-like technical progress will be ruled out, because it is well known that the combination of endogenous population and exogenous technical progress makes the system explosive—unless it is restrained by decreasing returns to scale or exhaustible natural resources.[4]

Assuming that technical improvements may result from experience, and that any act of production constitutes experience, we may write

$$\dot{Q} = F(K, L, Q) \tag{10}$$

where Q is cumulative output (the total number of units ever produced) and its time-derivative $\dot{Q}$, represents the output flow.[5] At any moment, Q is fixed and the production possibilities open to the economy are thus represented by $F(\ , Q)$, which is a conventional production function and will be assumed to satisfy all the usual properties attributed to it by growth theorists, including constant returns to scale. Assuming also perfect competition, so that

$$r = F_K \text{ and } w = F_L \tag{11}$$

we can then equate income to the output flow,

$$Y = \dot{Q}. \tag{12}$$

In addition or as an alternative to costless learning, technical progress may be also the result of activities like research and education, which use resources. But if we stipulate that, at least in the long run, the rate of return will be the same for all forms of investment, then the introduction of these alternative uses of savings would make no qualitative difference to the aggregate behaviour of the economy. Costly technical progress may thus be accommodated, without changes to the formal model, by simply reinterpreting K as a composite asset, comprising scientific knowledge and human capital as well as physical investments.

Given (4)–(8) and (12), the conditions for the momentary equilibrium are simply

$$\dot{K} = \sigma Y \tag{13}$$

and

$$\dot{L} = \nu L, \tag{14}$$

where

$$\nu = n - m \tag{15}$$

is the rate of population growth, n is the natality rate, determined in general by (6), (7), and (8), and m is the mortality rate, assumed constant. We can now exploit this information to derive the behaviour of the model economy over time, and it is convenient to describe such behaviour in terms of ν and two new variables: the output–capital ratio,

$$\beta \equiv Y/K \tag{16}$$

and the growth rate of cumulative output,

$$\delta \equiv \dot{Q}/Q = Y/Q \tag{17}$$

which also stands for the rate of accumulation of experience.

By differentiating (16) and (17) logarithmically with respect to time and using (10), (13), and (14), we find the first two dynamic equations,

$$\dot{\beta} = -\alpha_2 \sigma \beta^2 + \alpha_3 \beta \delta + \alpha_2 \beta \nu \tag{18}$$

and

$$\dot{\delta} = \alpha_1 \sigma \beta \delta - (1 - \alpha_3) \delta^2 + \alpha_2 \delta \nu \tag{19}$$

where α_i is the elasticity of output with respect to the ith argument of F( ). Since n is, in general, a function of y, we can also write

$$\frac{\dot{\nu}}{\nu} = \eta \frac{\dot{y}}{y} \tag{20}$$

where η is the income elasticity of the demand for children. Logarithmic differentiation of (14), on the other hand, yields

$$\frac{\dot{y}}{y} = \alpha_1 \sigma \beta + \alpha_3 \sigma - \alpha_1 \nu \tag{21}$$

which, substituted into (20), gives us the third dynamic equation,

$$\dot{\nu} = \alpha_1 \eta \sigma \beta \nu + \alpha_3 \delta \eta n - \alpha_1 \eta \nu^2. \tag{22}$$

These equations tell us that the rates of change in the output–capital ratio, rate of accumulation of knowledge, and rate of population growth are all decreasing functions of their own level, and increasing functions of the levels of the other two. Since α_1, α_2, and α_3 are, in general, functions of (K, L, Q), it is clear that the dynamic system formed by (18), (19), and (22) is highly non-linear.

Long-term Properties

Let us start by enquiring whether the dynamic system formed by the equations (18), (19), and (22) admits a steady-state solution, defined as a situation where β (and, therefore, δ) and ν are constant in time. This type of solution is of particular interest, because any other kind would result in output, consumption, or the population becoming zero, and the economy thus vanishing, in finite time.

For $\dot{\beta} = \dot{\delta} = \dot{\nu} = 0$, the system reduces to

$$-\alpha_2 \sigma \beta + \alpha_3 \delta + \alpha_2 \nu = 0 \tag{23}$$

$$\alpha_1 \sigma \beta + (\alpha_3 - 1)\delta + \alpha_2 \nu = 0 \tag{24}$$

$$\alpha_1 \eta \sigma \beta + \alpha_3 \eta \delta - \alpha_1 \eta \nu = 0 \tag{25}$$

which has a non-trivial solution if and only if

$$\beta > 0 \tag{26}$$

and

$$\alpha_3 \eta = 0. \tag{27}$$

In other words—and keeping in mind that α_3 and η are, in general, variables—the occurrence of a steady state would imply that the economy had reached a stage of development where there was nothing else to be learned by mere experience ($\alpha_3 = 0$), or where the birth-rate had ceased to be affected by the level of income ($\eta = 0$). We shall see in a moment what the latter would entail in terms of family preferences, but let us first complete the characterization of this long-term equilibrium.

Since (23)–(25) forms a homogeneous system, it can determine only *relative* values of the variables. A steady-state solution will thus be of the form:

$$\beta = \beta^* \tag{28}$$
$$\delta = \sigma\beta^* \tag{29}$$

and

$$\nu = \frac{\alpha_2 - \alpha_3}{\alpha_2} \sigma\beta^* \tag{30}$$

where β^* is a constant to be determined by initial conditions. The steady state is, therefore, not unique—a property that leaves scope for policy intervention. The associated growth rate of income per adult is given by

$$\frac{\dot{y}}{y} = \frac{\alpha_3}{\alpha_2} \sigma\beta^* \tag{31}$$

which is also open to policy manipulation. Notice that, while the output–capital ratio and, therefore, the growth rates of total and per-adult output are necessarily positive, the rate of population growth may be positive or negative, depending on whether labour employment is more or less important than technical progress (α_2 larger or smaller than α_3) in the production process.

The impact of endogenous population can be seen most clearly by comparing the model's behaviour in this case with its behaviour in the case where the natality rate is exogenously determined. Taking ν as a parameter, (23)–(24) becomes a non-homogeneous system, which can be solved for the absolute values of β and δ:

$$\beta = \frac{\alpha_2}{\alpha_2 - \alpha_3} \frac{\nu}{\sigma} \tag{28'}$$

$$\delta = \frac{\alpha_2}{\alpha_2 - \alpha_3} \nu = \sigma\beta \tag{29'}$$

and

$$\frac{\dot{y}}{y} = \frac{\alpha_3}{\alpha_2 - \alpha_3} \nu = \frac{\alpha_3}{\alpha_2} \sigma\beta. \tag{31'}$$

The equilibrium relationships of δ and $(\hat{y}/y)$ with β are thus the same, whether ν is endogenous or exogenous, but in the second case β is uniquely determined by σ.[6] Notice also that in the absence of endogenous technical progress (28') would reduce to the familiar Harrod–Domar equilibrium condition.

If the rate of population growth is exogenously determined, there is thus a unique equilibrium growth rate and, at any instant, a unique equilibrium level of income per adult for any given ratio of savings to income.[7] Conversely, if the population growth rate is allowed to vary endogenously, we can find different equilibrium levels and growth rates of income per adult associated with the same saving–income ratio. An important implication of endogenous population growth is, therefore, that it might be possible to influence both the level and the growth rate of income by a variety of different policies, whereas in the exogenous population case this can be achieved only by policies which affect the fraction of income saved.

Another important implication of endogenous population growth concerns the stability of equilibrium paths, that is whether the economy would tend to return to the original steady state after a small disturbance or, more generally, be attracted towards a steady-state path if it came close to one. For this to be true, the characteristic roots of the Jacobian matrix (formed by the partial derivatives of β, δ, and ν) must be negative in steady state, in turn implying

$$\alpha_3 - \alpha_2 < 1 \tag{32}$$

if population is endogenous, or

$$\alpha_3 - \alpha_2 < 0 \tag{32'}$$

if population is exogenous. Stability is thus more probable in the first case, where α_2 may be larger or smaller than α_3 and the population may thus be increasing, decreasing, or constant, than in the second case, where α_2 must exceed α_3 and the population must be forever increasing.

Let us now return to the condition for the existence of a long-term equilibrium with an endogenous population, (27), and see what this implies for the structure of the utility function. If we think that there will always be opportunities for costless learning (and, consequently, that living standards can go on increasing for ever), α_3 will be positive and η must consequently be zero. This means that the rate of population growth must be independent of income (though not necessarily of other economic variables) in the vicinity of a steady state. In other words, there must be no income effects on the demand for n. Since c and n enter the current expenditure constraint as a product, it also means that there must be no income effects on the demand for c. Therefore, the utility function must be weakly separable in (c, n),

$$u(a, c, n,) \equiv U(a, v(c, n)) \tag{33}$$

in a neighbourhood of the steady state.

If it is true that η vanishes in steady state, it must then be true that, for at least the combinations of a, c, and n which occur in such a state, the marginal rate of substitution between expenditure per child and number of children is independent of the level of adult consumption. The behavioural implication is that the family has a hierarchical decision procedure: after dividing its income between savings and current expenditure, the family proceeds to allocate current expenditure between adult consumption and child-related expenditure, and finally, as a last stage, decides how many children there are going to be and how much each child is going to cost.

Policy Implications

Suppose that income is taxed at the rate θ. On the face of it, that would reduce the equilibrium growth rate of output by $\theta\sigma\beta$, that of income per adult by $(\alpha_3\theta\sigma\beta/\alpha_2)$ and, if natality is endogenous, that of the population by $((\alpha_2 - \alpha_3)\theta\sigma\beta/\alpha_2)$, because the fraction of income saved by the families would now be $(1 - \theta)\sigma$ instead of σ. That, however, does not take account of the way the tax revenue is spent, nor of how the families would respond to these changes in their economic environment.

Consider, first, the case in which the rate of population growth is exogenously determined, as this is the easiest to deal with. If the revenue were spent on public investments, then the fraction of income invested would remain σ, thereby leaving the capital–output ratio and the rate of growth of income per adult exactly where they were. The only possible change might then be in the allocation of private expenditure between adults and children. Similarly, if the tax revenue were returned to the public in a lump sum (either the same for every adult, or in proportion to the number of children) or in the form of public goods (perfectly substitutable for private consumption, since we have only one commodity), the government would be giving back with one hand what it had taken away with the other, and nothing would change.

Not so if population change is endogenous, because, as we discovered, the output–capital ratio is not uniquely determined by the fraction of income saved. Furthermore, the effect of income taxation will be different not only according to whether the revenue is invested or redistributed, but also according to whether it is redistributed in equal amounts to every adult or in proportion to the number of children, which is now a choice variable.

To try and sort out these various effects, let us rewrite the budget constraint as

$$a + \tilde{z}n = (1 - \sigma)(1 - \theta)y + \psi \tag{34}$$

where

$$\tilde{z} \equiv b + c - \phi, \tag{35}$$

ϕ is the rate of child benefits[8] and ψ is a lump-sum payment. As remarked in the first section, the comparative-statics effects of parameter changes are generally ambiguous when n is a variable. But it we impose that the utility function must be weakly separable as in (33), that gives us just enough structure to sign unequivocally the changes of a and n:

$$\frac{\partial a}{\partial y} = (1 - \sigma)(1 - \theta)i_a > 0 \tag{36}$$

$$\frac{\partial a}{\partial \theta} = -(1 - \sigma)yi_a < 0 \tag{37}$$

$$\frac{\partial a}{\partial \phi} = ni_a > 0 \tag{38}$$

$$\frac{\partial a}{\partial \psi} = i_a > 0 \tag{39}$$

$$\frac{\partial c}{\partial y} = \frac{\partial c}{\partial \theta} = \frac{\partial c}{\partial \psi} = \frac{\partial n}{\partial y} = \frac{\partial n}{\partial \theta} = \frac{\partial n}{\partial \psi} = 0. \tag{40}$$

$$\frac{\partial c}{\partial \phi} = -\frac{\partial c}{\partial b} = -S_{cn} \tag{41}$$

and

$$\frac{\partial n}{\partial \phi} = -\frac{\partial n}{\partial b} = -S_{nn} > 0 \tag{42}$$

where S_{cn} and S_{nn} are, respectively, the cross- and direct-substitution effects of an increase in the cost of n. The income effect on adult consumption i_a has to be positive, because that is the only item of expenditure affected by a change in disposable income. The cross-substitution effect, on the other hand, can have any sign.

All that has to do with the demand side of the economy. To get the full picture we must look at what happens on the supply side too. Given (4), (12) and constant returns to scale, we can write

$$y = F\left(\frac{y}{\beta}, 1, Q\right). \tag{43}$$

Thus at any instant

$$dy = \alpha_1\left(dy - y\frac{d\beta}{\beta}\right) \tag{44}$$

or

$$\frac{dy}{y} = -\frac{\alpha_1}{\alpha_2}\frac{d\beta}{\beta}. \tag{45}$$

But, in steady state,

$$\frac{dv}{v} = \frac{d\beta}{\beta} \, . \tag{46}$$

Therefore,

$$\frac{v}{y} \frac{dy}{dv} = -\frac{\alpha_1}{\alpha_2} < 0. \tag{47}$$

we have thus established that income per adult and consumption per child will fall as the number of children per adult rises.[9]

We are now equipped to analyse the *instantaneous* effects of government intervention when n and, therefore, v are endogenously determined in accordance with economic theory. If the government taxes income to pay for public investment, then the fraction of output invested, the rate of population growth, the level of output per adult, and the level of expenditure per child remain the same. All that changes is the level of expenditure per adult, which will decrease by the precise amount of the tax. Not even adult consumption would change if the proceeds of the tax were redistributed in lump sums ($\psi = \theta y$).

If, on the other hand, the income tax serves to subsidize births ($yd\theta = nd\phi$), then the rate of population growth will rise in accordance with (42), while income per adult will fall by

$$\frac{\delta y}{\partial \phi} = \frac{\partial y}{\partial v} \frac{\partial n}{\partial \phi} = \frac{\alpha_1}{\alpha_2} \frac{y}{v} s_{nn} < 0 \tag{48}$$

and consumption per adult will rise by

$$\frac{\partial a}{\partial \theta} = \frac{y}{n} \frac{\partial a}{\partial \phi} = \sigma y i_a > 0. \tag{49}$$

But that implies that c has fallen by more than n has risen: in long-term equilibrium the 'quantity' and the 'quality' of children are highly substitutable for each other (s_{cn} positive and large). The subsidization of children has thus the expected effect of encouraging procreation, but it also encourages parents to consume more and spend less (per child and in total) on their offspring.

These are only instantaneous effects, in the sense that they show changes in equilibrium expenditures at a point in time, but they are all that happens if the tax revenue is invested or redistributed in lump sums. If, on the other hand, the tax revenue is redistributed in the form of child benefits, we must take account of the fact that the growth rate of y will rise in proportion to v. Hence if θ and ϕ were held constant over time at their new levels, the level of y would eventually become higher than it would have been without the policy change. Given the high degree of substitutability of n for c, this implies that adult consumption will become higher and higher, while expenditure per child will remain constant at its lower level. It is thus clear that the widespread practice of subsidizing child-bearing and taxing income cannot be judged by the Pareto criterion, because it raises adult consumption and lowers expenditure per child in all generations. Strong value-judgements are required for the justification of such a policy.

Conclusion

We set out in this chapter to examine the consequences of grafting an economic theory of fertility on to a simple model of economic growth. Our first discovery was that the existence of a sustainable equilibrium with growing per capita income imposes certain local restrictions on the form of the utility function. By exploiting those restrictions we were able to derive firm conclusions about the effects of government intervention on the long-term behaviour of the model economy. The most striking of those conclusions was that a policy of taxing income and redistributing the proceeds to the families in proportion to the number of children would increase income, consumption, and the number of children per adult, but would permanently reduce the amount spent on each child. By contrast, income taxation would have no macroeconomic effects, no matter how the proceeds are spent, if population were exogenous.

Strong results obtained with a highly stylized model must be taken with the proverbial pinch of salt, particularly so when they concern complex phenomena like fertility. But the approach followed in this discussion, namely inferring the properties of the utility function from the conditions for a sustainable equilibrium and then seeing how these properties affect the comparative statics and dynamics of the system, appears to be promising. It might even be that some of the steady-state results would carry over to models with a variable saving rate and a more detailed age structure.

Endnotes

1. See Becker (1960). A more up-to-date statement incorporating also the contributions of other authors and reviewing some of the empirical evidence is Becker (1981). See Ermisch (1979) for an assessment of this body of theory in relation to the UK experience.
2. A broad outline, without a formal model, is in Nerlove (1974). There are also endogenous population models, like those discussed in Cigno (1981, 1984*b*) or in Pitchford (1974), which may be consistent with a microeconomic theory of fertility but are not actually based on one.
3. As in much of the theoretical literature on the subject, I am implicitly assuming that the birth-rate is instantaneously controllable by the parents and, furthermore, that children become adults after an instant, so that number of births and number of children can be taken as synonymous.
4. In that case, however, output and consumption per capita are constant in the long run, irrespective of whether the rate of technical progress is exogenously or endogenously determined; see Cigno (1981, 1984*b*).
5. This is a generalization of Arrow (1962), where total output is proportional to capital and knowledge is measured by the cumulative output of investment goods only. See Cigno (1984*a*) for further discussion of the rationale and properties of this function.
6. The second result is standard. The first depends on the fact that the rate of technical progress is

endogenous. If the rate of technical progress were a given constant, the growth rate of income per adult would be independent of the saving–income ratio, as in the basic neo-classical model.
7. To be sure, there could be a distributional effect on families with different incomes and number of children—indeed, that would be the purpose of the operation—but so long as the aggregate saving ratio was not affected that would have no macroeconomic implications.
8. The motivation for government intervention in that sphere may be to alter the intergenerational distribution of consumption, as in Cigno (1983a), or the distribution of consumption between families, as in Cigno (1986).
9. The left-hand side of (47) is *not* the reciprocal of η. The latter describes the response of a category of agents, the families, to an exogenous change in their income, all other things being equal. The former is an equilibrium relationship between two simultaneously determined variables, y and n, when all the other variables change so as to maintain the economy in steady state.

References

Arrow, K. J. (1962), 'The Economic Implications of Learning by Doing', *Review of Economic Studies*, 29.

Becker, G. S. (1960), 'An Economic Analysis of Fertility' in A. J. Coale (ed.), *Demographic and Economic Change in Developed Countries*, Princeton University.

——(1981), *A Treatise on the Family*, Harvard University Press.

——'On the Interaction between the Quantity and Quality of Children', *Journal of Political Economy*, 81.

Cigno, A. (1981), 'Growth with Exhaustible Resources and Endogenous Population', *Review of Economic Studies*, 48.

——(1983a), 'On Optimal Family Allowances', *Oxford Economic Papers*, 35.

——(1984a), 'Further Implications of Learning by Doing', *Bulletin of Economic Research*, 36.

——(1984b), 'Consumption vs. Procreation in Economic Growth' in G. Steinmann (ed.), *Economic Consequences of Population Change in Industrialized Countries*, Springer-Verlag.

——(1986), 'Fertility and the Tax-Benefit System: A Reconsideration of the Theory of Family Taxation, *Economic Journal*, 96.

Ermisch, J. P. (1979), 'The Relevance of the Easterlin Hypothesis and the "New Home Economics" to Fertility Movements in Great Britain', *Population Studies*, 33.

Nerlove, M. (1974), 'Toward a New Theory of Population and Economic Growth', *Journal of Political Economy*, 84.

Pitchford, J. D. (1974), *Population in Economic Growth*, North-Holland.

Willis, R. J. (1973), 'A New Approach to the Economic Theory of Fertility Behaviour', *Journal of Political Economy*, 81, supplement (March/April).

Part 3

Population and Demand Patterns

Introduction: Demand Patterns

GERRY RODGERS

Economists have long been concerned with the impact of demographic factors on consumption, saving, and aggregate demand. There is a large literature in economics dealing with these issues, of which the two chapters in this Part occupy rather highly specialized corners. For this reason, it may be particularly helpful to give a brief overview of the broader area.

Most models of consumer behaviour are based on some concept of utility-maximization by the consuming unit, and if all consuming units were identical, fairly simple-minded models would probably suffice. It seems to be an acceptable simplification to regard 'households' as the basic consuming units, although this is inaccurate in many detailed respects. But households vary greatly in size, and in age and sex composition, and these variations modify the relationship between consumption and utility, for many reasons: needs vary by age and sex; there may be economies of scale in consumption; household formation, or the choice of household type, may also be a source of utility, so that consumption patterns and the size and structure of the consuming unit may be jointly determined; similar considerations apply to procreation.

Traditionally, it is age and sex composition which has generated the greatest concern, and a good deal of effort has gone into estimating adult equivalence scales of one sort or another. Prais and Houthakker's seminal contributions (1971) have generated a good deal of empirical research, most of it econometrically unsatisfactory, which attempts to estimate such scales from observed behaviour. In order to obtain satisfactory estimates it is necessary to impose implausible restrictions, for example treating responses to household size as quasi-price responses (Barten, 1964; Muellbauer, 1977), or regarding particular types of expenditure (alcohol or tobacco, for instance) as concerning only a subset of age–sex categories (Deaton, 1981). Attempts have also been made to measure perceived utility directly in households of different types, and hence permit the direct adjustment of the relationship between expenditure and utility (Kapteyn and Van Praag, 1976). Other approaches have focused on life cycle variations in consumption patterns and, most commonly, on some preconceived concept of differences in needs between individuals of different ages and sex.

The view now appears to be gaining ground that overall equivalence scales, and similar techniques for disposing of demographic factors by some process of adjustment, are inadequate. More detailed research into the implications for consumption levels and different expenditure items of particular demographic phenomena are likely to be more rewarding, especially where these examine jointly determinants of economic and demographic outcomes. The two chapters included in this Part are in this general tradition. Denton and Spencer are concerned with aggregate demand; their discussion shows that in a macroeconomic model, endogenizing fertility—and thus treating demographic and economic outcomes as jointly determined —makes a significant difference to model results, especially in the long term. Ermisch looks at a specific expenditure, that on housing, examining how demographic changes—in particular household formation rates—affect the housing market, and noting that household formation itself responds to the state of the housing market. Further detailed empirical studies of this type are likely to contribute in no mean degree to our understanding of the effects of demographic factors on demand patterns.

References

Barten, A. P. (1964), 'Family Composition, Prices and Expenditure Patterns' in P. E. Hart, G. Mills, and J. K. Whitaker (eds.), *Econometric Analysis for National Economic Planning*, Butterworth, London.

Deaton, Angus (1981), 'Three Essays on a Sri Lanka Household Survey', LSMS Working Paper No. 11, World Bank, Washington, DC.

Kapteyn, Arie and Bernard Van Praag (1976), 'A New Approach to the Construction of Family Equivalence Scales', *European Economic Review*, 7, 313–35.

Muellbauer, John (1977), 'Testing the Barten Model of Household Consumption Effects and the Cost of Children', *Economic Journal*, 87, 327; 460–87.

Prais, S. J. and H. S. Houthakker (1971), *The Analysis of Family Budgets*, Cambridge University Press, Cambridge.

8 Changing Demographic Patterns and the Housing Market with Special Reference to Great Britain

JOHN ERMISCH

Households occupy dwelling units, and it is through households that the various dimensions of housing demand are expressed. Thus the first part of this chapter considers the factors influencing the number of households formed out of the population. With this as a background, a measure of the change in the number of households purely attributable to age–sex distribution changes is derived. The second part of the chapter uses this measure in an econometric analysis of the effect of changes in the age–sex distribution of the population on house prices and public and private sector investment in housing. That is, the resource implications of demographically induced household growth are examined. This part also attempts to measure some feedback effects of the housing market on household formation, giving some tentative results. The third part of the chapter investigates the effect of demographic changes on the composition of housing demand, rather than just aggregate demand. A number of dimensions of housing demand are explored: dwelling size and type, housing tenure, quality attributes, and household expenditure on housing and residential location. More detailed measures of the effect of the age–sex distribution of the population on the size, type, and tenure dimensions of housing demand are constructed. In general it can be said that British housing markets are subject to considerable demographic pressure during the 1980s, but during the 1990s the demographic impetus to household growth and aggregate housing investment gradually fades away. During the next twenty years, demographic changes are increasingly shifting the pattern of housing demand in favour of owner-occupation, larger and higher-quality dwellings, and less-central locations.

Household Formation

It is not uncommon for housing analysts to examine the balance between the number of households and the number of dwellings as some gross indicator of excess demand/supply. In this case, as in many others, households are considered to be the demographic unit upon which to focus in analysing housing demand. While this focus is useful for some purposes it should be recognized that households are formed from more basic demographic units —individuals, couples, or nuclear families. Recognition of this is particularly important when analysing the implications of demographic change for housing demand.

Minimal Household Units

At the extreme, individuals are the basic unit of analysis, but economic decisions are often made by a larger unit—a couple or a family—and housing choices put into effect by this larger unit. One of these choices could be to set up a household with persons outside the unit. Recent work by Ermisch and Overton (1983) has suggested the concept of a Minimal Household Unit (MHU), which encompasses these various cases. An MHU is defined in purely demographic terms in the sense that an individual, over his/her lifetime, moves from one MHU type to another by means of a simple demographic transition or event. There are four basic types of MHU: (*a*) childless, non-married adults; (*b*) one-parent families; (*c*) childless married couples; and (*d*) married couples with dependent children. Clearly these various types of MHU are formed by traditional demographic events: ageing, marriage, child-bearing, divorce, and death. These types could be expanded: for example, single and previously married adults could be distinguished.

It appears appropriate to regard an MHU as an economic decision-making unit, particularly with regard to household formation and housing demand. Married couples make joint decisions about whether to live as separate households or whom to live with and make joint housing choices, and parents and their children can also be considered as a single unit, since parents make decisions for their dependent children. When young persons reach the age of majority (or perhaps earlier, when they leave school) they are also in a position to make their own housing choices, which include continuing to live in their parents' household. The number of MHUs in the population is the maximum number of households that could be formed from the population.

The propensity of individual MHUs to form separate households depends on the incomes and prices entering their budget constraints and on some of the demographic characteristics of MHUs. An economic theory of household formation has suggested how the earning capacities of members of an MHU, its non-earned income, and the price of housing affect an MHU's optimal household grouping, and an econometric application of the theory indicates that MHUs with higher income are significantly more likely to form a separate household, while a higher housing price reduces the probability of forming a separate household (Ermisch, 1981*a*, 1–9; Ermisch and Overton, 1984). The theory also predicts variation in the probability of forming a separate household by MHU type, with the presence of children in an MHU raising this probability and couples being more likely to form a separate household than individuals with similar income and of similar age. Econometric analysis confirms such variation, and it also indicates variation within MHU types in the probability of forming a separate household by age and sex of the 'head' of the MHU, holding income constant.

Thus the number of households operating in the housing market depends upon the number and composition of MHUs and the economic and housing market factors which affect their propensity to form a separate household. The number and composition of MHUs reflect ageing, family formation and dissolution, and death, which could be considered as purely demographic factors that are independent of housing market conditions. The impact of demographic change on the number of households could then be investigated by calculating the effect of changes in the number and composition of MHUs on the number of households, on the assumption that the probabilities that MHUs with particular demographic characteristics form a separate household are constant.

This approach is not adopted for a number of reasons. First, the focus of this chapter is on the impact of age distribution changes on the housing market rather than the impact of changes in patterns of family formation and dissolution. Second, there is evidence that housing market conditions affect marriage and fertility patterns (see Ermisch, 1981*b*; Ermisch and Joshi, 1983; Murphy and Sullivan, 1983, and subsequent unpublished work). This implies that if the impact of demographic change is to be measured, then it is necessary to sort out the feedback effects of the housing market on marriage and fertility, and that is a difficult task beyond the scope of this study. Third, there is interest in looking to the future, and although it is difficult to forecast marriage and fertility patterns the age distribution changes relevant to housing are easily forecast up to twenty years ahead. Finally, a proper study of the effect of changing family formation and dissolution patterns on the housing market would be based upon the MHU approach to studying household formation, but at this stage it has not been possible to construct the population of MHUs over time. It is nevertheless possible to measure the impact of age distribution changes on the housing market without measures of the MHU population.

Demographically Determined Household Formation

It has been noted how marital status, the presence of children, age, and earning capacity affect the likelihood of an MHU forming a separate household. Earning capacity varies systematically over the life cycle. Thus taken together these factors produce a life cycle pattern for the probability that an adult (with spouse, if married) is established as a separate household, changing as the adult ages and changes marital status. While the theory has been discussed in terms of MHUs this pattern is also apparent in more traditional perspectives on household formation, like that of household head-ship. Household headship rates express household heads as a percentage of the population in particular age–sex–marital-status groups. Such rates for Great Britain are shown in Table 8.1. The household headship concept has many disadvantages for the analysis of the factors influencing household formation: for instance, as noted above, it is often not individuals who are the decision-making unit, and it is household grouping that is chosen, not whether to be a 'head'. But being individual-based, the headship concept can be applied directly to available population distributions, and the sum of the rate by group products yields the number of households. The rates in Table 8.1 show the age and marital status patterns expected from the economic analysis and the expected sex pattern for the non-married. The different rates for married males and females merely reflect the convention about who is called 'head'. If estimates of the population of MHUs are lacking, these rates can be used to estimate the influence of the age–sex distribution on the number of households.

It has been demonstrated that income and housing market factors affect the incidence of households among particular types of MHUs. Further-more, income, and, to some extent, housing market factors influence the timing of marriage, thereby affecting the marital status distribution of the population (Ermisch, 1981*b*). Fertility and divorces are also affected by earnings growth (Ermisch, 1982*a*; Ermisch and Joshi, 1983; Becker, Landes, and Michael, 1977). Thus income, housing costs, and queues for subsidized housing influence the number of households formed out of a population of a given size and age structure. In other words, the number of households seeking accommodation from a given population cannot be characterized by a *number*, but rather a *schedule* relating the number of households to real income, housing costs, and queues.

In order to abstract from these economic influences on household forma-tion, a measure is constructed which isolates the effect of the age–sex distribution of the population on the number of households. This measure holds the proportions of men and women of particular ages in each of the marital status groups constant, and it also holds constant the propensities to head a household among men and women in each particular age and marital status group. When these weighted headship rates are applied to actual or projected changes in the age–sex distribution of the population, the outcome can be interpreted as net household formation attributable purely to demo-graphic change. As it depends upon the age/sex distribution of the adult population it can be forecast with considerable certainty fifteen or twenty years into the future. The year 1971 is taken as the base for the marital status proportions and the headship rates. Clearly this measure of net household formation attributable to demographic change is not invariant to the base chosen, but it is not particularly sensitive either; only general scaling up or down would probably be necessary. Another adjustment had to be made to

Table 8.1. Household headship rates, Great Britain (per cent of population usually resident in private households)

	Single		Married*		Widowed/divorced	
	1971	1981	1971	1981	1971	1981
Men aged:						
15–19	0.6	1.1	59.5	60.9	20.0	33.8
20–4	7.0	11.0	87.2	84.7	31.8	37.0
25–9	15.9	28.9	94.2	91.3	46.1	49.9
30–44	24.6	38.2	96.7	95.2	64.4	65.2
45–64	48.3	59.2	97.9	96.5	84.0	82.2
65–74	63.2	72.5	97.9	96.5	82.7	87.5
75 and over	63.0	74.0	96.6	95.0	73.6	82.2
Women aged:						
15–19	0.8	1.4	0.5	6.1	15.8	48.7
20–4	8.3	12.2	1.4	6.1	42.9	54.0
25–9	18.2	29.8	1.8	6.0	52.2	62.8
30–44	26.6	40.1	2.1	4.9	76.4	78.1
45–59	47.5	55.2	2.4	4.0	88.8	89.4
60–74	67.1	71.9	3.0	4.3	88.9	91.0
75 and over	71.4	77.1	4.6	7.4	77.6	83.3

*The designation of 'head of household' in the 1981 Census made it slightly more likely that the wife would be recorded as head.
Source: 1981 Census, National Report, Part I, Tables 7 and 35; and 1971 Census, Unpublished Tables DT 2049 and DT 2054.

facilitate the application of the weighted rates to the more readily available 'total enumerated population' rather than the usually resident private household population: heads were expressed as a percentage of the enumerated population in 1971, whereas Table 8.1 expresses them in terms of the usually resident private household population. A further adjustment had to be made after 1981 to compensate for the change from the total population to the 'usually resident population' for projection purposes.[1]

Table 8.2 shows that the average contribution of age–sex distribution changes to household growth has fallen slightly in successive decades of the post-war period, but it is about to rise again to a new post-war high. 'Other changes' reflect changes in the marital status distribution and in the propensities of MHUs to form separate households, which in turn partly reflect housing market and other economic influences such as income growth. These other changes contributed 50–60 per cent of the household growth during the 1950s and 1960s, but only 35 per cent in the 1970s. The large contribution of other changes during the 1960s was primarily due to the increase in the incidence of separate households in the individual age–sex-marital-status groups; changes in the marital status composition of the population only made a small positive contribution to household growth (perhaps because earlier marriage was offset by more divorce). The large amount of household fission during the 1960s is probably in part due to the historically high level of house-building activity during the 1960s (see Table

Table 8.2.   Households and dwellings, Great Britain, 1951–2001

| Period | Total | Changes in the number of households per annum (thousands), attributable to: | | Changes in the number of dwellings per annum (thousands) | Average housing starts per annum (thousands) |
		Age and sex distribution changes*	Other changes		
1951–61	163.5	90	73.5	—	294.5(1951–60)
1961–71	212.8	80	132.8	272.6	370.6(1961–70)
1971–81	117.5	75	42.5	218.5	283.5(1971–80)
1981–4		78			
1984–7		95			
1987–90		90			
1990–3		82			
1993–6		46			
1996–9		19			
1999–2001		16			

*The effect of changes in the numbers in each age–sex group if age–sex–marital-status-specific household headship rates and proportions in each marital status are held constant at 1971 levels; the rates were defined for five-year age groups.

8.2), alleviating the scarcity of dwellings relative to households existing in 1961. Relatively rapid real income growth during the 1960s probably also made an important contribution.[2]

The small contribution of 'other changes' to household growth during the 1970s has, however, a great deal to do with marital status changes. Changes in the marital status composition of the population between 1971 and 1981 offset 40 per cent of the growth in households arising from changes in the age–sex distribution of the population.[3] The large rise in the incidence of divorce and the large fall in marriage rates during the 1970s increased the proportion of the population in MHUs with relatively low probabilities of forming a separate household; between 1971 and 1981 the proportions of men in private households who were married fell in every age group less than 70, and the proportion of women married rose in every age group above 55. It is clear from Table 8.1 that these changes tend to reduce the number of households. Table 8.1 also shows that there was a substantial rise in household headship rates among the non-married during the 1970s, which more than compensated for the marital status composition changes.

It is clear from Table 8.2 that there is considerable demographic stimulus to household growth during the 1980s, peaking in the mid-1980s, but remaining above previous levels of demographic stimulus until the 1990s. During the 1990s, the demographic impetus to household growth decelerates significantly. If fertility remains at its present level, age distribution changes will start to reduce the number of households from about the turn of the century.

Thus the 1980s could be the last of the demographically inspired housing booms. Whether a boom materializes depends primarily upon whether the incidence of separate households among MHUs, particularly non-married persons, continues to rise, and also on trends in marriage and divorce. Without this other source of growth the building of, on average, 150,000 units per annum during the 1980s would take care of household growth and replacement requirements (see Ermisch, 1983, ch. 5, on calculation of replacement requirements). As comparison with past house-building activity indicates (Table 8.2), this level of building would hardly be of boom proportions.

The number of additional households actually formed depends therefore upon economic changes like income growth, autonomous trends in marriage and divorce, and the interaction of demand and supply in the housing market, which determines rents and housing queues. The next section considers the effect on housing markets of the purely demographic stimulus to household growth and the claim on real resources made by the resulting economic activity in the housing sector.

Resource Implications of Demographically Induced Household Growth

An important feature of housing in Great Britain is the large role of the public sector. Just over 30 per cent of households are in dwellings provided by local authorities (councils) at rents below the market value of the units. At these subsidized rents there is a continual excess demand for local authority housing units, and the units are rationed according to various criteria of 'housing need'. The entry rules generally give preference to families with children and pensioners, but once a family is in this housing sector it can remain, even though its circumstances change, and its seniority in the sector actually helps the family obtain better housing. Of the housing allocated by the private sector, about 85 per cent is currently owner-occupied, with the private rental sector now playing a small role in the provision of housing. At present only 13 per cent of households rent privately, and a large proportion of these pay rents which are controlled, and therefore below market value. Thus a large amount of privately rented housing is also rationed.

Through most of the post-war period, a housing shortage existed at the prevailing level of rents and house prices. Indeed, until the late 1960s the number of households exceeded the number of dwellings. Thus is took quite a while even to approach eliminating the acute housing shortage inherited at the end of the Second World War (in 1951 there were 750,000 more households than dwelling units in England and Wales). Another major development during the post-war period was the decline in the proportion of dwelling units rented privately from about half in 1951 to less than 10 per cent now. Rent controls were in operation, with varying degrees of severity, throughout this period. The analysis of the impact of demographically induced household growth first focuses on the only true housing 'market' that remains in Britain, the owner-occupied housing market. Demographic impacts on both the public and private sectors, and interaction between them, are then examined.

Owner-occupied Housing Market

An economic model of the British market for owner-occupied housing which incorporates net household formation attributable to age–sex distribution changes, measured in the same way as in Table 8.2, was estimated by Buckley and Ermisch (1982) over the period 1968–78 using quarterly data. The model is able to identify the demand function for owner-occupied housing. It is a disequilibrium model which allows for MHUs to adjust to earlier 'optimization errors' as well as current changes in economic and demographic variables. An important property of the model is that the derived equilibrium demand function is satisfied in equilibrium, but not at each point in time; only the *model*, and not the *data*, is forced to satisfy the equilibrium demand relationship. With the estimated parameters, the equilibrium demand function for owner-occupied housing is

$$ln P_H = 1.10.ln HH + 0.72\ ln S + 0.28\ ln B + 9.3\ g + b.ln(H^o/Q) + a \tag{1}$$

where P_H is the real price of an owner-occupied house (that is, relative to the consumption deflator); HH is net household formation attributable to age–sex distribution changes; S is the relative tax advantage of owner-occupied housing as a consequence of the tax exemption of its return (equal to the marginal income tax rate times the *nominal* interest rate); B is a mortgage-rationing variable; and g is the rate of growth of real disposable income.

Since g is positively related to permanent income, the g term in equation (1) represents the permanent income effect. Because the owner-occupied housing stock H^o and the difference between the number of households and the number of subsidized rental units available (Q) moved so closely together we were not able to identify their equilibrium influences (b).

It is clear from equation (1) that more rapid growth stimulated by age–sex distribution changes puts strong upward pressure on the demand for owner-occupied housing and house prices; the elasticity of real house prices with respect to demographically induced net household formation is about 1. This is the equilibrium effect, when all demand adjustments have worked themselves out and the rate of change in local authority house completions equals the rate of demographically induced household formation. Outside equilibrium, the direct impact on house prices of net household formation attributable to demographic change is enhanced (reduced) when it exceeds (lags behind) the addition to the local authority housing stock.

Thus the econometric model has quantified the unexceptional proposition that faster household growth due to demographic change puts upward pressure on house prices. It is clear from Table 8.2 that demographic changes put upward pressure on real house prices over the 1980s. What actually happens to house prices will depend upon other factors, particularly inflation, mortgage rates, income growth, building societies' ability to attract funds, and local authority house-building, but age structure changes provide considerable demographic impetus to house prices and private sector building activity during the 1980s. This impetus will be enhanced if local authority house-building is constrained. The extent to which this produces a boom in house-building and an eventual moderation of house price increases depends upon changes in building costs and development constraints, which affect the price elasticity of supply. Analysis in the next section attempts to incorporate supply responses, albeit in a much cruder housing model.

Aggregate Housing Investment

The model of the owner-occupied housing market indicated that the effect of household growth from demographic change on house prices depends upon the extent of alternative housing provision, particularly local authority house-building. The latter is determined by political decision, and these decisions may in part be determined by the government's satisfaction with the ability of the private sector to provide housing for various population groups. The public authorities may respond to demographically induced household growth (and other economic variables), but their responses may be influenced by private sector housing provision. The simple model outlined and estimated here tries to take into account this potential interaction between the private and public sector housing provision.

It is postulated that since the public authorities responsible for housing provision are constrained by the resources available to them, they are likely to be influenced by national income (from which taxes must be raised) and also by building costs. It is also assumed that they respond to 'housing need', which is presumed to be a function of the number of households and the size of the private sector housing stock. It also appears that Labour governments have a greater proclivity towards public housing provision than Conservative governments. Letting G^* denote the desired public sector housing stock, these assumptions can be summarized in the following functional relationship:

$$G^* = G(H^*, S^*, y, C, T) \tag{2}$$

where H^* is the total number of households; S^* is the private sector housing stock; y is real national income per 'demographically determined household' (see next paragraph); C is real non-land construction costs; and T is a dichotomous political party indicator (T = 1 if there is a Labour government, T = 0 if Conservative).

Drawing on the earlier analysis, the total number of households is assumed to be a function of real income (y), house prices (p), nominal interest rates (r), the demographically determined number of households (H), measured as in Table 8.2,[4] and the size of the public sector housing stock (G*).

The inclusion of the last variable reflects the fact that public sector rents are not relevant to household formation decisions at the margin because entry is determined by non-price rationing. For a given H, a larger public sector stock (G*) entails shorter queues for entry. In terms of our notation,

$$H^* = h(y, p, r, H, G^*) \tag{3}$$

The analysis of the demand for owner-occupied housing in the previous section suggests the following housing demand function in the private sector:[5]

$$D = D(y, p, r, G^*, H^*). \tag{4}$$

The inclusion of G* in (4) reflects the fact that if there are more subsidized rental units available for a given number of households, then fewer households may want owner-occupied housing.

On the supply side, builders' supply decisions will depend upon house prices relative to costs, including financing. Thus:

$$S^* = S(p, r, C) \tag{5}$$

The shape of the supply function S( ) reflects the elasticity of substitution between land and other inputs in the production of housing and the elasticity of land supply. Non-land production costs appear directly in the variable C.

The appearance of the nominal interest rate in (3), (4), and (5) may seem questionable. The nominal rate is the sum of the real rate and the expected rate of inflation. It would be more proper to include both of these separately, although the latter is difficult to measure. Buckley and Ermisch show both theoretically and empirically that the equilibrium demand for owner-occupied housing is a positive function of the expected inflation rate because a higher inflation rate lowers the real cost of owner-occupied housing services through the tax system, but nominal mortgage rates have a negative disequilibrium influence on demand because of borrowing/liquidity constraints on consumption.[6]

Changes in nominal interest rates can therefore have two opposing effects on housing demand, and both types of effect also probably operate in household formation decisions.

The system of equations (2)–(5) contains five endogenous variables: D, S*, p, H*, G*. The equilibrium solutions are obtained from the private sector equilibrium condition D = S*. By the usual application of the implicit function theorem, we can solve for the endogenous variables in terms of the exogenous variables:

$$S^* = f^S(y, r, C, H, T) \tag{6}$$
$$H^* = f^H(y, r, C, H, T) \tag{7}$$
$$G^* = f^G(y, r, C, H, T) \tag{8}$$
$$p = f^P(y, r, C, H, T) \tag{9}$$

Annual measures of H^* are not very reliable and are not always available; thus the empirical analysis will concentrate on S^* and G^*. The relations (6)–(9) are equilibrium ones. There are, however, likely to be adjustment lags on both the demand and supply sides. To allow for this, a stock adjustment model is assumed. Thus gross housing investment in the private (I_S) and the public sector (I_G) are given by:

$$I_{St} = a_S(S^*_t - S_{t-1}) + d_S S_{t-1} \tag{10}$$
$$I_{Gt} = a_G(G^*_t - G_{t-1}) + d_G G_{t-1} \tag{11}$$

where t is a time index and the a_js and the d_js are speed of adjustment and depreciation parameters respectively; $0 < a_j < 1$ and $0 < d_j < 1$.

Econometric analysis of the model faces a problem which is difficult to overcome fully. Each of the equilibrium reduced-form equations of the housing model (6)–(9) reflects the parameters of the public sector housing equation (2). Even without changes of government, it is highly likely that the parameters of the public sector equation will not be stable over time, since housing policies change. Shifts in policy could also cause parameter changes in the other structural equations as well, but equation (2) is most susceptible, particularly over the long period considered here, 1959–80. In basing the econometric analysis on the reduced form, this potential parameter instability is spread to all the equations to be estimated. It may therefore be preferable to estimate the structural forms (2)–(5) for many purposes, and the preceding section has done that for the demand function for owner-occupied housing. But the data available and structural instability make the estimation of (3)–(5) difficult; yet it would be useful to have some idea of the total effect on housing investment of demographically induced household growth, which is manifested through the interaction of the private and public sectors.

Because of the potential parameter instability just mentioned, the estimated effects should be interpreted as average responses over the estimation period.[7]

Two approaches to examining the total effect of demographically induced household growth through the interaction of public and private sectors are followed. The first simply adds the optimal private and public stocks, $S^* + G^* = K^*$, and focuses the analysis on the total stock. Previous analysis over the period 1959–76 found the demographic impact (i.e., of H) on total net housing investment to be robust with respect to the remainder of the econometric specification (Ermisch, 1982*b*). A stock adjustment model is again assumed, and since there are direct estimates of annual depreciation of the housing stock available for the total stock, net housing investment (I_{Nt}) is taken as the dependent variable:

$$I_{Nt} = a(K^*_t - K_{t-1}) \tag{12}$$

$$K^*_t = S_t^* + G^*_t = g(y, r, C, H, T) \tag{13}$$

Estimation of the model in (12) and (13) must also allow for the fact that real income y is probably not exogenous since housing investment is a large part of total investment expenditure. 'Autonomous expenditure' (A), consisting of exports plus domestic fixed capital formation other than investment in dwellings plus public authorities' current expenditure, divided by H is used as an instrument for real income y. It has the properties of a good instrument: its correlation with y is 0.995 and it is exogenous. The resulting equation:

$$I_{Nt} = ag(A/H, r, C, H, T) - aK_{t-1} \tag{14}$$

can be interpreted as either a 'full reduced form' in the context of the housing model and a simple macroeconomic model, or as only the housing market reduced form with A/H as an instrument for y.[8] Measures of the variables are given in Appendix 8.I. A linear approximation of the function $g(\ )$ is used in the estimation.

Not surprisingly in light of the countervailing effects of the nominal interest rate mentioned above, its coefficient is insignificantly different from zero. Dropping the nominal interest rate from the equation yields the following estimated equation, which is statistically superior in that the standard error of the equation is smaller, and most coefficients are better-determined.

$$I_{Nt} = 0.668\,H_t - 19.57\,C_t + 1.486\,(A/H)_t + 180.4\,T_t$$
$$\quad (2.32) \qquad (5.43) \qquad (4.01) \qquad\qquad (4.95)$$
$$\quad - 0.068\,K_{t-1} - 8{,}635$$
$$\quad (3.60) \qquad\quad (1.78)$$
$$\text{SE} = 73.59 \;\; R^2 = 0.905 \;\; F = 39.34 \;\; \text{DW} = 1.71 \; (1959\text{--}80)$$

(t-statistics in parentheses).

An extra household attributable to demographic change raises net investment in dwellings by £668 (1970 prices), but this is only the short-run effect. The long-run effect depends upon the speed of adjustment a, which is the coefficient of K_{t-1}. In the long run, an additional household raises the housing stock by £9,825 (1970 prices).

The effects of the other variables are as expected. Higher real construction costs lower the housing stock, and a Labour government invests £180 million more per annum in housing than a Conservative one, all else equal. If autonomous expenditure is taken as an instrument for income, the results are consistent with an income elasticity of the housing stock of about 0.65. When it is noted that the income elasticity of the housing stock is generally much less than the income elasticity of housing demand, then this estimate is within the range of outcomes expected on the basis of other housing demand studies.[9] This income elasticity would include the effect of income on marriage and on the probability of forming a separate household. During 1959–80, growth in real income and household growth from age–sex distribution change contributed almost equally to the growth in the housing stock.

The second approach to investigating the impact of demographically determined household growth returns to equations (10) and (11). Substituting from (6) and (8) into these:

$$I_{S_t} = a_S f^S (y, r, C, H, T) + (d_S - a_S)S_{t-1} + u_{S_t} \qquad (16)$$

$$I_{G_t} = a_G f^G (y, r, C, H, T) + (d_G - a_G)G_{t-1} + u_{G_t} \qquad (17)$$

where stochastic terms u_{S_t} and u_{G_t} have been added to the equations. In order to account better for the public–private sector interaction, equations (16) and (17) should be estimated jointly, allowing for correlation between the stochastic terms, which capture unobserved influences. This is accomplished by using Generalized Least Squares, after again using autonomous expenditures as an instrument for income and approximating $f^S(\ )$ and $f^G(\ )$ by linear functions. These equations could be considered as 'full reduced forms', as noted above, or reduced forms in the housing market with A/H as an instrument for y. The measures of the variables are described in Appendix 8.1; all monetary variables are in constant 1975 pounds, rather than 1970 pounds, which was the case in equation (15).

Estimates of the parameters of (16) and (17) are shown in Table 8.3. The low asymptotic t-values of some of the coefficients in specification (1) suggest that the equations may be able to be simplified by dropping some variables. A prime candidate is the political taste variable T, which has a t-value of only 0.07 in the private sector equation. In both equations, the demographically determined household variable H has a coefficient with a t-value just over unity. Exclusion of the variable with the lowest t-value in each equation yields the specification (2) in the table, and in terms of the summary statistics this specification is superior to the first, and indeed to other specifications: it has the lowest standard error and the highest R^2. Specification (3) also did quite well; it differs from (2) in exluding the nominal interest rate rather than H in the public sector equation.

In none of the specifications of the public and private sector investment equations is the effect of household growth from age–sex distribution changes particularly well determined. According to the 'statistically preferred' specification (2), an additional household affects only private sector housing investment, increasing it by £816 in the short run, but the standard deviation of this effect is £577. The long-run effect is harder to identify

Table 8.3. Generalized least-squares estimates of private and public sector housing investment, 1959–80 (£ million, 1975 prices)

Independent variables	(1) Private	Public	(2) Private	Public	(3) Private	Public
H_t	0.693	0.493	0.816	—	0.623	0.689
(thousands)	(1.09)	(1.11)	(1.41)		(1.06)	(1.58)
C_t	−24.19	−32.00	−23.12	−34.20	−25.78	−27.08
(1970 = 100)	(2.67)	(5.37)	(2.68)	(6.09)	(2.99)	(5.42)
$(A/H)_t$	87.82	82.69	82.77	95.05	89.34	77.25
(£ hundreds)	(2.38)	(2.48)	(2.35)	(3.04)	(2.52)	(2.26)
T_t	−4.9	395.0	—	410.4	—	390.3
	(0.07)	(6.43)		(7.08)		(6.36)
G_{t-1}	—	−0.044	—	−0.026	—	−0.046
(£ million)		(1.86)		(1.49)		(1.91)
S_{t-1}	−0.043	—	−0.047	—	−0.042	—
(£ million)	(1.43)		(1.69)		(1.51)	
r_t	−33.26	28.17	−34.81	34.94	−25.17	—
(per cent)	(1.42)	(1.41)	(1.54)	(1.84)	(1.15)	
Constant	−7,563	−5,344	−9,639	3,165	−6,266	−9,143
	(0.71)	(0.70)	(1.00)	(6.04)	(0.64)	(1.23)
Asymptotic *t*-statistics in parentheses.						
Summary statistics*						
SE	147.4	124.9	142.5	124.8	142.5	129.2
$\bar{R}^2$	0.740	0.889	0.758	0.890	0.758	0.882
F	10.50	27.77	13.50	33.22	13.50	30.80
DW	1.73	2.17	1.73	2.14	1.73	1.94

*Based on residuals of first-stage regressions.

because the coefficients only give us an estimate of $d_S - a_S$. On the assumption that $d_S = 0.02$, the long-run effect of an additional household from demographic change is to increase the private sector housing stock by £12,180 (1975 prices). In 1975 prices, the estimate of the effect of an additional household on total net housing investment from equation (15) is almost double that. The mean total effect estimated from specifications (1) and (3) are closer to the effect estimated from equation (15), but the standard error of the estimated total effect is quite large as well. In these latter two cases an additional household affects housing investment in both the public and private sectors by about the same amount, on average. Perhaps the large standard deviation associated with the average response to additional households is due to policy changes, as suggested earlier. Another result favouring specifications (1) and (3) over (2) is the very high long-run income elasticity of the public sector stock indicated by specification (2); an income elasticity of 1.4.

On the basis of estimates of the price elasticities of housing demand and supply and the income elasticity of housing demand by households, an income elasticity of the housing stock in excess of unity is highly unlikely.[10] Thus the income elasticity of 1.4 in the public sector equation of specification (2) suggests that the exclusion of H from the equation is improper.

Because of the high correlation between H and A/H or y (0.985), the exclusion of the former artificially inflates the estimated effect of the latter. For a similar reason, we have not reported any two-stage least-squares estimates. The income elasticities from this estimation procedure were 1.6 in the total net housing investment equation (i.e., from (12) and (13)), 1.4 in the private sector equation (16), and 2.0 in the public sector equation (17). These high income elasticities emerge because of the large coefficient of H on y in the first stage of the estimation. The instrumental variable estimates of the income elasticity, with A/H as instrument, have therefore been favoured; alternatively, these equations with A/H can be interpreted as 'full reduced forms,' with no income elasticity interpretation.

With one possible exception, the other variables have the expected effects. The long-run income elasticities of the housing stock are about 0.5 in the private sector and about 0.8 in the public sector, according to specifications (1) and (3). All else equal, annual gross public investment in housing is around £400 million higher when a Labour government is in office, and higher real construction costs reduce both the private and public sector housing stocks. Higher nominal interest rates tend to lower private sector housing investment, but raise public sector investment (according to specifications (1) and (2)). The latter result is somewhat surprising, but since these are housing market reduced-form equations it could represent efforts by the public housing authorities to compensate for lower private sector investment.

The housing policy stance conditions both the public and private responses to demographically induced household growth. Variation in this stance may be the cause of the relatively high standard deviation of the mean responses in the public and private sector housing investment equations in Table 8.3. On the assumption that the average responses during the next twenty years are similar to those during 1959–80, it is possible to assess the resource implications of household growth arising from age–sex distribution changes over the remainder of the century. Between 1981 and the turn of the century age distribution changes add about 1.25 million households to the housing market of Great Britain. On the basis of equation (15), in which the effect of an additional household is better-determined, these additional households would bring forth an increase in the total housing stock of £27,000 million (1975 prices), an increase of about 17 per cent.[11] The larger percentage increase in the housing stock than in the number of households arises because the marginal cost of accommodating an additional household exceeds the average cost (the value of the housing stock per household). It is for this reason that it is inappropriate to use the average value of the housing stock per household to gauge the impact of additional households on the size of the housing stock.

Household Formation and the Number of Dwelling Units

In order to obtain further information concerning the effect of income and housing costs on the number of households, the relationship between the demographically determined number of households and the number of dwelling units is examined. Real income and the cost of housing primarily affect the size and quality of the dwelling unit demanded, but the effect on the number of dwelling units per household would appear to be small in an advanced economy; although of course the demand for second homes would tend to rise with real income, this effect may be small. Thus changes in the number of dwellings units per demographically determined household (D/H) would tend primarily to reflect changes in the number of households formed out of a population of a given size, age, and sex structure. It has been stressed throughout that such changes are a function of income and housing costs and quantity constraints. Let us assume that this function is log-linear, so its parameters can be interpreted as elasticities:

$$ln(D/H) = Q_D + b_1 \, lny + b_2 \, lnP \qquad (18)$$

where D is the number of dwelling units and P is the price of housing; the other variables are defined as before. On the supply side, the number of units supplied (S) is a function of the price of housing and non-land construction costs:

$$lnS = Q_S + a_1 \, lnP + a_2 \, lnC \qquad (19)$$

In equilibrium, D = S, and it is easily derived that:

$$lnD = Q + d_1 lnH + d_2 lny + d_3 \, lnC \qquad (20)$$

where the parameters Q and the d_js are functions of the parameters of the demand and supply functions in (18) and (19).[12] Of particular importance is that $d_1 = 1/(1 - b_2/a_1)$. The parameter a_1 is the price elasticity of housing supply and b_2 is the price elasticity of the number of dwellings per demographically determined household; the former is greater than zero and the latter is less than or equal to zero.

Equation (20) is an equilibrium relationship, but we are unlikely to observe the equilibrium relationship directly. This is formalized by assuming a special case of a first-order rational lag model:

$$\Delta lnD_t = Q + c_1 \Delta lnH_t + c_2 \Delta lnC_t + c_3 \Delta lny_t + \lambda_1 lnH_{t-1}$$
$$+ \lambda_2 lnD_{t-1} + \lambda_3 lnC_{t-1} + \lambda_4 lny_{t-1} + v_t \qquad (21)$$

where v_t is an independently distributed random variable and $\Delta ln_t = ln \, X_t$ lnX_{t-1}. This equation can be interpreted as stating that current changes in the number of dwellings reflect both current demographic and economic changes and adjustment to the disequilibrium situation prevailing at the beginning of the period. These disequilibrium terms are those with the λ_j coefficients.

Annual estimates of the number of dwellings do not go back beyond 1964. In order to expand the sample and also make the application of only a first-order lag formulation more appropriate, equation (21) was estimated using a pooled cross-section of the ten British planning regions over the periods 1961–6, 1967–72, and 1973–8; thus the changes refer to changes over these five-year periods and the lagged levels refer to values at the beginning of the period. Real male weekly earnings were used to approximate y, but this variable never approached statistical significance, so it was dropped. The measure of C is as before, and it did not vary over region, only over time. The demographically determined number of households was estimated as before using regional household headship rates in 1971 as weights (the size of Q_D and Q reflects the base). The estimated equation is:

$$\Delta lnD_t = 0.975 + 0.920\ \Delta lnH_t + 0.369\ \Delta lnC_t + 0.277\ lnH_{t-1}$$
$$(3.27)\quad (8.15) \qquad\qquad (2.72) \qquad\qquad (3.89)$$

$$- 0.280\ lnD_{t-1} - 0.197\ lnC_{t-1}$$
$$(3.88) \qquad\qquad (3.01)$$
$$F = 32.85\ R^2 = 0.846\ SE = 0.00914\ DW = 2.20$$

(Absolute value of t-values in parentheses). (22)

In equilibrium, $\Delta lnD_t = \Delta lnH_t = \Delta lnC_t = 0$, and the equilibrium equation (20) can be derived from (22):

$$lnD = 3.482 - 0.704\ lnC + 0.989\ lnH \tag{23}$$

Comparison of (20) and (23) indicates that $d_1 = 0.989$. Estimates of the price elasticity of housing supply in Britain indicate a value of a_1 of 0.6; thus $b_2 = -0.007$; if $a_1 = 2$, as some American estimates suggest, then $b_2 = -0.022$. Thus it appears that household formation is only very weakly responsive to the price of housing, but these results should only be taken as tentative estimates that rely on a very crude model of the housing market.[13]

A corollary of the results in equation (23) is that the primary determinant of regional variation in house-building is demographically induced changes in the number of households in the region: at the mean value of real construction costs, $D = 1.2\ H^{0.989}$. These estimates have assumed that the regional demographic changes are not a function of housing market developments. That may not be a bad assumption, since the vast majority of interregional moves are for job rather than housing reasons,[14] but the potential endogeneity of migration, and therefore the exogeneity of H, is still open to question.

Multiple Dimensions of Housing Demand

When one buys housing services, either through rental or purchase, one acquires more than shelter in a structure of a particular size. The dwelling is at a particular geographical location, which implies that it is in a particular position relative to other activities (for example work, entertainment) and is characterized by a particular physical and social environment. As with other goods, the dwelling unit also has other, non-locational 'quality' attributes associated with it. In addition, the housing tenure chosen, particularly owner-occupation versus local-authority-owned housing, has implications for net housing costs, asset accumulation, and the mobility of the household. These various dimensions of housing choice are powerfully influenced by the demographic characteristics of the household, particularly age, marital status, the presence and number of children, and the age of the youngest child. Changes in these characteristics follow a relatively regular pattern through the life cycle.

An individual marries, or he/she may leave the parental home to form a separate household alone or with other young adults and marry later; has children; the children age; the children leave home; one of the spouses dies. The passage between these stages affects housing needs and preferences, and accompanying the life cycle progression there are changes in labour force participation by household members and in household income. The increasing incidence of divorce adds another stage at an indeterminate point in the life cycle after marriage, and the duration of each of these stages can change as a result of decisions about the age of marriage and the timing and number of children. This part of the chapter examines how changes in age structure affect the pattern of housing demand.

Dwelling Size and Type

Life cycle factors have one of their clearest effects on the size of the dwelling within which the household resides. For instance, the mean number of bedrooms occupied by a household tends to rise with the age of the head of the household until the head's 50s, reflecting family formation and the ageing of children, and then it declines, as children leave home. Mirroring this pattern, the proportion of households living in a flat has the shape of an inverted J over the life cycle. These patterns in the size and type of dwelling reflect changing space requirements, both in terms of the number of rooms and access to private outdoor space. In Britain, these patterns come about through choices made by owner-occupiers and private tenants and through the housing allocation rules of local authorities, but the choice of tenure is also intimately connected with the size of dwelling demanded. To obtain more space one must usually purchase a house or queue for local authority housing. Which one of these two tenures is chosen depends upon marriage and family formation patterns.

Tenure Choice

Entry into owner-occupied housing at marriage is strongly related to age at marriage. For instance, couples in which the woman married as a teenager are less than half as likely to achieve owner-occupation at marriage than those in which the woman marries later (Holmans, 1981). An important reason for the sharp difference in tenure pattern at marriage between women marrying as teenagers and those marrying later is the family-building patterns of the former. In the late 1960s and in the 1970s, almost 40 per cent of women marrying in their teens were either pregnant at marriage or had given birth before marriage, while only about 15 per cent of women marrying at later ages were in this situation. Couples with a child early on in marriage would find it more difficult to save to purchase a dwelling and easier to obtain a local authority dwelling.[15]

The likelihood of a couple becoming an owner-occupier rises as their anniversaries pass, but at each marriage duration women marrying earlier are less likely to have entered owner-occupation, even after controlling for child-bearing and other factors.[16] This age-at-marriage differential appears to arise in part because of the relationship between age and earnings and constraints on borrowing without collateral. Couples marrying at earlier ages tend to have lower earnings at each duration of marriage than their counterparts who marry when they are older. The variation in the likelihood of becoming an owner-occupier with age at marriage may also arise because women with higher earning capacity and motivation toward working marry later; with a higher earning capacity and a firmer attachment to working, they earn more and thereby can more easily afford to purchase a house with their husband when they marry. The counterpart of the relationship between age at marriage and entry into owner-occupation is that at each marriage duration a lower age at marriage is associated with a higher probability of entry into local authority accommodation, and this effect persists after controlling for family formation patterns.

The timing of child-bearing within marriage also affects tenure choice. All else equal, the effect of a first birth is to reduce substantially the probability of entry into owner-occupation and to increase the probability of entering local authority housing.[17] This reflects the effect of a child on saving and the allocation procedures of local authorities, which give priority to couples with children. The birth of a second child does not have a significant effect on tenure choice, but a third birth has a very large effect, substantially raising the probability of obtaining local authority housing. The combination of the effect of children on saving mentioned above and the allocation rules of local authorities probably accounts for these large child effects. There is also a strong tendency for one-parent families to live in local authority housing (see Ermisch and Overton, 1983).

These effects of child-bearing on tenure choice are not only important because of their strength, but also because there is little movement between the two major tenure groups: achievement of one of these two types of tenures greatly reduces the chances of entering the other tenure subsequently (Murphy, 1983). Thus choices made early in marriage have a very strong effect on a couple's lifetime housing situation.

These relationships between housing tenure and family formation patterns help produce an age–sex profile of housing tenure among heads of households, and this will be exploited when examining the implication of age distribution changes. But these relationships also indicate that the family formation patterns of a birth cohort will have lasting effects on their tenure.

Residential Location

Location is bound up with the size, type, and quality of the dwelling demanded as well as the pattern of labour force participation and household income over the life cycle. The location of existing local authority housing obviously dictates the location of many who acquire housing through this sector, although in some cases this sector may be chosen because local authority housing is in a desirable location (for example New Towns). In general it is difficult for local authority tenants to move outside the jurisdiction of their local housing authority. Effecting transfers between authorities is often difficult, and some parts of the country (for example many London suburbs) have a very small local authority sector housing stock into which to move. Thus while local authority tenants do not have a lower propensity to move house than owner-occupiers, the direction and scope of their movement is limited (Gordon *et al.*, 1982).

In owner-occupied housing there is a tendency to move away from city centres as one progresses through the life cycle. This tendency arises because the cost of space declines with the distance from the city centre, and with a given level of household income one must locate further from the city centre in order to acquire the extra space needed as the household expands over the life cycle. Before marriage one's space requirements are small; while space requirements expand somewhat when one marries, if both spouses continue to work commuting costs will dictate a location close to centres of employment. If and when the couple has a family there will be an incentive to move further out from the centre in order to economize on the costs of the additional space required; since the wife will probably also drop out of the labour force at this time household income will be reduced and the need to minimize commuting time lessened, both of which enhance the incentive to acquire housing further from the city centre. While the re-entry of the wife into the labour force and the exodus of children from the home may produce an economic incentive to move back toward the city centre, locational ties in the suburban area generally thwart this move.

An important implication of these locational tendencies is that factors which increase the demand for space by households in the private sector increase outward movement from the city centres. In addition, a larger demand for owner-occupied housing causes the metropolitan area to grow extensively, with new house-building on the suburban fringe (or further out). Demographically inspired household growth or household growth induced by income growth therefore encourage growth of the suburbs, and income growth and family building also encourage suburbanization by increasing the demand for space. Thus the age composition of household heads also affects location patterns. In particular, when the age composition favours the demand for family dwellings, it also favours suburban locations.

Impact of Changing Age Distribution

Changes in the age distribution of the population affect the composition of housing demand through the life cycle patterns discussed above. An attempt is made here to measure the influence of changes in the age distribution on the following dimensions of housing demand: number of bedrooms, type of dwelling, tenure, and household size. The measures are based on the changes in the distribution of households by the age and sex of the household head attributable to changes in the age and sex distribution of the population, and the changes in the distribution of heads are calculated using the same method as was used in calculating the effect of changes in the age–sex distribution of the population on the number of households in Table 8.2. Thus the estimates of the effects of the age–sex distribution on the number of households and on their distribution by age and sex of the head have the same foundation. In order to convert the latter distribution into estimates of the effect of the age–sex distribution of the population on the composition of housing demand it is necessary to apply weights for each dimension of housing demand to the distribution of households by the age and sex of the head.

These weights are based on the composition of housing demand for each age–sex group of household heads in the 1980 General Household Survey. In drawing the weights from a cross-section survey rather than a true life cycle pattern, errors arise because of trends over periods and cohorts in patterns of family formation and dissolution and in the composition of housing demand. Trends in family formation and dissolution particularly affect the weights for the size (number of bedrooms) and type of dwelling and for households size. There is nevertheless a clear life cycle pattern which is probably only slightly disturbed by these trends. The strong trend toward owner-occupation across cohorts does, however, make it difficult to infer the life cycle pattern of housing tenure, and so it seemed appropriate to adjust the proportions observed among age–sex groups of heads in 1980. Since few owner-occupiers move to another tenure and since owner-occupiers have lower mortality than tenants, it has been assumed that the proportion of owner-occupiers rises with age to a plateau (from age 35 for

Table 8.4. Effect of age–sex distribution on the size and composition of housing demand

	1971–81	1981–90	1990–9
Demographic increase in the number of households per annum (thousands)	75	88	49
Per cent of demographic increase in households in housing with particular characteristics			
Bedrooms			
1	19.4	13.4	– 7.8
2	33.1	29.5	7.3
3	42.1	48.5	74.1
4	4.5	7.1	20.8
5 or more	0.9	1.6	5.5
Type of dwelling			
House	75.2	76.6	108.0
Flat	24.4	22.6	– 9.4
Tenure			
Owner-occupied	57.7	57.4	85.1
Local authority tenant	31.9	29.7	23.9
Other tenant	10.4	13.0	– 8.9
Persons per household			
1	37.0	21.4	2.1
2	28.4	27.2	7.1
3	8.9	15.0	19.0
4	18.6	22.5	41.1
5 or more	7.1	13.9	30.7

male heads, 45 for female heads), and never declines. The weights at the plateau and in the approach to it are taken from the 1980 General Household Survey. Actually, the plateau probably occurs a bit later in the life cycle, but there was no way of discerning where (in the cross-section, the proportion of heads who were owner-occupiers fell after age 35 (men) or 45 (women)).

The estimates of the effect of the age–sex distribution of the population on the composition of housing demand shown in Table 8.4 must be treated with some caution because of the potential errors in the weights just mentioned, particularly the effect on housing tenure. From Table 8.4 it appears that during the 1980s the growth in the number of households arising from age–sex distribution changes will be dominated to a lesser extent by small households than was the case in the 1970s, although almost half of the net increase in households is still made up of one- or two-person households. Similarly, small residences (one or two bedrooms) make up quite a large proportion of the net increase in the demand for residences in the 1980s, but less than in the 1970s. At the same time, the composition of demand tends to shift away from the main two types of tenure towards private rental. These patterns, particularly the shift toward private rental, reflect the growing number of persons in their twenties during the 1980s, and in conjunction with the diminishing supply of private rental accommodation, in part attributable to the Rent Acts (MacClennan, 1974), they put substantial upward pressure on rents in the private sector. There may be some overspill of this demand into the purchase of flats, but most young single people have little desire to own (or co-own) a flat at this stage in their life, when they are very mobile, and privately rented accommodation is an important temporary arrangement for young couples, with about a third moving into it at marriage (Holmans, 1981). Nevertheless, with additional supply of private rental units discouraged by rent control and tenants' security legislation, many young people will either have to enter other tenures or not form separate households. The tendency toward a larger proportion of households in private rental accommodation is, therefore, unlikely to be realized.

The shift in the composition of housing demand in favour of larger households and dwellings during the 1980s arises from the growth in the number of households headed by persons aged 30–44. Since households with heads of these ages are having fewer children than in the past and are more likely to contain a wife strongly attached to the labour force they will probably be increasingly interested in owner-occupation rather than local authority housing, and they will generally demand higher-quality dwelling units with easier access to employment centres. But a still-large minority of this growing number of family households cannot afford or do not desire to purchase a dwelling, and the numbers in this category will probably be enhanced by the higher incidence of long-term unemployment during the 1980s. In the current British housing scene, local authority or housing association dwellings are the only choices open to them, so if considerable family hardship is to be avoided family housing provision through these channels will also need to be increased.

Over the last decade of the century, housing demand shifts dramatically toward larger dwellings: all the net increase in households arising from age–sex distribution changes tend to want three bedrooms or more, and the demand for one-bedroom units and flats actually declines (see Table 8.4). It appears that over 90 per cent of this net increase in households have three or more persons, although numbers of persons per household are somewhat exaggerated by using the 1980 weights, which partly reflect the higher fertility of the mid-1960s. Nevertheless, the shift in demand towards larger dwellings appears to reflect primarily life cyle stage, and is unlikely to be much reduced by the lower average family sizes likely to prevail in the 1990s relative to 1980.[18]

These compositional trends are in sharp contrast to the 1970s and 1980s. In addition, the net increase in households is strongly biased towards owner-occupation, and because of the upward trend across cohorts in owner-occupation, the bias toward owner-occupation will actually be more than Table 8.4 indicates. The demand for private rental accommodation actually declines in the 1990s. This pressure of demand for larger, family dwellings arises because the number of persons aged 30–59 expands rapidly. At the same time the demand for flats and small residences for rental plummets because the small birth cohorts of the 'baby bust' years are leaving home to set up separate households and the number of persons over pensionable age declines.

Summary

Considerable attention has been given to measuring the change in the number of households attributable to age distribution changes. As a background to such measurement, the factors influencing household formation were briefly examined. A measure of net household formation purely attributable to changes in the age–sex distribution of the population was then derived. This measure was used in the econometric analysis of the effect of changes in the age–sex distribution on house prices and private and public sector investment in housing. During 1959–80, household growth arising purely from age distribution changes and real income growth contributed about equally to the growth in the housing stock.

The analysis paints a picture of housing markets subject to considerable demographic pressure during the 1980s. During the mid-1980s the demographic stimulus to household growth has indeed been one of the largest during the post-war period. As a consequence, there will initially be strong upward pressure on house prices and rents in the private sector and a lengthening of local authority housing queues. How much housing investment will materialize in response to these price incentives and pressures on local authority housing depends upon housing policies; these policies condition both the public and private responses. On the basis of responses in the past, the 1.25 million households added to the housing market of Great Britain between now and the turn of the century by age–sex distribution changes would bring forth an increase in the total housing stock of £27,000 million (1975 prices), or about 17 per cent. Because of shifts in policies, the standard error of this estimate is, however, large.

During the 1990s, the demographic impetus to household growth and housing investment gradually fades away. Thus the 1980s could be the last of the demographically inspired housing booms. Whether such a boom occurs depends upon income growth and other factors affecting the incidence of separate households among non-married persons, trends in marriage and divorce, and the responsiveness of builders to price incentives and of the public housing authorities.

The pattern of housing demand in terms of type and size of dwelling, housing tenure, and residential location are also affected by age distribution changes. Previous fluctuations in births produce a swing in the demand for flats for rental, peaking in the late 1980s. Other trends in the age distribution entail a steadily increasing demand for larger, family dwellings for owner-occupation, which may, however, be of a slightly smaller size than family dwellings in the past, and which would generally be of higher quality, in suburban or non-metropolitan locations. But a still-large minority of family households will need to rely on the local authorities for housing. Research on the implications of trends in family formation and dissolution patterns for the pattern of demand would be helpful in filling out the picture, but in general it can be said that demographic changes are shifting the pattern in favour of owner-occupation, larger and higher-quality dwellings, and less-central locations, but with easier access to employment centres.

Appendix

Measurement of the variables in the housing investment models

I_N: Gross domestic fixed capital formation in dwellings less capital consumption, dwellings (£million, 1970 prices).

K: Gross capital stock in dwellings at 1970 replacement cost (£million).

I_G: Gross domestic fixed capital formation in dwellings by the public sector (£million, 1975 prices).

I_S: Gross domestic fixed capital formation in dwellings by the private sector (£million, 1975 prices).

G: Gross capital stock in public sector dwellings (£million, 1975 prices).

S: Gross capital stock in private sector dwellings (£million, 1975 prices).

A in equation (14), exports plus public authorities' current expenditure plus domestic fixed capital formation other than I_N (£million, 1970 prices).

A in equations (16) and (17) exports plus public authorities' current expenditure plus domestic fixed capital formation other than I_G or I_S (£million, 1975 prices).

All the above are from *National Income and Expenditure*, various years; the constant price series of each variable was compiled by linking the implicit deflators for the variable in the years in which the Central Statistical Office did not publish values at those prices.

H: Sum of the products of the 1971 household headship rate for each age–sex group and the population in that age–sex group in that year; population figures are UK total population from the *Annual Abstract of Statistics*, various years (thousands).

A/H measured in £.

r: Weighted average of the Bank rate (minimum lending rate) for that year, from *Economic Trends Annual Supplement 1982* (per cent).

C: Index of Cost of New Construction (*Housing and Construction Statistics*) divided by the implicit deflator for gross domestic product at factor costs (*National Income and Expenditure*) (1979 = 100).

T: T = 1 if a Labour government in power for that year: T = 0 if a Conservative government (T = 0.5 in 1970 when each party was in power for half the year).

Means and standard deviations

	Mean	Standard deviation
I_N	1,062.2	239.4
I_G	1,648.5	375.4
I_S	2,095.9	289.3
K_{t-1}	49,985.7	8,996.6
S_{t-1}	78,561.9	11,915.1
G_{t-1}	43,766.7	10,278.3
A/H		
in (14)	£1,508.0	£287.3
in (16) & (17)	£2,962.6	£572.5
T	0.5	0.5
C	107.3	87.8
H	19,239.2	531.6
r	8.04%	3.31%

Endnotes

1. The 1981 ratio of the enumerated population to the usually resident population estimated by the Government Actuary's Department (GAD) in each age–sex group was used to adjust the headship rates. For the latter population estimates, see *OPCS Monitor* (1982 and 1983). The population projections for Great Britain were kindly provided by GAD.
2. On the assumption of an income elasticity of 0.2 suggested by the analysis above and by Hickman, *op. cit.*, about a quarter of the household growth during 1961–71 could be attributed to growth in real personal disposable income per adult.
3. This calculation was based on the population usually resident in private households.
4. That is, the age–sex-specific household headship rates in 1971 are applied to the actual age–sex distribution of the population each year to yield the 'demographically determined number of households'.
5. The mortgage-rationing variable B which appeared in equation (1) was deleted because it was statistically insignificant in the econometric analysis of annual changes in housing investment during 1959–80 reported later in the section.
6. Liquidity constraints could also have an equilibrium influence on housing demand: see R. Schwab (1982), 143–53, but Buckley and Ermisch (1982) found no evidence of such an equilibrium effect in Britain, only a disequilibrium effect.
7. The effects could be thought of as 'random coefficients', although no use has been made of the random coefficient estimation techniques.
8. Ermisch (1982b) for the nesting of (12) and (13) in a simple macroeconomic model. As explained below, when two-stage least squares were used to estimate (12) and (13) from such a system of equations, the estimates produced implausibly high income elasticities; thus it seemed preferable to stick with A/H as the instrument.
9. The income elasticity of housing demand is $(1 - e_d/e_s)$ times the income elasticity of the housing stock, where e_d is the price elasticity of housing demand and e_s is the price elasticity of housing supply. Estimates for Britain suggest that $e_d = -0.5$ and $e_s = 0.6$; thus the income elasticity of the housing stock is about 0.55 times the income elasticity of housing demand. The latter has been estimated to range from 0.6 to about 1 for British households, but these exclude the effect of income on household formation, which would be included in our estimate.
10. As the relation derived in the previous note indicates, the income elasticity of housing demand would have to be about 1.8 for the income elasticity of the housing stock to be unity.

11. Specifications (3) and (1) of Table 8.3 suggest increases of £26 million and £36 million respectively, but these estimates have quite large standard errors.
12. $d_2 = b_1/q$, $d_3 = -b_2 a_2/a_1 q$, $d_1 = 1/q$, and $Q = (Q_D Q_s - b_2/a_1)q$, where $q = 1 - b_2/a_1$.
13. For instance, there is no distinction in the model between private and public sectors, and in the latter sector rationing is not by price, but by queues. This affects the interpretation of d_1 and b_2.
14. A. I. Harris and R. Clausen (1967). Other analysis suggests, however, that a quarter of inter-regional migrants do *not* change their workplace; I. Mohlo (1982), 283–97. Recent unpublished estimates by Ian Gordon indicate that only 12 per cent of interregional migrants do *not* change their workplace.
15. An American longitudinal study shows that the arrival of young children in the early years of marriage depresses savings (including the increase in equity in a home): the principal channel through which children reduce savings is the decline in the wife's earnings associated with child-induced withdrawal from the labour force; J. P. Smith and M. P. Ward (1980), 241–60.
16. M. Murphy uses a proportional-hazards lifetable model to investigate the effects on the probability of entering owner-occupation and of entering local authority housing of: husband's occupational group prior to marriage (manual/non-manual); housing tenure and whether sharing at marriage; entry into other tenures after marriage; births since marriage and age at marriage; marriage at the age of 25 produces the highest probability of entering owner-occupation, but the subsequent downturn in the age-of-marriage effect merely reflects the fact that couples marrying at greater ages are more likely to have been in owner-occupation at marriage (see M. Murphy, 1983).
17. The results reported in this paragraph are from Murphy (1983).
18. The proportion of household heads in three-bedroom dwellings is almost at its peak for heads aged 30–34 in 1980. Heads of these ages had their children mainly in the low-fertility years of the 1970s. Generally, the heads were the husbands, their wives being about two years younger. Women aged 28–32 in 1980 produced fewer children by the age of 29 than other cohorts born since the early 1930s.

References

Becker, G. S. (1977), E. Landes, and R. Michael, 'An Economic Analysis of Marital Instability', *Journal of Political Economy*, 85 (November/December), 1141–87.

Buckley, R. and J. F. Ermisch (1982), 'Government Policy and House Prices in the United Kingdom: An econometric analysis', *Oxford Bulletin of Economics and Statistics*, 44 (November), 273–304.

Ermisch, J. F. (1981*a*), 'An Economic Theory of Household Formation', *Scottish Journal of Political Economy*, 28 (February), 1–9.

——(1981*b*), 'Economic Opportunities, Marriage Squeezes and the Propensity to Marry: An Economic Analysis of Period Marriage Rates in England and Wales', *Population Studies*, 35 (November), 347–56.

——(1982*a*), 'Economic Models of Period Fertility in Britain', Policy Studies Institute Working Paper, Policy Studies Institute, London.

——(1982*b*), 'Demographic Changes and Housing and Infrastructure Investment' in *Population Change and Social Planning*, D. Eversley and W. Koellmann (eds.) Edward Arnold, London.

——(1983), 'Demographic Swings in Housing Demand' in *The Political Economy of Demographic Change*, Heinemann, London.

——and H. Joshi (1983), 'Modelling Fertility Patterns over Time: A Progress Report', Policy Studies Institute Working Paper, Policy Studies Institute, London.

——and E. Overton (1984), *Minimal Household Units: A New Perspective in the Demographic and Economic Analysis of Household Formation*, Policy Studies

Institute Research Report, Policy Studies Institute, London.

——(1985), 'Minimal Household Units: A New Approach to the Analysis of Household Formation', *Population Studies*, 39 (March).

Gordon, I., D. Lamont, R. Vickerman, and A. Thomas (1982), *Opportunities, Preferences and Constraints on Population Movement in the London Region*, final report to the Department of the Environment, Urban and Regional Studies Unit, University of Kent at Canterbury.

Harris, A. I. and R. Clausen (1967), *Labour Mobility in Great Britain 1953-63*, Government Social Survey SS333, Her Majesty's Stationery Office, London.

Hickman, B. G. (1974), 'What Became of the Building Cycle?' in *Nations and Households in Economic Growth: Essays in Honor of Moses Abramovitz*, P. David and M. W. Reder (eds.), Academic Press, London.

Holmans, A. (1981), 'Housing Careers of Recently Married Couples,' *Population Trends* 24, 10-13.

MacClennan, D. (1974), 'The 1974 Rent Act: Some Short Run Supply Effects', *Economic Journal*, 88, 331-40.

Mohlo, I. (1982), 'Contiguity and Inter-Regional Migration Flows in Great Britain', *Scottish Journal of Political Economy*, 29 (November), 283-97.

Murphy, M. J. (1983), 'The Influence of Fertility, Early Housing Career and Socio Economic Factors on Tenure Determination in Contemporary Britain', working paper, London School of Economics.

——and Sullivan, O. (1983), 'Housing Tenure and Fertility in Post-War Britain', Centre for Population Studies Research Paper No. 83-2, London School of Hygiene, University of London.

——*OPCS Monitor* Ref. PP1, 82/2 (Sept. 1982) and 83/1 (March 1983).

Schwab, R. (1982), 'Inflation Expectations and the Demand for Housing', *American Economic Review*, 72 (March), 143-53.

Smith, J. P. and M. P. Ward (1980) 'Asset Accumulation and Family Size', *Demography*, 17 (August), 241-60.

9 Endogenous versus Exogenous Fertility: What Difference for the Macroeconomy?

FRANK T. DENTON AND BYRON G. SPENCER

The traditional approach to population in long-run macroeconomic model-ling and forecasting has been to treat it as exogenous. Either the population growth rate is assumed to be exogenous directly or it is taken as the outcome of exogenously determined fertility, mortality, and migration rates applied to some initial population. Given the time-path of population, the path of the labour force is determined, and hence the supply of labour for input into an aggregate production process. The production–income–expenditure linkages are modelled explicitly so that the major macroeconomic variables of the system are jointly determined and the capital stock moves through time in response to endogenous investment. Labour force participation rates may or may not be determined endogenously but however they are treated there is no feedback from the economy to the population. The direction of influence is all in one direction in the traditional approach.

It is obviously not that economists have been unaware of the fact that economic variables can interact with demographic variables. Malthus is much too firmly established in the history of economic thought for anyone to think that. The economic study of migration has always taken account of the influence of geographic differences of income, and in principle at least the effects of standard of living levels on morbidity and mortality have long been recognized. However, such influences have tended to be ignored in the construction of formal theoretical and econometric macroeconomic models (at least in the mainstream of such activity). It is one thing to say that economic variables affect demographic variables, or are jointly determined along with them; it is quite another to specify an explicit and credible

This chapter is a revised version of a paper prepared for presentation at the IUSSP–IIASA Workshop on the Economic Consequences of Population Composition in Developed Countries, held in Laxenburg, Austria, 12–14 December 1983. The authors express their thanks to Christine H. Feaver, who carried out all the programming and related computer work. The study on which the chapter is based is part of a larger one supported by the Social Sciences and Humanities Research Council of Canada under the terms of a grant awarded jointly to the authors and to Victor W. Marshall for research on the economic and social implications of an ageing population.

mechanism that can be incorporated into a complete mathematically defined economic–demographic macromodel for use in long-run analysis or forecasting, and perhaps as a guide to important decisions of policy. Some very interesting ideas have been put foward as to how the population and the economy may interact with each other but strong empirical evidence of their validity is difficult to compile and much of the literature must be regarded as intellectually stimulating but highly conjectural. Given this state of affairs it is not surprising that the builders of macroeconomic and macroeconometric models have tended to 'play it safe' by sticking with the traditional assumption of demographic exogeneity.

An important question to ask is how much difference it makes to practical economic analysis and forecasting if one assumes demographic exogeneity when in fact population change is jointly determined with macroeconomic change. If in quantitative terms it matters little for the time-path of the economy, economists may accord the issue less weight in their list of worries than they would if there were large effects. The task that we have set ourselves in this chapter is to provide some analytical results that bear on this question.

Our particular concern is with the treatment of fertility. Various authors, including ourselves, have explored the macroeconomic effects of fertility change under the assumption that the latter is determined exogenously.[1] Other authors have treated fertility as endogenous.[2] In the types of model proposed originally by Richard Easterlin, for example, fertility is a function of the income level of young adults, which in turn is a function of young adult cohort size, and hence of past fertility. Another type of endogenous fertility model is one in which household fertility, labour supply, and consumption are jointly determined in a life cycle planning framework and are subject to a lifetime budget constraint. We have proposed and experimented with such a life cycle model elsewhere (Denton and Spencer, 1983, 1984b). In the present chapter we juxtapose exogenous fertility and life cycle models and report some comparative simulation experiments which provide information about the differences in the implications of the two types of models for the time-path of the macroeconomy and its theoretical steady state.

The plan of the chapter is as follows. The first three sections are devoted to specification of the endogenous fertility model: the first section discusses the basic idea of fertility as a life cycle choice variable, the second provides an explicit formal model of household optimization, and the third presents a complete economic–demographic macromodel based on the optimization model. This macromodel is referred to as Model A. Model B is the alternative macromodel based on the assumption of exogenous fertility, and it is described in the next section of the chapter. Models A and B are then brought together in the context of some simulation experiments in the following section. The implications of the experiments for the endogenous versus exogenous fertility issue are considered next, by examining the differences in results when the two alternative macromodels are run in parallel. Some further research possibilities and extensions of the work reported here are then considered, and a final statement of conclusions is provided in the last section.

Fertility as a Life Cycle Choice Variable

Let us assume a population in which each married couple plans the way in which it will allocate its lifetime wealth and does so at the time of marriage. The husband and wife anticipate their future real income, as best they can, by forming expectations about future wage and tax rates and by coupling these with planned labour force participation rates. The rates of labour force participation depend on the amounts of leisure[3] that they plan to enjoy during their lives and on the number of children that they plan to have. Each unit of time that they allocate to leisure represents some income (and hence consumption) foregone, and each child implies some time subtracted from leisure or income-earning time and some sacrifice of consumption goods by the parents. The actual amount of time required to care for a child and the actual volume of consumption by the child are functions of the child's age, younger children being assumed to require more care and less consumption than older ones. Thus the total expected cost of having children is determined by the planned level of fertility and the anticipated age schedule of child care and consumption requirements. Viewed as a problem of life cycle planning, the problem for the husband and wife is to weigh the utilities from consumption, leisure, and children against the expected opportunity costs of each and to choose an optimum combination. We may think of the couple as calculating its lifetime potential wealth as its initial wealth plus the present value of expected future earnings and unearned net transfers, under the assumption of maximum labour force participation at every age. An optimum plan is then chosen by allocating the potential lifetime wealth between consumption, leisure, and the rearing of children so as to maximize a lifetime utility function. (There may also be allowance for a bequest or contingency fund, as discussed later.) In general, the optimum plan will involve labour force participation at less than maximum rates in order that the couple may have some time for leisure and child-rearing. The concept of lifetime wealth that we have in mind thus differs from the conventional concept, which is based on *realized* market income rather than *potential* market income.

The foregoing assumes that fertility is entirely planned and may be regarded as a life cycle choice variable, along with planned leisure and consumption. In practice, of course, fertility may include an unplanned component, either positive or negative, but we ignore this. We have in mind a 'typical' or 'average' couple and also ignore differences in individual household preferences and the probability distribution of actual fertility around average fertility.

People change their plans in the real world as they grow older and as they come to perceive that actual circumstances differ from what they had anticipated. However, decisions about fertility must be made at a relatively early age in the life cycle of a household because of biological factors and of obvious social constraints on the ability of a couple to reduce its number of children should it decide that it has too many. To the extent that labour force participation is linked to fertility, the participation pattern is also subject to early determination. In any event, for reasons of simplification it is convenient to assume (*a*) that each couple makes an initial decision about its lifetime fertility, leisure, and consumption, and (*b*) that only its consumption plan can be changed subsequently. In our framework, the couple is stuck with its initial choices of lifetime fertility and leisure patterns no matter how the future unfolds.

A Formal Specification of the Household Optimization Problem

Let us assume that each household comes into being when the husband and wife are both of age 18 (the age at which children become adults and leave home). We may think of a cohort consisting of a large number of 18-year-old households, with all households having identical tastes and labour skills. Let there be a real interest rate r and a proportional tax rate τ which is levied on all household income, both wage and non-wage. Let the annual wage and unemployment rates for sex i and age j be w_{ij} and u_{ij}, and let the annual amount of inheritance received be h_{ij}. The effective rate of return on wealth is then $r' = r(1 - \tau)$ and the effective rate of return for market labour is $w'_{ij} = (1 - \tau)(1 - u_{ij})w_{ij}$. Assuming the maximum possible labour force participation rate[4] for sex i and j to be $\tilde{p}_{ij}$, and that both the husband and wife expect to live until age J, the household calculates the present value of its potential wealth as

$$V = \sum_{j=18}^{J} (1 + r')^{18-j} \sum_{i=1}^{2} (\tilde{p}_{ij}w'_{ij} + h_{ij}). \tag{1}$$

Its total potential wealth having been calculated, the household then allocates the total among the following components:

V_0 present value of lifetime consumption by husband and wife combined;

V_1 present value of husband's leisure over his lifetime;

V_2 present value of wife's leisure over her lifetime;

V_3 present value of costs of raising children;

V_4 present value of contingency allowance (to allow for uncertainty about the terminal age J) or planned bequest.

The five components must be non-negative and must account for the whole of the potential wealth, so that $V_0 + V_1 + V_2 + V_3 + V_4 = V$. We consider the components in turn.

Lifetime Consumption

For simplicity, assume that the husband and wife plan their consumption to be the same at every age and that their shares are equal. If each is to consume an amount C^* per year, the combined present value of their lifetime consumption is

$$V_0 = \pi_0 C^* \tag{2}$$

where π_0 is the present value shadow price of consumption, as given by

$$\pi_0 = 2 \sum_{j=18}^{J} (1 + r')^{18 - j}. \tag{3}$$

Lifetime Leisure

Assume that R_{ij} is the fraction of a year taken as leisure by an individual of sex i and age j. Leisure may be viewed as consumption foregone and therefore as having a current annual shadow price of w'_{ij}, which is the annual wage rate adjusted for taxes and unemployment. In principle, optimization would involve a choice of leisure for every age. However, for simplicity we reduce the choice to a single one for each sex by assuming a fixed allocation rule. If R_i is the chosen total lifetime leisure for sex i, the rule is $R_{ij} = b_{ij} R_i$, where the b_{ij} are age-specific constants. Under this rule, the present value of leisure is

$$V_i = \pi_i R_i \qquad (i = 1, 2) \tag{4}$$

where the present value shadow prices π_1 and π_2 are given by

$$\pi_i = \sum_{j=18}^{J} (1 + r')^{18 - j} b_{ij} w'_{ij} \qquad (i = 1, 2) \tag{5}$$

Child-rearing

The cost of rearing children has two components, both of which may vary with age. One component is associated with time spent in child care, the other with foregone adult consumption. Assuming that all child care is provided by the wife, the implicit cost of care for a child of age k when the wife is of age j is $c_k w'_{2j}$. Assuming further that children's consumption is determined by social norms, we may take it that a child of age k will be allowed to consume $a_k \bar{C}$, where $\bar{C}$ is average adult consumption in the cohort to which the household belongs and a_k is some constant between 0 and 1. Letting f_j

be the fertility rate (annual live births per woman) at age j and F the total fertility rate, we impose a constant age distribution on fertility by writing $f_j = \phi_j F$, where the proportion ϕ_j is invariant to the choice of F. Noting that the number and age distribution of children in a household at any given time is a function of the household's fertility history, and ignoring child mortality, the present value of children is given by

$$V_3 = \pi_3 F \tag{6}$$

where π_3 is interpreted as the present-value shadow price associated with the planned total lifetime fertility rate, and is defined by

$$\pi_3 = \sum_{j=18}^{J} (1 + r')^{18-j} \sum_{k=0}^{17} \phi_{j-k}(c_k w'_{2j} + a_k \bar{C}). \tag{7}$$

The Bequest–Contingency Fund

The present value of the amount to be given at death or to be used for the household's own subsequent consumption should it turn out that the husband and/or wife survive beyond age J is

$$V_4 = \pi_4 Z \tag{8}$$

where Z is the physical amount of wealth (expressed in units of real income or consumption) and π_4, the present-value shadow price associated with Z, is given by

$$\pi_4 = (1 + r')^{18-J} \tag{9}$$

It will be convenient later to establish a relation between Z and C* so that when the household is allowed to reoptimize C* as it grows older there will be an automatic revision of Z. To this end we introduce the variable v_j, the ratio of the planned bequest–contingency fund, evaluated at age j, to the (constant) planned level of adult consumption:

$$v_j = V_4(1 + r')^{j-18}/C^* = (Z/C^*)(1 + r')^{j-J} \tag{10}$$

Utility Maximization

We assume now a utility function in C*, R_1, R_2, F, and Z of the Cobb–Douglas form

$$U = (C^*)^{\gamma_0}(R_1)^{\gamma_1}(R_2)^{\gamma_2}(F)^{\gamma_3}(Z)^{\gamma_4}. \tag{11}$$

U is the household's lifetime utility as it perceives it at age 18, viewed as a function of the choices that it makes about consumption, leisure, fertility, and the amount to be reserved for bequest–contingency purposes. The parameters γ_s ($s = 0, 1, 2, 3, 4$) are positive and restricted by the normalization rule $\Sigma\gamma_s = 1$. The household can be thought of as maximizing U by choosing (C^*, R_1, R_2, F, Z) subject to the wealth constraint $V = \Sigma V_s$, *with all prices* π_s $(s = 0, 1, 2, 3, 4)$ taken as fixed. An alternative but exactly equivalent form of utility function is

$$U = \Gamma(P_0)^{\gamma_0}(P_1)^{\gamma_1}(P_2)^{\gamma_2}(P_3)^{\gamma_3}(P_4)^{\gamma_4} \qquad (12)$$

where $P_s = V_s/V$ $(s = 0, 1, 2, 3, 4)$ and

$$\Gamma = V\left(\prod_{s=0}^{4} \pi_s^{\gamma_s} \right)^{-1} \qquad (13)$$

The household's optimization problem may therefore be defined alternatively as choosing the vector $P = (P_0, P_1, P_2, P_3 P_4)$ that maximizes U in equation (12), subject to the constraint $\Sigma P_s = 1$. The optimum vector is easily seen to be $P^* = (\gamma_0, \gamma_1, \gamma_2, \gamma_3, \gamma_4)$. The result then is that the household allocates its potential wealth among the five utility-producing categories in the proportions γ_s $(s = 0, 1, 2, 3, 4)$. The latter may be referred to as *taste parameters*.

Labour Force Participation

The household's decisions about labour force participation are implied by its choices of leisure and fertility. For males, the annual participation rates are obtained by subtracting annual leisure from the maximum participation rates; for females, a further subtraction is required for time spent in child care:

$$p_{1j} = \tilde{p}_{1j} - R_{1j} = \tilde{p}_{1j} - b_{1j}R_1 \qquad (14)$$

$$p_{2j} = \tilde{p}_{2j} - b_{2j}R_2 - F \sum_{k=0}^{17} \phi_{j-k}c_k. \qquad (15)$$

The last term in equation (15) makes use of the fact that if child mortality is ignored the number and age distribution of children in the household at any time is exactly determined by the total fertility rate (F) and the distribution of fertility by age of mother (as represented by the ϕ parameters). The justification for ignoring child mortality can be either that it is negligible or that the husband and wife ignore it in making their lifetime choices.

Total Household Consumption

The total consumption of the household is the consumption of the two adults plus the consumption of their children. Under the assumption that children's consumption varies with age but bears a fixed ratio at any age to cohort adult consumption ($\bar{C}$), the household total when the husband and wife are of age j is given by

$$C_j^{**} = 2C^* + \left(F \sum_{k=0}^{17} \phi_{j-k} a_k \right) \bar{C} \qquad (16)$$

where we have again used the fact that the number and age distribution of children is determined by F and the ϕ parameters. With all households having identical tastes and circumstances, adult consumption may now be taken as the same in every household. Thus $\bar{C} = C^*$, and we may rewrite (16) as

$$C_j^{**} = \left(2 + F \sum_{k=0}^{17} \phi_{j-k} a_k \right) C^*. \qquad (17)$$

The Complete Solution for All Household Variables

The optimum values of C^*, R_1, R_2, F, and Z can be found in a straightforward manner if values are specified for the rate of interest (r), the tax rate (τ), the age–sex-specific wage rates (w_{ij}), the age–sex-specific inheritances (h_{ij}), and the terminal age for life cycle planning (J). V is first calculated from equation (1) and V_0, V_1, V_2, V_3, and V_4 are obtained from $V_s = \gamma_s V$. Equations (2)–(9) are then solved for C^*, R_1, R_2, F, and Z. The p_{ij} are derived from equations (14) and (15) and the C_j^* from equation (17).

Reoptimization of Consumption as the Household Ages

As noted above, we assume no revision of the initial fertility and leisure plans but we do allow the household to reoptimize its consumption as it ages and receives new information from year to year. Aside from other considerations, the expected age of death rises as the husband and wife grow older, and for those households that survive to age $j' > 18$ reoptimization is based on a terminal age $J' > J$. The revised consumption plan is determined by the condition that the present value of consumption over the anticipated remaining years of life must be equal to the present value of future earnings and inheritances, plus current actual wealth, minus the current value of the bequest–contingency fund. As a simplifying rule of behaviour, we assume that the household adheres to its original ratios of bequest–contingency fund to consumption, as represented by the v_j, defined in equation (10). Hence if C^* is revised, the bequest–contingency fund (which is $v_{j'} C^*$ at age j') will be revised in the same proportion. If W stands for actual current wealth, the condition may be written as

$$C^* \sum_{j=j'}^{J'} (1 + r')^{j'-j} \left(2 + F \sum_{k=0}^{17} \phi_{j-k} a_k \right)$$

$$= W_{j'} + \sum_{j-j'}^{J'} (1+r')^{j'-j} \sum_{i=1}^{2} (p_{ij}w'_{ij} + h_{ij}) - v_{j'}C^* \qquad (18)$$

where it is understood that r', w'_{ij}, and h_{ij} are now based on revised expectations which reflect any relevant new information that has become available. Since all the other variables in equation (18) have values which were determined once and for all at the time of the household's initial plan, the new value of C^* can be calculated easily. The new value of Z can then be calculated using equation (10) and the new values of C_j^{**} using equation (17).

Model A: An Economic–Demographic Macromodel with Endogenous Fertility

We proceed now to develop Model A, a complete macromodel of the population and the economy in which the household life cycle model just described is the key behavioural component. Model A is neo-classical with regard to production and the determination of factor returns. The economy produces a single commodity which serves for both consumption and capital formation. All income, expenditure, and wealth variables are in real terms, being measured in units of the commodity. There is a single aggregate production function into which labour and capital enter as inputs. The economy is always at full employment, although frictional unemployment is allowed for and the rate of unemployment is permitted to vary by age and sex. The economy is strictly closed: there is no commodity trade and no migration. There is a government sector which absorbs some of the gross national product but only for consumption purposes; all capital formation takes place in the private sector. The model is intended for use in simulation experiments and is designed to move forward in time by annual increments; all calculations involving cohorts are therefore carried out by single years of age. The economic and demographic time paths of each cohort are tracked from birth to the age of 109, the oldest age at which anyone is still alive in the model. The endogeneity of fertility comes about because of the joint determination of fertility, consumption, and leisure (and hence labour force participation). Every cohort consists of identical households and summation over cohorts yields the relevant aggregates at the macrolevel. Thus household decisions influence the aggregate labour supply, investment, wage rates, the interest rate, and other macroeconomic variables, which in turn feed back on the individual households and affect the microlevel optimizing decisions at the next round.

The equations of Model A are set forth in Appendix 9.1 and a statement of definitions of all variables and parameters is provided. The equations of the model are organized into eight blocks, and we now discuss each of these blocks in detail.

Population

The determination of its lifetime total fertility rate is made by each cohort when it reaches the age of 18. This is represented by equation (A.1) in which opt{·} is used to symbolize the household optimizing calculation based on expected values of w, h, r, and τ, as described in the previous section. Age-specific fertility rates are determined in equation (A.2) for all ages 18 and over, under the assumption that the specific rates for any cohort vary in proportion to its total rate. Some births occur before the age of 18 and allowance is made for this in equation (A.3) by linking the rates for women aged 15, 16, and 17 in each year to the total fertility rate chosen by the new 18-year-old cohort in that year. Fertility rates for women under 15 and 50 or over are set to zero in equation (A.4). The total number of live births is determined in equation (A.5) by the application of fertility rates to female population, with averaging of consecutive years to allow for intra-annual ageing of the child-bearing population. Assuming a fixed sex ratio, births are distributed between males and females in equation (A.6). The population aged 1 and over is obtained in equation (A.7) by ageing the previous year's population one year and subjecting it to a fixed set of age–sex-specific mortality rates. The population under 1 year of age is obtained in equation (A.8) by applying appropriate mortality rates to male and female births within the year. The combined male and female population at each age is calculated in equation (A.9) and the total population in equation (A.10).

Labour Force and Employment

As with its fertility rates, the age–sex-specific rates of labour force participation of each cohort are the result of household optimizing decisions made when the cohort is of age 18, and this is indicated by the opt{·} function in equation (A.11). For ages 15, 16, and 17 the participation rates are set equal to the rates for the previous year plus a fraction of the change in the 18-year-old rate, in equation (A.12). The labour force of each age and sex is calculated in equation (A.13) as the product of participation rate and population, and the employed labour force is calculated in equation (A.14) by adjusting for unemployment. The aggregate labour force is calculated in equation (A.15) and the aggregate employed labour force in equation (A.16).

Production

Output is produced by a Cobb–Douglas production function with constant returns to scale, as specified in equation (A.17). The inputs are labour and capital. The capital input is represented by the total stock of capital. The labour input is represented by a weighted sum of the components of the employed labour force, the weights representing age–sex-related differences in productivity, as indicated by equation (A.18). (For purposes of the present chapter we abstract from technical progress and therefore make no allowance for it in the production function.)

Income and Factor Returns

Labour is assumed to receive its marginal product and the age–sex-specific and overall average wage rates are determined accordingly in equations (A.19) and (A.20). The rate of interest is identified with the net rate of return to capital, and is derived in equation (A.21) under the assumption that capital also receives its marginal product. The annual income before tax of each population cohort (males and females combined) is calculated in equation (A.22) as the cohort's wage income plus the annual interest return on its current wealth. Aggregating over all cohorts in equation (A.23) yields the net national income.

Private Consumption and Saving

Average household consumption is determined in equation (A.24), again using opt$\{\cdot\}$ to represent the household optimizing choice. However, unlike the fertility and labour force participation choices, which are made once and for all at age 18, the consumption choice is subject to revision each year as the households within a cohort age and receive new information. Total consumption for each cohort 18 and over is obtained in equation (A.25) by multiplying average consumption by the number of households (which is equal to half the population of the cohort, since each household in the model has two adult members of identical ages). In practice, individuals under 18 have non-zero labour force participation rates and hence non-zero incomes; however, this bit of awkwardness is circumvented in equation (A.26) by assuming that cohorts aged 15, 16, and 17 consume all of their after-tax incomes, and that such consumption is independent of the children's consumption paid for out of adult income. Net annual saving is calculated for each cohort in equation (A.27) by subtracting consumption from the cohort's after-tax income. For the economy as a whole, aggregate consumption and net saving are determined by adding across cohorts in equations (A.28) and (A.29). For equation (A.30), total gross saving is calculated as net saving plus total depreciation on the capital stock.

Wealth and Inheritance

The model keeps track of each cohort's total wealth in equation (A.31). A cohort's wealth at the start of any year is its wealth one year earlier plus net saving and net gains through inheritance. As indicated by equation (A.32), each cohort starts its adult life at age 18 with zero wealth. Its losses through transfers at death are proportional to the number of its members who die, as indicated by equation (A.33). Its gains from inheritance are calculated as a share of all transfers at death in the population as a whole, the shares varying according to the cohort's age. (The inheritance share proportions are represented by the ξ parameters in equation (A.31); these parameters necessarily sum to 1 over all ages.) The total wealth in the economy is found by summing over all cohorts in equation (A.34).

Investment and Capital Stock

The equality of gross investment and gross saving for the economy as a whole is represented by equation (A.35), and the equality of the capital stock and aggregate wealth is represented by equation (A.36). The capital stock at the beginning of any year is also equal to the remainder (after depreciation) of the stock in existence a year earlier plus the gross investment of the previous year, as in equation (A.37). (Only one of equations (A.36) and (A.37) is needed to obtain a solution when the model is used for simulation; the other equation is redundant for that purpose but included in the list of equations as an aid to understanding the model.)

Government Consumption and Taxes

All government expenditure is for consumption purposes. Government consumption is determined as a fraction of total gross output in equation (A.38), with provision for lags of up to five years to reflect institutional delays in response when the output level changes. The government budget is always in balance, as represented by the equality of taxes and government consumption in equation (A.39). The income tax rate is calculated in equation (A.40) as that rate which will provide the total tax yield necessary to balance the budget.

Model B: An Alternative Macromodel with Fertility Treated as Exogenous

The alternative model, Model B, is defined with reference to Model A. The new equations are listed following the Model A listing and definitions; the ones that are dropped and those that are retained are noted. The new symbols introduced in Model B are noted also.

The essential difference of Model B from Model A is that the life cycle choice mechanism has been eliminated. Equation (B.1), which replaces (A.1), states simply that the overall total (period) fertility rate in any given year has an exogenously specified value denoted by the symbol $\bar{F}$, and equation (B.2) states that all age-specific fertility rates vary in proportion to the total rate. Fertility is thus entirely independent of everything else in Model B.

Similarly, equation (B.11), which replaces (A.11), states that all age–sex-specific labour force participation rates have exogenously determined values, symbolized by $\bar{p}$, and in fact that the rate for every age–sex category is constant over time.

Private consumption is determined only at the macrolevel in Model B. As indicated by the new equation (B.28), aggregate private consumption is assumed to be a constant fraction ρ of gross output less the portion of output claimed by the government through taxes. Net saving is now also determined only at the aggregate level, as indicated by equation (B.29). Private consumption is responsive directly to annual income (output) in Model B, rather than to potential wealth, and is no longer jointly determined with fertility and labour force participation.

Other features of Model B are as follows. The equations for determining births and population (given the fertility rates) are unchanged, and so too are the equations for determining the labour force and employment (given the participation rates). The production function and the labour input equation are the same as before. The equations for determining income and factor returns are also retained, although the wage and interest rates that were so important in the calculation and allocation of potential wealth in Model A no longer play any role in determining the economic aggregates in Model B: the rates are derived in the same way as before but have no influence on other variables. All of the cohort-specific equations are dropped from the private consumption and savings block, since consumption and saving are now determined only in the aggregate. The wealth and inheritance equations disappear entirely since wealth, as such, no longer plays a role in the determination of consumption and saving, and since cohort wealth can no longer be calculated in any event, owing to the fact that cohort consumption and saving are no longer calculated. The investment, capital stock, government consumption, and tax equations remain unchanged.

Comparative Simulations with Models A and B

Models A and B represent the tools for addressing the question of how much difference it makes for the macroeconomy if fertility is treated as exogenous, on the one hand, or as endogenously and jointly determined within the fertility–leisure–consumption life cycle framework, on the other. We address this question by conducting a series of simulation experiments in which the two models are run 'in parallel'. Alternative initial conditions and exogenous shocks are specified and the two models are compared with regard to their dynamic responses and their final steady states. We discuss the strategy of the simulation experiments in this section, and in particular what we mean by running the models 'in parallel'. The results of the experiments are analysed in the next section.

The ultimate determinants of Model A are its parameters. The model is non-stochastic and completely closed or self-determining, once its parameter values have been specified: there are no variables operating on it exogenously from outside, random or otherwise. To subject it to a shock, therefore, we need to introduce a change of parameter values. We do this by assuming an exogenous change in household tastes, and this change is embodied in a shift in the parameters γ_s (s = 0, 1, 2, 3, 4) of the lifetime utility function (as defined either by equation (11) or equation (12)). Specifically, we assume a shift in household preferences for children, as represented by γ_3. However, we cannot change γ_3 alone, because the five γ parameters necessarily sum to unity. If household preferences for children change, that implies a change in the planned fraction of lifetime potential wealth to be devoted to the rearing of children. A greater or lesser proportion of the potential wealth total is therefore available for other uses, and we must specify the changes in the other γ parameters that accompany the change in γ_3.

The bench-mark state for Model A is a stationary state which has a number of features broadly reflective of a developed economy. The bench-mark values for the γs are chosen in such a way as to produce a stationary-state total fertility rate of approximately 2.1 and labour force participation rates roughly similar to recent Canadian rates.[5] Unemployment, leisure, and mortality rates are also based on Canadian data, and so too are the fertility age distribution parameters. The stationary population is that of the 1975–7 Statistics Canada life tables and the ages of death assumed by households for planning purposes are based on life expectancies from these tables. The age–productivity weights are based on 1971 Canadian census earnings data. The 'equivalent adult unit' (EAU) consumption weights start at 0.25 at age 0 and rise linearly to 1.0 at age 18. Child care weights start at 0.3 for a newborn infant (that is to say, the child requires three-tenths of a person-year of care in its first year of life); they then decline linearly to about 0.12 by age 6, and to 0 by age 15. (The setting of these child care weights draws on an econometric study using Canadian data by Spencer (1973), with subsequent scaling of the weights to make them consistent with the fertility and female labour force participation rates specified for the model.) The inheritance share parameters (the ξs) are set arbitrarily so as to rise from 0 at age 18 to a maximum at age 50, and then to decline linearly to 0 again by age 75. (The shares sum to 1 over all ages, of course.) It is assumed that households expect future wage, interest, and tax rates to be the same as the most recently observed ones (the ones for the previous year). Expectations about inheritances are based on backward-looking 50-year averages. The parameter β of the aggregate production function is set at 0.3, implying capital and labour income shares of 30 per cent and 70 per cent respectively. The rate of depreciation of capital (δ) is set at 0.05 per annum. The government expenditure parameters (the Θs) are set so that the government claims 20 per cent of the gross national product through taxes in the stationary state. Additional detail pertaining to the setting of parameter values is provided in Denton and Spencer (1983).

The values of the utility function parameters that were found to yield a 'realistic' bench-mark stationary state are as follows: $\gamma_0 = 0.5754$; $\gamma_1 = 0.0639$; $\gamma_2 = 0.1044$; $\gamma_3 = 0.1568$; $\gamma_4 = 0.0995$. We interpret these values as meaning that households plan to allocate some 58 per cent of their lifetime wealth to adult consumption, 6 per cent and 10 per cent to male and female leisure, respectively, and 16 per cent to the raising of children; 10 per cent is then left over as a bequest or contingency fund.

We shock Model A for experimental purposes by allowing γ_3 to increase or decrease and making compensating adjustments to the other γs. This induces a time-path for each of the economic and demographic variables of the model. To obtain a parallel run with Model B we then do the following: (*a*) We take the Model A time-path of the total fertility rate and treat it as exogenous input into Model B. The time-path of F is thus the same for both models in any given experiment, the only difference being that it is endogenously determined in the one case and exogenously imposed in the other. We next, (*b*), fix the levels of all labour force participation rates in Model B at their initial levels; the rates respond dynamically in Model A in any given experiment but are constant in Model B. We then, (*c*), do the same for ρ, the aggregate propensity to consume: the value of ρ is calculated for the initial state (from $\rho = C/(Q - T)$) and then held constant in Model B throughout an experiment. (ρ plays no role as a parameter in Model A but the ratio $C/(Q - T)$ varies with time in that model, whereas in Model B it does not.) All other parameters of Model B are the same as their counterparts in Model A. These procedures imply that both models will generate the same initial states for the economic–demographic system and the same time-paths for all fertility and population variables, but that the time-paths of the economic variables will differ. Our interest is in studying the nature and extent of the differences in economic time-paths.

We report here two parallel-run experiments of the kind just described.[6] Experiment 1 assumes an initial stationary state with γ values as specified above. In this experiment γ_3 is increased from 0.1568 to 0.2613, implying a sharp shift towards greater preference for children. The shift in preferences is assumed to affect only the incoming cohorts of 18-year-olds, older cohorts being unaffected. The shift takes place linearly over a period of a decade: the 18-year-olds of year 1 have a γ_3 of 0.1672; the 18-year-olds of year 2 have a γ_3 of 0.1777; and so on, until the 0.2613 level is reached for the 18-year-olds of year 10, and remains in force for all subsequent new adult cohorts. The increased preference for children implies less lifetime wealth available for adult consumption, leisure, and bequests. The assumption made is that the compensating reduction is evenly distributed between adult consumption and leisure (evenly distributed in the sense that γ_0, γ_1, and γ_2 are all reduced in the same proportion, the proportion being determined by the restriction γ_0

$+ \ \gamma_1 + \gamma_2 + \ \gamma_3 + \ \gamma_4 \ = \ 1$), but that the contingency allocation is unchanged.

Experiment 2 starts off from an initial steady state in which household preferences are such as to produce a total fertility rate far above the stationary level, and hence a rapidly growing population. The shock in this experiment takes the form of a preference shift in the direction of fewer children, such that ultimately zero population growth results. Thus, whereas Experiment 1 represents a transition from stationary to rapid-growth steady states, Experiment 2 represents a transition in the opposite direction—from a rapid-growth steady state to a statutory or no-growth state. In the latter experiment, as in the former one, the shifts in the γ parameters affect only incoming 18-year-old cohorts, and are phased in linearly over ten years. Experiment 2 might be regarded as roughly representative of situations such as those observed in North America and other developed areas in the past quarter-century, with fertility rates falling from very high levels to levels that are very low by historical standards, assuming that these low levels were to be maintained in the future.

The exact specification of the utility function shocks to Model A which define the two experiments are set forth in Table 9.1. The values of the γ parameters before and after the shocks are reported in the table ('after' meaning year 10 and later, by which time the entire shift in parameters has occurred). The experiments may be summarized as follows:

Table 9.1.   Experimental shifts in utility function parameters

	Experiment 1		Experiment 2	
	Year 0	Year 10	Year 0	Year 10
γ_0	0.5754	0.4945	0.4945	0.5754
γ_1	0.0639	0.0549	0.0549	0.0639
γ_2	0.1044	0.0898	0.0898	0.1044
γ_3	0.1568	0.2613	0.2613	0.1568
γ_4	0.0995	0.0995	0.0995	0.0995

Note: Parameter values for years between 0 and 10 are obtained by linear interpolation; values are constant after year 10.

Experiment 1: Transition from zero growth to rapid growth; increased preference for children in Model A offset by reduced preferences for consumption and leisure.

Experiment 2: Transition from rapid growth to zero growth; reduced preference for children in Model A offset by increased preference for consumption and leisure.

An Appraisal of the Simulation Results

We have selected sixteen variables of interest in reporting the results of the simulation experiments. These variables are displayed in Tables 9.2 and 9.3 for the two experiments and a subset of six of the variables is displayed graphically for each experiment in Figures 9.1 and 9.2. For each of the economic variables, the results for Models A and B are juxtaposed. (For the demographic variables there are no differences between the two models.) In the tables, results are reported at ten-year intervals for the first half-century after the initial shock, at twenty-five-year intervals for the next half-century, and for the final steady state. In the figures, the selected variables are plotted continuously over the first 200 years after the shock.

Experiment 1: Zero to Rapid Population Growth

The shock in the case of Experiment 1 results in a very large increase in the total fertility rate: the rate rises from 2.1 in the initial stationary state to a final steady-state level of 3.5. There is a sharp rise in the first two or three decades, then some falling off, followed again by an increase: the time path exhibits a damped cyclical pattern as the fertility rate wends its way towards the ultimate steady-state level. The annual rate of population growth also rises markedly in the early decades but the cyclical pattern is less pronounced. The same is true of the crude birth-rate. At the same time, the age distribution shifts markedly, as indicated by the changes in the proportions under 15 years of age and 65 and over. The under-15 component increases from 20.0 per cent of the total to 34.0 per cent by the time of the final steady state, and for all intents and purposes the increase is complete after the first fifty years. Concomitantly, the 65-and-over component drops from 17.0 to an ultimate 7.4 per cent, although here the transition requires a longer period to become virtually complete.

The initial and ultimate rates of growth of all variables in the system are identical but the paths of transition are quite different. The labour force grows less rapidly than the population (or even declines) in the early decades but the rate then catches up and surpasses the population rate for a time. The labour force growth rates behave in a roughly similar fashion over most of the transition period whether Model A or B applies. There are some differences between the growth rates of the weighted labour input and the (unweighted) labour force, reflecting the shifts in labour force age–sex distribution interacting with the age–sex-differentiated productivity parameters. However, by and large the time-paths of the rates are similar, and the differences between Model A and Model B that show up for the one series show up also for the other.

The differences between the annual GNP growth rates in Models A and B are relatively small, as evidenced by Table 9.2 and more especially by Figure

Table 9.2.   Simulated transition from zero to rapid population growth based on Models A and B (Experiment 1)

Variable	Model	Year in simulation period								
		0	10	20	30	40	50	75	100	∞
Total fertility rate (per woman)	Both	2.1	2.7	3.8	3.9	3.8	3.6	3.3	3.5	3.5
Crude birth rate (per thousand population)	Both	13.6	16.8	22.3	22.9	26.3	26.7	26.0	26.0	26.7
Population under 15 (per cent)	Both	20.0	20.9	26.3	30.5	32.1	34.4	33.7	33.1	34.0
Population 65 + (per cent)	Both	17.0	16.8	15.6	14.0	12.2	10.3	6.8	7.6	7.4
Annual growth rates (per cent):										
Population	Both	0.0	0.3	1.0	1.1	1.6	1.8	2.0	2.0	2.0
Labour force	A	0.0	-0.2	-0.2	1.0	1.7	2.1	2.0	1.7	2.0
	B	0.0	0.0	0.1	1.0	1.6	1.9	2.0	1.8	2.0
Weighted labour input	A	0.0	-0.1	-0.1	0.7	1.5	2.0	2.1	1.7	2.0
	B	0.0	0.1	0.0	0.6	1.5	1.9	2.1	1.8	2.0
Gross national product (GNP)	A	0.0	-0.1	-0.2	0.3	1.0	1.6	2.2	2.0	2.0
	B	0.0	0.0	0.0	0.5	1.1	1.6	2.0	1.9	2.0
Capital stock	A	0.0	0.1	-0.2	-0.6	-0.2	0.5	2.6	2.7	2.0
	B	0.0	0.0	0.0	0.1	0.4	0.8	1.8	1.9	2.0
Annual interest rate (per cent)	A	1.9	1.8	1.8	2.1	2.9	3.8	4.6	3.3	3.3
	B	1.9	1.9	1.9	2.0	2.4	3.0	4.2	4.4	4.5
Labour productivity (index)	A	100.0	100.3	100.6	98.5	94.0	89.8	86.6	92.3	92.3
	B	100.0	100.0	100.0	99.2	96.6	93.6	88.1	87.5	86.8
Capital-output ratio	A	4.4	4.4	4.4	4.2	3.8	3.4	3.1	3.6	3.6
	B	4.4	4.4	4.4	4.3	4.0	3.7	3.3	3.2	3.1
GNP per capita (index)	A	100.0	98.6	90.6	81.6	76.2	72.8	77.0	80.1	80.1
	B	100.0	98.8	92.0	84.6	80.4	77.4	78.9	78.5	76.4
Consumption per capita (index)	A	100.0	98.0	92.0	86.1	80.9	77.1	75.6	72.9	76.4
	B	100.0	98.8	92.0	84.8	80.9	78.0	79.8	79.4	77.2
Consumption per EAU* (index)	A	100.0	98.8	95.8	91.4	87.0	83.8	81.9	78.7	82.9
	B	100.0	99.6	95.9	90.0	86.9	84.9	86.4	85.6	83.8
Net saving rate (percentage of GNP)	A	0.0	0.2	-1.3	-2.3	-0.3	2.1	8.2	9.9	7.4
	B	0.0	0.2	0.0	0.5	1.8	3.3	5.8	6.1	6.4

*Equivalent adult units.

Table 9.3. Simulated transition from rapid to zero population growth based on Models A and B (Experiment 2)

Variable	Model	Year in simulation period								
		0	10	20	30	40	50	75	100	∞
Total fertility rate (per woman)	Both	3.5	3.0	2.0	1.9	1.9	2.0	2.2	2.2	2.1
Crude birth rate (per thousand population)	Both	26.7	22.8	16.8	16.3	14.5	13.5	13.7	14.4	13.6
Population under 15 (per cent)	Both	34.0	33.0	27.7	23.1	22.0	20.1	20.0	21.3	20.0
Population 65 + (per cent)	Both	7.4	7.5	8.1	9.1	10.3	12.1	18.2	16.8	17.0
Annual growth rates (per cent):										
Population	Both	2.0	1.6	1.0	0.9	0.6	0.4	0.0	0.1	0.0
Labour force	A	2.0	2.3	2.2	1.1	0.4	0.1	-0.1	0.3	0.0
	B	2.0	2.0	2.0	1.2	0.6	0.3	-0.2	0.2	0.0
Weighted labour input	A	2.0	2.2	2.0	1.4	0.7	0.2	-0.1	0.2	0.0
	B	2.0	2.0	2.0	1.4	0.8	0.4	-0.2	0.1	0.0
Gross national product (GNP)	A	2.0	2.1	2.2	1.7	1.1	0.6	-0.1	-0.1	0.0
	B	2.0	2.0	2.0	1.6	1.0	0.6	-0.1	0.1	0.0
Capital stock	A	2.0	2.0	2.3	2.5	2.1	1.5	-0.1	-0.8	0.0
	B	2.0	2.0	2.0	1.9	1.6	1.2	0.3	0.1	0.0
Annual interest rate (per cent)	A	3.3	3.3	3.4	3.0	2.3	1.7	0.7	1.4	1.9
	B	3.3	3.3	3.3	3.1	2.8	2.3	1.3	1.1	0.9
Labour productivity (index)	A	100.0	99.6	99.3	101.2	105.4	109.8	117.7	111.8	108.4
	B	100.0	100.0	100.0	100.7	102.8	105.4	112.4	114.0	115.2
Capital-output ratio	A	3.6	3.6	3.6	3.7	4.1	4.5	5.3	4.7	4.4
	B	3.6	3.6	3.6	3.7	3.9	4.1	4.8	4.9	5.0
GNP per capita (index)	A	100.0	101.8	111.8	124.4	132.5	137.2	131.5	128.6	124.8
	B	100.0	101.5	109.8	120.1	126.5	131.0	127.6	128.1	132.7
Consumption per capita (index)	A	100.0	102.5	110.5	118.6	123.6	126.6	128.9	140.1	130.9
	B	100.0	101.5	109.8	119.8	125.8	130.0	126.1	126.7	131.2
Consumption per EAU* (index)	A	100.0	101.6	105.7	111.2	115.0	116.6	118.8	130.0	120.6
	B	100.0	100.6	105.0	112.4	117.2	119.8	116.2	117.6	120.9
Net saving rate (percentage of GNP)	A	7.4	7.1	8.4	9.3	8.3	6.6	-0.9	-3.9	0.0
	B	7.4	7.4	7.4	7.0	6.0	4.8	1.4	0.6	0.0

*Equivalent adult units.

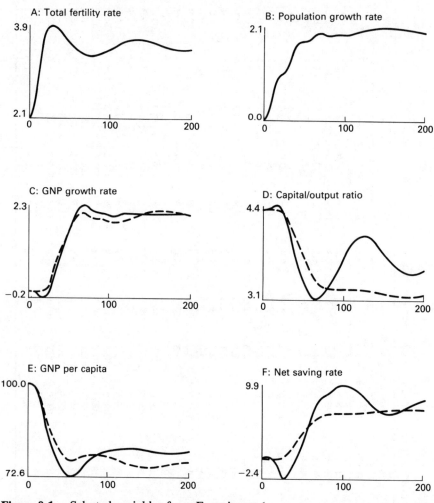

Figure 9.1.   Selected variables from Experiment 1
The total fertility rate and population growth rate are the same for Models A and B.
For other variables, the Model A series is indicated by the solid line and the Model B
series by the broken line.

9.1(C). However, even small differences can have a substantial cumulative
effect, and this is indicated by comparisons of the per capita GNP series. The
ultimate steady-state level of GNP per capita is (*a*) lower than the initial level
(for both models) and (*b*) lower in Model B than in Model A. The general
reduction in per capita GNP is associated largely with the increased proportions of children in the population and with the younger average age of the
labour force, and hence the reduced average productivity level. The fact that
the ultimate reduction is less for Model A than for Model B reflects the
ability of households in Model A to respond to price signals by reallocating
their lifetime budgets, and in particular by adjusting their labour force parti-

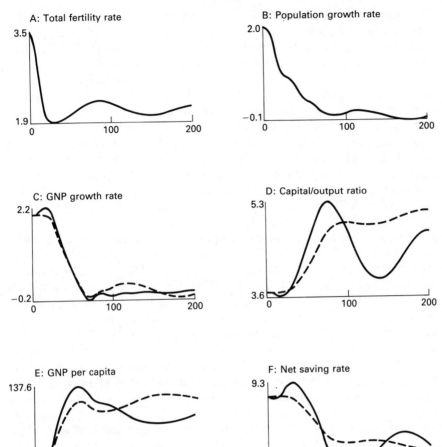

Figure 9.2. Selected variables from Experiment 2
The total fertility rate and population growth rate are the same for Models A and B.
For other variables, the Model A series is indicated by the solid line and the Model B
series by the broken line.

cipation rates. (In Model B they are locked into a fixed set of participation
rates.) Although the per capita GNP level is ultimately higher for Model A
than for Model B, this is not true at all points along the transition path. As
indicated most clearly by Figure 9.1(E), the per capita time series lines cross
over during the transition. The Model A path is more volatile than the Model
B path, and this reflects a general feature of the comparative simulation
results: in general, there is a greater tendency towards cyclical volatility in
Model A, although both models exhibit long-run stability, at least under the
assumptions of the experiments reported here.

The consumption series show a pattern rather different from that of the

GNP series. Two consumption series are shown in the tables: one is consumption per capita (total consumption divided simply by total population); the other is consumption per 'equivalent adult unit' (EAU). In the latter, account is taken of the lower consumption levels of children, and total consumption is expressed relative to the total number of consumption-weighted units in the population. The average level of consumption declines in the experiments but the decline is less in the case of consumption per EAU than in the case of unweighted consumption per capita.

Whether one looks at weighted or unweighted consumption per capita, it is apparent that the differences between the Model A and Model B results need not be in the same direction for consumption as for GNP. The ultimate GNP per capita index is higher for Model A than for Model B (80.1 compared with 76.4), whereas the ultimate consumption per EAU index is lower (82.9 compared with 83.8). These differences reflect the differences in savings rates and hence in the consumption–investment allocation of GNP.

The net rate of saving (the proportion of GNP saved) and the capital-output ratio are subject to marked variation, as evident both from Table 9.1 and from Figures 9.1(D) and 9.1(F). This is true of both models, but the series are especially volatile in the case of Model A, thus revealing again the greater tendency towards cyclical behaviour in the case of that model. The differences in savings rates become apparent much sooner than the differences in capital–output ratios; indeed, several decades are required before the latter differences become pronounced. The differences in savings rates are reflected also in the different patterns of growth of the capital stock in the two models. In Model A, the annual rate of growth of the stock is negative after two decades and is still negative after four. It then enters the positive range, where it undergoes damped oscillation until finally reaching a steady-state level of 2.0 per cent per annum. In the case of Model B, on the other hand, the rate is never negative: it remains at or close to zero for the first three decades, and then moves gradually towards the same steady-state level as in Model A.

There are notable differences also in the labour productivity and interest rate series generated by the two models. In Model B, there is no change in the annual interest rate until after year 20; by year 30 the rate has started to rise and it continues along a (more or less) monotonic time path until reaching a steady-state level more than double its initial one (4.5 compared with 1.9). In the case of Model A, the interest rate effects show up sooner, although they are small at first. The rate rises well beyond its ultimate steady-state level, falls back again, and then moves along a path of damped oscillation until finally coming to rest. That Models A and B can generate quite different steady-state interest rates is also clear: the steady-state rates are 3.3 and 4.5 per cent respectively.

The average wage rate moves with the labour productivity index in both models, by virtue of their common production function and the assumption that factors of production receive their marginal products. The labour productivity index declines after the first two decades, and ultimately settles some 8–13 per cent below its initial level, depending on the model. These declines represent the obverse of the increases in interest rates and reflect the shift in relative factor returns towards capital and away from labour that necessarily accompanies an increase in the growth rate if the economy has standard neo-classical production–distribution features.

Experiment 2: Rapid to Zero Population Growth

In some degree, Experiment 2 may be viewed as representative of the sharp declines in fertility that occurred in North America and elsewhere during the 1960s and 1970s. At the beginning of each experiment the population and the economy are in steady-state growth with high fertility. (The initial total fertility rate is 3.5.) Household tastes then shift away from large families, and the total fertility rate declines and ultimately comes to rest at the replacement level of 2.1. The results of the experiment are recorded in Table 9.3 and Figure 9.2.

The population and the economy ultimately settle into a stationary or zero-growth state but the paths of transition exhibit cyclical patterns, as in the previous experiment, and again the cycles are considerably more pronounced for Model A than for Model B. Indeed, most of the earlier general observations about the transition paths carry over to Experiment 2, except of course that the long-run trajectories of demographic and economic growth rates are downward rather than upward. The volatility of the savings rate and the capital–output ratio in Model A are again in evidence. GNP per capita now increases with both models, although the extent of increase differs substantially between models. Consumption per capita and per equivalent adult unit also increases, but with little difference between the two models. Aside from other considerations, the experiment indicates clearly that a shift towards fewer children both raises the feasible per capita level of output of the economy and makes possible a greater proportionate allocation to consumption. Whether the full potential increase in national product in fact occurs and is taken in the form of conventionally defined consumption goods (which are measured in the market and reflected in the national accounts), or whether instead the gains are taken as leisure (which is not) is a matter of social choice or the collective implication of individual household decisions.

The age distribution of the population shifts towards the older end in Experiment 2, of course, just as it is now shifting in North America and other areas of the world in which fertility has declined. The total fertility rate drops very rapidly in the first two decades of the experiments and by year 30 it has fallen to 1.9, which is below the long-run replacement level; it then rises, falls, and so on as it cycles towards the stationary level of 2.1. A point of interest is that North American rates have also fallen below the replacement level. Can one infer from the experiments with Model A that the time series patterns observed in actual North American (and other) rates are consistent with long-run population stationarity?

The capital–output ratio rises in Experiment 2 and so does the labour productivity index. As necessary concomitants (given the nature of the models), wage rates increase and the rate of return to capital (the interest rate) falls. This pattern of shift in factor returns is consistent with standard neo-classical growth theory.

Further Research Possibilities

No model, however complex, allows for the exploration of all matters of possible interest. Our Model A is no exception. Even though it appears well suited to the exploration of a number of phenomena of interest in the context of longer-term interactions involving the population and the economy, there are several ways in which the model might be modified to permit the exploration of still other phenomena.

Model A is highly stylized in a number of respects. For example, it makes no allowance for general technological advance; it treats all members of each cohort as homogeneous, thereby ignoring all diversity within cohorts, including diversity of income distribution. No doubt each of these assumptions could be relaxed, at the price of greater complexity in the model, and some further insights might result. Also, other specifications of the utility function and of the aggregate production process could be incorporated, as could other mechanisms of expectations formation and of inheritance, with similar costs and possible benefits.[7]

Worthy of note is the failure of Model A, in its present form, to allow households to rethink their fertility decisions in response to any discrepancies between expectations and realizations, once their lifetime plans have been made. Reoptimization of fertility decisions (and labour force participation decisions as well) could be introduced into the model, and could even occur each year. However, this would greatly increase the already high computer costs of running the model, and would probably provide little additional insight, since economic conditions change only slowly in the model and changes in fertility plans are increasingly bounded by biological and social considerations as time passes and individual cohorts age.

The implications of Model A have been explored in rather specialized experiments designed to focus on the macro consequences of endogenous fertility. Clearly, the model could be used to explore other implications of endogenous fertility (for example, with alternative values of key parameters other than those relating to tastes), and could also be used to address other issues. Furthermore, it could, with substantial modification, but while retaining its broad outline, be used for the purpose of making longer-term forecasts about the population and the economy.

Conclusions

We have employed two types of model in this chapter. One is based on the idea that consumption–leisure–fertility choices are made jointly by households, that fertility should therefore be regarded as an endogenous variable, and that the population and the economy should be viewed as an interactive macrosystem. The other takes the more conventional view that fertility can be regarded as exogenous and that the direction of influence can be thought of as entirely from the population to the macroeconomy. Model A employs a particular lifetime utility function, and certainly other functions could be specified and experimented with. Both Model A and Model B employ a particular (simple) type of production function, and here too there are obviously other forms of function to be considered. However, the models and experiments do provide information as to how much difference the alternative approaches can make in artificial experiments and, by implication, how much difference they might make in a practical forecasting context. We now summarize what we think are the principal issues and conclusions identified by the model specification and analysis.

The first issue is whether it makes sense to view fertility, consumption, and leisure as jointly determined and subject to an overall lifetime budget constraint in the context of a developed economy. To the extent that fertility is controllable by individuals and subject to household planning, we think that it makes very good sense. The rearing of children uses up real resources, in the form of both time and consumption goods. Wealth that is devoted to the rearing of children is not available for other uses, and this unavoidable constraint applies both to individual households and to the economy as a whole. If fertility can be planned, and if households do any planning at all, they cannot avoid choosing between more or fewer children, greater or lesser labour force participation, and higher or lower levels of consumption. At that level of generality there seems to be as strong a case for applying consumer budget theory to choices about fertility as to choices about leisure and commodities, as conventionally defined. Of course, that does not argue for any particular narrowly defined model but merely for a general approach that would recognize the interdependence.

As a practical matter, does it make much difference whether one adopts the one approach rather than the other? Will forecasts that take account of the interdependence differ much from forecasts that ignore it? Readers can form their own opinions after looking at the results of the experiments, but our reading of the results is that the differences can be very large. To some extent one cay say that the differences between the two models are less pronounced in the first two or three decades after a major fertility shift, and one might take some consolation from that: after all, no one really believes in the accuracy of forecasts several decades into the future, regardless of how elegant the arguments and models on which they are based. However, the very sharp fall in North American fertility rates in the 1960s and 1970s, for example, might be viewed as a fertility shock of the first magnitude that commenced about a quarter of a century ago, and one would like to be able to predict the course of its continuing effects over the next quarter-century. In any event, demographic events have long-run implications, and one would like to have as full an understanding of these implications as one can. We view the experimental results as indicating the importance of recognizing the interdependence of fertility, consumption, and labour force participation for such an understanding.

That demographic shocks have echo effects which induce long cycles is well known, although the role of economic factors in the cyclical mechanism is open to debate. The type of model pioneered by Richard Easterlin and developed by him and others represents one way of viewing the underlying economic–demographic interactions. A life cycle budget model of the kind on which our Model A rests represents another. Both types of models can produce marked cyclical patterns in fertility and economic variables. That our Model A can do so is evident from the results presented here. However, it should be noted that the sensitivity of fertility to economic influence in Model A is highly dependent on the nature of the production function and the assumptions that are made about the degree to which age–sex-specific wage rates respond to cohort size. Incorporation into Model A of a production–income mechanism in which wage rates were more sensitive to the numbers of workers of particular ages and sexes would undoubtedly produce a greater tendency towards cyclical volatility in that model.

In sum, we think that the results presented here support the case for viewing the population and the economy as a dynamic interactive macrosystem rather than as a system in which fertility is taken to be exogenous. We think also that a life cycle planning approach to the modelling of fertility–leisure–consumption choices provides a promising foundation for macroanalysis and that further work in this direction is desirable, both at a theoretical level and in the development of practical methods for incorporating the approach into long-run economic and demographic forecasting.

Endnotes

1. See, for example, Coale and Hoover (1958), Denton and Spencer (1973, 1975, 1981), Enke and Zind (1969), Enke (1971), and Simon (1976).
2. Easterlin (1962, 1966a, 1966b, 1968, 1969, 1973, and 1978) suggested a model for the US which has been variously elaborated, formalized, extended, and disputed by others: see, for example, Ahlburg (1982, 1983), Ben-Porath (1975), Butz and Ward (1979), Denton and Spencer (1975 chs. 3, 10), Easterlin and Condran (1976), Easterlin, Wachter, and Wachter (1978a, 1978b), Lee (1976, 1981), Moffit (1982), Samuelson (1976), Wachter (1975), and Ward and Butz (1980). Anker and Knowles (1983) and Barlow and Davies (1974) developed simulation models for

developing countries with fertility endogenous.
3. 'Leisure' is used to mean all time not spent in the labour force or in caring for children.
4. The maximum possible participation rate is not necessarily 1. Institutional restrictions or physical incapacity may make it impossible to work at some ages or to work a full year.
5. The maximum participation rates required by the model ($\bar{p}$) are inferred (somewhat arbitrarily) from observed actual Canadian rates. As stated in note 4, the maximum rates need not be 1 at all ages, and in fact the $\bar{p}$ values used in the simulations are always set below 1 (even for young and middle-aged adults) in order to allow for physical incapacity in some fraction of each cohort. For the elderly population the rates are well below 1 and eventually tail off to zero, reflecting both physical incapacity and institutional restrictions on the employment of older people.
6. These and other experiments are reported in an earlier version of this chapter; see Denton and Spencer (1984*b*).
7. The production function in the present model makes no provision for changes in technology. We have done some preliminary experiments with Model A in which we allow the scale parameter in the production function to shift. These experiments suggest that while there is some impact on fertility its general time path is far less sensitive to shifts in technology than it is to shifts in household tastes. However, considerably more work would be required to reach firm conclusions in this regard.

Appendix 9.1. Model A

Population

$$F_{jt} = \text{opt } [F\,|\,E(w, h, r, \tau) \text{ at age 18 in year } t - j + 18] \qquad (j \geq 18) \quad \text{(A.1)}$$
$$f_{jt} = \phi_j F_{jt} \qquad (18 \leq j < 50) \quad \text{(A.2)}$$
$$f_{jt} = \phi_j F_{18,\,t} \qquad (j = 15, 16, 17) \quad \text{(A.3)}$$
$$f_{jt} = 0 \qquad (j \leq 14; j \geq 50) \quad \text{(A.4)}$$

$$B_t = \sum_{j=15}^{50} [1/2(f_{jt} + f_{j-1,\,t-1}) \cdot 1/2(N_{2jt} + N_{2,\,j-1,\,t-1})] \qquad \text{(A.5)}$$

$$B_{1t} = \left(\frac{s}{1+s}\right) B_t; \quad B_{2t} = \left(\frac{1}{1+s}\right) B_t \qquad \text{(A.6)}$$

$$N_{ijt} = (1 - d_{ijt})N_{i,\,j-1,\,t-1} \qquad (i = 1, 2; j \geq 1) \quad \text{(A.7)}$$
$$N_{i0t} = (1 - d_{i0t})B_{it} \qquad (i = 1, 2) \quad \text{(A.8)}$$
$$N_{jt} = N_{1jt} + N_{2jt} \qquad (j \geq 0) \quad \text{(A.9)}$$

$$N_t = \sum_{j \geq 0} N_{jt} \qquad \text{(A.10)}$$

Labour Force and Employment

$$p_{ijt} = \text{opt}[p_{ij}\,|\,E(w, h, r, \tau) \text{ at age 18 in year } t - j + 18] \quad (i = 1, 2; j \geq 18) \quad \text{(A.11)}$$
$$p_{ijt} = p_{ij,\,t-1} + \eta_{ij}(p_{i,\,18,\,t} - p_{i,\,18,\,t-1}) \qquad (i = 1, 2; j = 15, 16, 17) \quad \text{(A.12)}$$
$$L_{ijt} = p_{ijt}N_{ijt} \qquad (i = 1, 2; j \geq 15) \quad \text{(A.13)}$$
$$L'_{ijt} = (1 - u_{ij})L_{ijt} \qquad (i = 1, 2; j \geq 15) \quad \text{(A.14)}$$

$$L_t = \sum_i \sum_{j \geq 15} L_{ijt} \qquad \text{(A.15)}$$

$$L'_t = \sum_i \sum_{j \geq 15} L'_{ijt} \qquad \text{(A.16)}$$

Production

$$Q_t = \alpha(K_t)^\beta (L_t^*)^{1-\beta} \tag{A.17}$$

$$L_t^* = \sum_i \sum_{j \geq 15} q_{ij} L_{ijt}' \tag{A.18}$$

Income and Factor Returns

$$w_{ijt} = (1 - \beta)(Q_t/L_t^*)q_{ij} \qquad\qquad (i = 1, 2; j \geq 15) \quad \text{(A.19)}$$
$$w_t = (1 - \beta)(Q_t/L_t') \qquad\qquad\qquad\qquad\qquad\qquad \text{(A.20)}$$
$$r_t = \beta(Q_t/K_t) - \delta \qquad\qquad\qquad\qquad\qquad\qquad \text{(A.21)}$$

$$Y_{jt} = \sum_i w_{ijt} L_{ijt}' + r_t W_{jt} \qquad\qquad\qquad (j \geq 15) \quad \text{(A.22)}$$

$$Y_t = \sum_{j \geq 15} Y_{jt} \tag{A.23}$$

Private Consumption and Savings

$$C_j^{**} = \text{opt} \, [C_j^{**} \,|\, E(w, h, r, \tau) \text{ at age } j \text{ in year } t] \qquad (j \geq 18) \quad \text{(A.24)}$$
$$C_{jt} = 1/2(N_{jt} C_{jt}^{**}) \qquad\qquad\qquad\qquad\qquad\qquad (j \geq 18) \quad \text{(A.25)}$$
$$C_{jt} = (1 - \tau_t)Y_{jt} \qquad\qquad\qquad\qquad\qquad (j = 15, 16, 17) \quad \text{(A.26)}$$
$$S_{jt}' = (1 - \tau_t)Y_{jt} - C_{jt} \qquad\qquad\qquad\qquad\qquad (j \geq 15) \quad \text{(A.27)}$$

$$C_t = \sum_{j \geq 15} C_{jt} \tag{A.28}$$

$$S_t' = \sum_{j \geq 15} S_{jt}' \tag{A.29}$$

$$S_t = S_t' + \delta K_t \tag{A.30}$$

Wealth and Inheritance

$$W_{jt} = W_{j-1, t-1} + S_{j-1, t-1}' + \xi_j \sum_{k > 18} H_{kt} - H_{jt} \qquad (j > 18) \quad \text{(A.31)}$$

$$W_{jt} = 0 \qquad\qquad\qquad\qquad\qquad\qquad\qquad\qquad (j \leq 18) \quad \text{(A.32)}$$

$$H_{jt} = \left[\left(\sum_i d_{ijt} N_{i, j-1, t-1} \right) / N_{jt} \right] \left[W_{j-1, t-1} + S_{j-1, t-1}' \right] \qquad (j > 18) \quad \text{(A.33)}$$

$$W_t = \sum_{j > 18} W_{jt} \tag{A.34}$$

Investment and Capital Stock

$$I_t = S_t \tag{A.35}$$
$$K_t = W_t \tag{A.36}$$
$$K_t = (1 - \delta)K_{t-1} + I_{t-1} \tag{A.37}$$

Government Consumption and Taxes

$$G_t = \sum_{k=1}^{5} \theta_k Q_{t-k} \tag{A.38}$$

$$T_t = G_t \tag{A.39}$$

$$\tau_t = T_t / Y_t \tag{A.40}$$

Symbols Used in Model A

Greek symbols

α	production function scale parameter
β	production function distribution parameter
δ	annual depreciation rate
η	participation rate adjustment parameter
θ	government expenditure parameter
ξ	inheritance share parameter
τ	income tax rate
ϕ	fertility parameter

Latin symbols

B	annual live births
B_1	male live births
B_2	female live births
C	private consumption
C**	private consumption per household unit
d	mortality rate
E	expectation operator
F	total cohort fertility rate
f	age-specific fertility rate
G	government consumption
H	cohort wealth transfer at death
h	inheritance received per person
I	gross investment
i	sex subscript (male 1, female 2)
j	age subscript
K	capital stock (start of year)
k	supplementary subscript for age or time lag
L	labour force
L'	employed labour force
L*	productivity-weighted labour input
N	population
opt	life cycle optimization operator
p	labour force participation rate

Q	gross output (or income)
q	age–sex productivity weight
r	interest rate (net return to capital)
S	gross saving
S	net saving (before depreciation allowance)
s	male–female birth ratio
T	total taxes
t	time subscript
u	unemployment rate
W	wealth (start of year)
w	wage rate
Y	net income (before tax)

Appendix 9.2.   Model B

(The model is defined with reference to Model A.)

Population

The following equations replace equations (A.1) and (A.2):

$$F_t = \bar{F}_t \tag{B.1}$$
$$f_{jt} = \phi_j F_t \qquad\qquad (15 \leq j \leq 50) \quad \text{(B.2)}$$

Equation (A.3) is dropped. Equations (A.4)–(A.10) are retained.

Labour Force and Employment

The following equation replaces equation (A.11):

$$p_{ijt} = \bar{p}_{ij} \qquad\qquad (i = 1, 2; j \geq 15) \quad \text{(B.11)}$$

Equation (A.12) is dropped. Equations (A.13)–(A.16) are retained.

Production

No changes: equations (A.17) and (A.18) are retained.

Income and Factor Returns

No changes: equations (A.19)–(A.23) are retained.

Private Consumption and Savings

The following equations replace equations (A.28) and (A.29):

$$C_t = \rho(Q_t - T_t) \tag{B.28}$$
$$S'_t = (1 - \tau_t)Y_t - C_t \tag{B.29}$$

Equations (A.24)–(A.27) are dropped. Equation (A.30) is retained.

Wealth and Inheritance

This block is eliminated entirely: equations (A.31)–(A.34) are dropped.

Investment and Capital Stock

No changes: equations (A.35)–(A.37) are retained.

Government Consumption and Taxes

No changes: equations (A.38)–(A.40) are retained.

Symbols Used in Model B

All symbols used in Model B are the same as ones used in Model A except for the following:

ρ	propensity to consume out of after-tax gross income
F	period (annual) total fertility rate
$\bar{F}$	exogenous value assigned to F in a given year
$\bar{p}$	exogenous (constant) value assigned to labour force participation rate.

References

Ahlburg, D. A. (1982), 'The New Kuznets Cycle: A Test of the Easterlin–Wachter Hypothesis' in *Research in Population Economics*, 4, 93–115.
——(1983), 'A Macroeconometric Economic–Demographic Forecasting Model for the United States', unpublished manuscript, University of Minnesota.
Anker, Richard and Knowles, James C. (1983), *Population Growth, Employment and Economic–Demographic Interactions in Kenya*, St Martin's Press, New York.
Barlow, R. and Davies, G. W. (1974), 'Policy Analysis with a Disaggregated Economic Demographic Model', *Journal of Public Economics*, 3, 43–70.
Ben-Porath, Yoram (1975), 'First Generation Effects on Second Generation Fertility', *Demography*, 12, 3, 397–405.
Butz, W. P. and Ward, M. P. (1979), 'The Emergence of Countercyclical US Fertility', *American Economic Review*, 69, 3, 318–28.
——(1980), 'Completed Fertility and its Timing', *Journal of Political Economy*, 88, 5, 917–40.
Coale, A. J. and Hoover, E. M. (1958), *Population Growth and Economic Development in Low Income Countries*, Princeton University Press, Princeton, NJ.

Denton, F. T. and Spencer, B. G. (1973), 'A Simulation Analysis of the Effects of Population Change on a Neo-Classical Economy', *Journal of Political Economy*, 81, 2, 356–75.

—— ——(1975), *Population and the Economy*, DC Heath, Westmead, England.

—— ——(1981), 'A Macro-economic Analysis of the Effects of a Public Pension Plan', *Canadian Journal of Economics*, 14, 4, 609–34.

—— ——(1983), 'Macroeconomic Aspects of the Transition to Zero Population Growth' in Christopher Garbacz (ed.), *Economic Resources for the Elderly*, Westview Press, Boulder, Colorado, 81–111.

—— ——(1984*a*), 'The Time Path of the Economy as the Population Moves Towards a Stationary State' in Gunter Steinmann (ed.), *Economic Consequences of Population Change in Industrialized Countries*, Springer–Verlag, Berlin–Heidelberg–New York–Tokyo, 109–31.

—— ——(1984*b*), 'Endogenous vs. Exogenous Fertility: What Difference for the Macroeconomy?', McMaster University Program for Quantitative Studies in Economics and Population Research Report No. 90.

Easterlin, R. A. (1962), 'The American Baby Boom in Historical Perspective', National Bureau of Economic Research Occasional Paper 79.

——(1966*a*), 'Economic–Demographic Interactions and Long Swings in Economic Growth', *American Economic Review*, 56, 5, 1063–104.

——(1966*b*), 'On the Relation of Economic Factors to Recent and Projected Fertility Changes', *Demography*, 3, 131–53.

——(1968), *Population, Labor Force and Long Swings in Economic Growth: The American Experience*, Columbia University Press, New York.

——(1969), 'Towards a Socioeconomic Theory of Fertility: A Survey of Recent Research on Economic Factors in American Fertility' in S. J. Behrman *et al.*, *Fertility and Family Planning: A World View*, University of Michigan Press, Ann Arbor, 127–56.

——(1973), 'Relative Economic Status and the American Fertility Swing' in E. B. Sheldon (ed.), *Family Economic Behavior: Problems and Prospects*, J. B. Lippincott, Philadelphia, 170–223.

——(1978), 'What Will 1984 Be Like? Socioeconomic Implications of Recent Twists in Age Structure', *Demography*, 15, 4 (November), 397–432.

——and Condran, G. A. (1976), 'A Note on the Recent Fertility Swing in Australia, Canada, England and Wales and the United States' in H. Richards (ed.), *Population, Factor Movements and Economic Development*, University of Wales Press, Cardiff, 139–51.

—— Wachter, M. L. and Wachter, S. M. (1978*a*), 'Demographic Influences on Economic Stability: The US Experience', *Population and Development Review*, 4, 1 (March), 1–22.

—— —— ——(1978*b*), 'The Changing Impact of Population Swings on the American Economy', *Proceedings of the American Philosophic Society*, 122, 119–30.

Enke, S. (1971), 'Economic Consequences of Rapid Population Growth', *Economic Journal*, 81, 800–11.

—— and Zind, R. G. (1969), 'Effects of Fewer Births on Average Income', *Journal of Biosocial Sciences*, 1, 41–55.

Lee, R. D. (1976), 'Demographic Forecasting and the Easterlin Hypothesis', *Population and Development Review*, 2, 3/4, 459–68.

——(1981), 'A Stock Adjustment Model of US Marital Fertility', *Research in Population Economics*, 3, 67–91.

Moffit, R. A. (1982), 'Postwar Fertility Cycles and the Easterlin Hypothesis: A Life Cycle Approach', *Research in Population Economics*, 4, 237–52.

Samuelson, Paul A. (1976), 'An Economist's Non-linear model of Self-generated Fertility Waves', *Population Studies*, 30, 2, 243–47.

Simon, J. L. (1976), 'Population Growth may be Good for LDCs in the Long Run: A Richer Simulation Model', *Economic Development and Cultural Change*, 24, 309–37.

Spencer, B. G. (1973), 'Determinants of the Labour Force Participation of Married Women: A Micro-study of Toronto Households', *Canadian Journal of Economics*, 6, 2, 222–38.

Wachter, M. L. (1975), 'A Time-series Fertility Equation: The Potential for a Baby-boom in the 1980s', *International Economic Review*, 16, 3, 609–24.

Index

labour market (*cont.*)
  in United States
    baby boom and 42–3
labour supply
  Kondratieff cycles and 9
Lamont, D. 182
Landes, E. 158, 181
Lapkoff, Shelley 90, 103, 105
Lee, Ronald D. 1, 109, 134, 137, 214
leisure
  household optimization and 187
  labour force participation and 185
less-developed countries
  population growth rates in 2
Lewis, H. Gregg 137, 140
life cycle choice variable
  fertility as 185–6
life cycle factors
  household dwelling size and type and 172
life expectancy
  in developed countries 1

MacClennan, D. 176, 182
Malthus 9
marital status
  household formation and 157–8
marriage
  housing booms and 161
  housing tenure and 173
  owner-occupied housing and 173–4
Martin, Linda G. 11, 59–61, 64, 74
McNicoll, Geoffrey 109, 110, 134, 137
Merrilees, W. 84, 86
Michael, R. 158, 181
migrant workers
  in developed countries 2
military service
  labour market in Israel and 23–6
Mills, G. 154
Mincer, J. 58
Modigliani, Franco 107, 138
Moffit, R. A. 215
Mohlo, I. 182
mortality
  household size and 2
  transfer schemes and 96
Muellbauer, John 153, 154
Murphy, Kevin 10, 11, 39, 58
Murphy, M. J. 157, 182

Nerlove, M. 150
new home economics 139–49
  growth model in 141–3
  household sector in 139–41
nuptiality
  overlapping-generations model and 110

Ogawa, Naohiro 11, 59, 60, 75
Okuno, Masahiro 137

overlapping-generations model 106–36
  balanced and golden-rule equilibria and 116–18
  competitive equilibrium and 112–15
  equilibrium rate of interest and 118–21
  supply of capital and 121–7
  supply of credit and 127–9
Overton, E. 156, 181

Pissarides, C. 81, 86
Pitchford, J. D. 150
Plant, Mark 10, 11, 39, 58, 64
policy
  economic growth and 146–9
  educational
    baby boom and 9
  public sector housing and 165
population
  endogenous fertility and 192
population growth
  endogenous
    implications of 144–6
  welfare effects of
    intergenerational transfers and 134–5
population growth rates
  in developed countries 2
  in less-developed countries 2
  social security schemes and 103
Prais, S. J. 153, 154
production
  endogenous fertility and 192–3
production sector
  savings and 114–15
public sector
  elderly and 20
  housing in Great Britain and 161–2
  in Israel 18–23

quasi-interest
  transfer schemes and 95

Razin, Assaf 110, 135, 138
regression analysis
  wage ratios in Japan and 68–73
Rodgers, Gerry 153

Samuelson, Paul A. 89, 106–8, 110, 117–19, 135, 138, 215
Sato, R. 86
savings
  alternative uses of
    economy and 142
  capital stock growth and 204
  child-rearing and 134
  endogenous fertility and 193
  individual sector 113–14, 120
  production sector 114–15
Schwab, R. 182